TONY CHRISTIE

THE SONG INTERPRETER

THE OFFICIAL AUTOBIOGRAPHY

WITH CHRIS BERRY

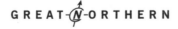

GREAT NORTHERN

Great Northern Books Limited
PO Box 1380, Bradford, BD5 5FB

www.greatnorthernbooks.co.uk

ISBN: 978-1-912101-08-5

Design and layout: David Burrill

CIP Data
A catalogue for this book is available from the British Library

I dedicate this book to
my dear mum Iris, my dear dad Paddy,
my dear brother Neal,
my lovely wife Sue,
my mother and father in law
Irene & John Ashley,
all our beautiful children and their partners,
and all our amazing grandchildren.

CONTENTS

TONY CHRISTIE

THE SONG INTERPRETER

INTRODUCTION

The Song Interpreter

If you're looking for a story of sex 'n' drugs 'n' rock 'n' roll, I'm afraid you will be mightily disappointed with this book. But if you want to read of a singer's career and how someone can come from a working-class background to have hit records and play great venues all over the world in the '70s, have an amazing second career in Europe in the '80s and '90s, a remarkable UK comeback in the 2000s and come through it all with a fabulous marriage to a wonderful woman and having grown a fantastic family, then stay tuned.

As anyone who knows me will tell you, I'm a man of generally few words, happy to let my singing voice take the lead. I'm an interpreter of songs, that's why I chose the book title. I don't claim to be an inventor. Songs can make people happy and joyful or sad and reflective. I've been very fortunate in having some of the best songwriters in the world give me some amazing songs that more than fulfil both those ends of the spectrum.

I will always be grateful to Neil Sedaka and Howard Greenfield for writing 'Amarillo'. The song has been an absolute blessing and I've said several times over the years I wish he'd given me another one or two like it. There are so many big names in this business that don't have that one song, but I've been blessed to have had many more hits throughout the world and to have recorded some of the finest material of my career since coming back to the UK from Spain after Peter Kay's *Phoenix Nights* set the ball rolling again.

My career has ebbed and flowed like any other, but it has given me far more than I ever expected when I was growing up in South Yorkshire. I've known what it is like to struggle and have to work my backside off just to pay the rent and I've made some right royal mistakes along the way. I'm certainly no businessman. I've been fleeced by some unscrupulous tour promoters. I've been embarrassed by my attempt at going into the nightclub business. I should have earned more from my record deals, but you know, I've had a fantastic time, met some amazing people, had a great life — and it's still progressing.

There are not many who have the good fortune to live abroad for 15 years and then come back to the UK and have the success I've continued to enjoy for the past 14 years. And there are not many who can have a second career in mainland Europe playing songs that very few in the UK have ever heard of, and yet 'Sweet September' remains a favourite of my fans in Germany, Austria and Switzerland.

One person has remained constant throughout. She's my rock, my soulmate. She's been with me all the way. This book is as much about Sue as it is about me. We are one. I hope you enjoy reading. See you at a concert soon!

CHAPTER 1

Anthony Fitzgerald enters the world 25 April 1943

I'm not the only person in my family to have had a share of fame. Back when I was a young lad, before I knew singing was to be my future, there was someone else who was much more famous and landed far more hits than I've ever had.

There would be a knock at the door around teatime, or you might call it dinner if you're being posh and come from somewhere other than Yorkshire. Whoever was there would say, 'Does Percy Wall live here? I've come from Barnsley (although it could have been a multitude of other places) and I understand he's a bit of a street fighter.'

Granddad was famous. He used to work down the pit before later becoming a fireman and then a fire chief and had built up this invincibility others were always eager and willing to challenge. I've played golf with boxing champions John Conteh and John H. Stracey who, if they'd come up against him, may have met their match.

I remember my granddad putting down his knife and fork, having just sat down for his evening meal and he'd say to my mum, 'Iris, put that in the oven, I won't be long.' Then he'd go and knock seven bells out of this bloke in the street, all with his fists, no gloves, no kicking, none of that, come back in and finish his dinner. He was a proper street fighter and such was his reputation and prowess that men from all over South Yorkshire and out of the area would come to offer him outside for a fight.

Mum would never let me see any of them and when he'd finished he'd just walk back in without a scratch on him, no black eye, no cut lip. He'd sit back down and she'd get out his dinner again, place it in front of him and he'd finish it as though nothing had happened. You might think this would only have taken place maybe once or twice because it sounds so crazy now, but in the early 1950s it really was like that in the heart of the coal mining community where we lived in Conisbrough, and Granddad would take it all in his stride. He would be offered out maybe six or seven times a year. And it wasn't for money either. In those days, all pit villages had gangs and they'd fight each other. It was as much a sport as anything else.

Granddad was very fit, he'd always take me on walks and he gave me my first real interest in nature and wildlife that I've kept up with ever since. He liked the birds and yes, I know all the connotations that phrase can bring, especially among those in my line of business, but these were the feathered variety. We would go through the woods near an area known as the Crags that went down to Denaby and he'd point out all the different bird species. I learned a lot, became an ornithologist for a while and still have books all around the house. Every day, when I'm home, I feed the birds. They get to know that yours is the house to come to and will often let me know if I'm late.

I didn't see my dad, Patrick Joseph Fitzgerald, known to everyone as Paddy, until I was about three or four years old, so if you're wondering about Granddad getting top billing it's because I was close to him and my uncles right from the start. We all lived in the same house. When Dad came home from his time in the RAF, I remember cowering behind my mum wondering who this strange man was.

He'd had two choices of job. He could either go down the pit or work in the munitions factory where they made barrels for guns. He obviously made the right choice with the latter as that's where he met Mum and they married. He joined the RAF and wanted to be a pilot, but couldn't become one on account of being colour blind. His time in the RAF saw him handling administrative work while stationed in India and Egypt, which was why I didn't see him. When he came back, he was stationed at RAF Spitalgate, Grantham in Lincolnshire and I went to school there for a short while before we moved back home.

I found out not so long ago, from Mum, that Dad was too brainy to go down the pit. She told me about it one day as I was driving her back home to Conisbrough from where we live in Lichfield. She said, 'You know the teachers hated your dad at school. He was always correcting them.' He had about 10 'O' levels, or whatever they called them in those days. He was even barred from some quiz nights as he'd stand at the bar without being part of a team, but giving out the answers. My brother Neal, who's five years my junior, is great with facts and figures too and became a schoolteacher. Not me. My brain's from a different universe.

Dad was from Maltby, Freddie Trueman-land if you're a cricket lover, but as you can probably tell by his name he was from Irish descent and my family on his side is from the west coast of Ireland in County Mayo. It's that connection that led to one of my most recent releases, *The Great Irish Songbook*, with the excellent band Ranagri who have supported me on tour. Dad always liked us to sing Irish songs as I grew up with them at home and that clearly rubbed off on me.

Music was always around me at home and with Dad's family. I listened to the radio all the time from being six or seven years old and I remember the Fitzgerald clan would come over from Maltby to visit on a Sunday. At about nine years old, Dad would stand me on a chair and I would sing the songs I'd heard on the radio while he played piano. I remember singing 'Here in My Heart' by Al Martino, who many years later I was fortunate to meet and we became good friends.

My grandmother Mary Anne, on Dad's side, played the fiddle in a ceilidh band and my granddad Martin Fitzgerald played the squeezebox, which I still have today. My uncle Jack was a good singer. He sounded a bit like Richard Tauber when he was shaving and one song I recall him singing was 'You're Breaking My Heart 'Cause You're Leaving' that Vic Damone sang in the '50s. Vic turned out to be my doppelganger, or I was his, as we both found out much later.

At home we had an upright piano and next to it was a melodeon that my grandfather Percy played. He could play but couldn't read music, but my dad read and he would go out and buy the sheet music so he could play and I could sing. I suppose the die was cast back then of my love of big band singers, especially Frank Sinatra. Dad sent me for piano lessons to Miss Bairstow in Conisbrough. I was fine sitting next to her hearing and seeing what she was playing because I could work out the notes and could play what she played, but I never learned to read music. Maybe I should have, but it hasn't held me back. By the time I was 14, I knew singing in front of a big band was something I would love if ever the chance came.

Dad eventually gave me his record collection he'd collected in Egypt and India, a stack of 78s that included Glenn Miller, Frank Sinatra, Ella Fitzgerald (no relation by the way) and all the great singers of the '40s and '50s like Peggy Lee, Nat King Cole, Tony Bennett and Vic Damone — all proper singers. I'm into voices and there are some very good ones around today. Lady Gaga is a proper singer who would also have been a big star in the '40s and '50s, and Paloma Faith too, who I've appeared alongside in concert. It's Lady Gaga's phrasing that sets her apart. Phrasing and interpreting a song is everything.

Those proper singers were my real education as I wasn't very good at school. It didn't help that we had a history teacher who just told us to read something and would then disappear, but I really can't blame anyone. I just couldn't get interested unless it was music lessons where we'd sing or if we were playing sport. After Denaby Junior School, I went to Northcliffe Secondary Modern School in Conisbrough that is now called the De Warenne Academy.

It was once I left school that I became a reader, in my mid-teens, and I went through a patch of heavy reading, taking in the classics like Charles Dickens and the Brontes because I thought I'd perhaps missed out. I went through a massive catching up time, to such an extent Mum even said it was time I got out again.

Miss Mills was my music teacher in primary school. She was great in every respect as she was pretty and I loved her lessons. I could sing and hit pitch right from the start and was sat next to a boy who was tone deaf. I thought he was brilliant and yet it was weird because we were singing all sorts of fantastic songs and whatever he sang it was all one note, so I tried to copy him.

One day, the lovely Miss Mills came down the classroom because she'd heard my voice and said, 'You go to the front, you can sing.' We were singing hymns at the time and I still enjoy hymn singing today. I met her years later when I was playing at Southport Theatre and she came backstage with her husband. She said I probably wouldn't remember her, but I said, 'Oh yes I do, I had a schoolboy's crush on you.' I hope she wasn't too embarrassed.

15 Montague Avenue was a well-stocked council house. By that I mean there were plenty of us. Mum, Dad, Granddad, who was with us as Grandma had died, my uncles Roy and Jack who both worked down the pit, uncle Joe and auntie Jean — all from Mum's side. Then there was me and five years on from my arrival, my brother Neal. Numbers varied a bit over the years, but there were eight of us at one time in the 3-bedroomed terraced council house with a ginnel where we played cricket with stumps chalked on the coalhouse wall.

I never knew what it was like to get into a cold bed for years, as I shared with my uncles who worked on shifts at the pit, so when they'd get out to go on nightshift I'd get into a nice warm bed. Granddad had his bed in the front room downstairs and eventually, as Joe, Jack and Jean all married and left, I eventually had my own room.

Mum had black hair and was very pretty, extremely glamorous. She was what I call a provider. Her mum, my granddad Percy's wife, had died during the war when I was a baby and she'd had to look after her dad and her siblings that also included another brother, Joe, at one time until he married. She worked all the time — baking, cooking, washing, cleaning, mending — looking after everyone. I loved her cooking and particularly my favourite: sheep's brains. I once went to a restaurant over in Holmfirth with the famous Yorkshire artist Ashley Jackson, who is a good friend, and couldn't believe it when I saw it on the menu. I'd not had it since Mum cooked for us.

Roy and Jack had racing pigeons and one of my earliest memories was looking down from the bedroom window to where they kept them in a pigeon loft. They'd take them down the crags to the railway station, put them on a train to Doncaster where they would then be transferred to a truck to France where they'd be released and fly back. Actor Donald Pleasence's father was once station master at Conisbrough. Now there's a fact.

I had a pet magpie for a while and my dad couldn't stand it. Looking back, I can understand why he may have been upset, because I used to keep it in a kitchen cupboard. I'd had it from it being a baby after it had fallen out of a tree in the woods and a schoolmate had found it. What really got my dad going was when he would sit down for his breakfast and it would fly out and steal the yolk from his egg. I can hear him now going wild shouting, 'Get that bloody bird out of here!'

When we had come back from our brief exile in Grantham, which I'd hated because I was away from all my friends, I always loved playing in the woods and in the street like most kids. We'd play football, cricket, sledge down the crags in winter, go exploring in the woods, congregate at the top of the street and play marbles. I wasn't bad at marbles. I'd pick out one in the circle that I really wanted to add to my collection. All normal kids' stuff.

I was a happy child and of course in those days it was safe to play anywhere. When I was about six or seven, I would pretend I was going to the pit and Mum would make me a snap tin that included a bottle of water in a milk bottle and a jam sandwich. I'd play on the crags walking around as though I was working in a pit. There were three or four pits in the area, including Denaby Main Colliery and Cadeby Main Colliery, so for young kids it was natural to play at being a miner.

But I was also an accomplice to a felony when I was around eight or nine years old, acting as lookout for local gamblers. Funnily enough, I may have ended up playing for some of them in my casino shows as an adult years later.

Not far from the end of our street was a valley near the reservoir where men would play cards, gambling for cash, and because gambling was illegal in those days they would ask if I would keep an eye out for police on their way from Denaby. When I shouted they would all grab the money and scatter as the police chased them. It was just like watching a film.

Granddad also took me fishing. It's one of those things that you either like it or you don't, there's no in-between. I liked it and we would get the train to Doncaster and then another to the Selby-Goole area. I remember going to the village of Keadby on the bank of the River Trent and next to the Stainforth and Keadby Canal. We'd take a tent and stop overnight. We'd also fish while on holiday when we went to places like Skegness and Cleethorpes when we'd go by Billy's Coaches in Mexborough or by train.

I've always enjoyed sport — playing and watching. Dad took me to watch Doncaster Rovers every home game from being nine years old until I was in my teens. I played in midfield for my school team when I was at Denaby as I could distribute the ball. It was six miles to the Belle Vue ground where Rovers played until moving to the Keepmoat Stadium not so long ago. We would all meet up at the Lord Conyers Hotel pub where we would get on the coach to the game. During that time, we had Harry Gregg in goal before he joined Manchester United. He became one of the 'Busby Babes' who survived the Munich air disaster. Our centre half was the man who went on to be a well-liked TV comedian, Charlie Williams, who was born in another pit village, Royston.

Our outside right was a Scottish lad, Johnny Mooney, and we had an amazing young centre forward called Alick Jeffrey who made his debut at 15 and broke his leg at 17 when playing for England U23. At the time, he was all set to sign for Manchester United and was tipped to make the full England team. His broken leg was so bad it looked as though it would end his career, but he returned to Rovers in the '60s and did really well.

I've followed both Sheffield teams over the years, having lived in the city, but I will always watch out for Rovers' results just as much as Sheffield Wednesday and United. They were good days and I was a big footie fan.

Running and cycling were my other two sporting activities at the time, and they are where I got my power from and my breathing when singing. I've always been slim and have never put on any weight. Even when I later drank six or seven pints on a night, I'd always burn it off by running when I was living in Sheffield.

I was a late developer, as some call it, and quite enjoyed cross-country running. I found it a bit more interesting than the track at school, but throughout my teenage years cycling was my thing.

I became a member of a cycling club and had a racing bike that my mum and dad had bought me. I'd cycle to school with my friend Geoff who I think became a lawyer. My bike had a 6-gear derailleur. I joined the Conisbrough Ivanhoe Cycling Club next to the old crisp factory and the Red Lion Hotel. I had the same bike for years, would cycle in time trials and regularly clocked up around 30 miles per night. Weekend cycling was great and there would be a group of 20 of us go to Northumberland, stopping overnight in youth hostels. Other times we'd be into Derbyshire and the Peak District.

When I left school at 15, I really didn't know what I was going to do. Yes, I'd had dreams of singing with a big band, but there was nothing more to it than that at the time. I used to walk home from school with my mate Dave Bramley who had a pretty good voice and we'd sing together. I could sing harmony, so he'd sing the tune and I'd harmonise and that was the start of my singing journey, or to put it more appropriately, how I drifted into singing.

Trad Jazz was popular in the '50s and I bought a banjo. I went for a few lessons, but found playing the guitar was easier and had more range when I took that up on leaving school. The first songs I learned were 'Peggy Sue' by Buddy Holly and some of the Everly Brothers hits like 'All I Have to Do Is Dream' and 'Bye Bye Love'. The first record I ever bought was 'Walk Right Back'. We had a red Dansette record player.

We moved out of Montague Avenue and into Cadeby Avenue when I was 16. Granddad and Uncle Roy moved with Mum, Dad, me and Neal, but that was it by then, just the six of us, with Uncle Joe and his wife living across the road. It was a newer house, a bit bigger, still 3-bedroomed, but a semi-detached house a third of a mile from

Montague Avenue.

I've been back to where we all lived together in those early days and it looks very tiny, yet when I was a kid it all felt massive. It was a whole different world sixty and seventy years ago, but it didn't do me any harm and through singing at home with family, Miss Mills at school and then with Dave, it set me on my way to what has turned out to be an amazing life in music and with a wonderful family of my own that means more to me than anything. Let's crack on.

CHAPTER 2

The Grant Brothers enter the world at the Ivanhoe WMC in 1961

Baker and Bessemer were my first employers. Their steelworks were in Swinton near Mexborough. I used to get what was called the 'trackless', otherwise known as a trolleybus, that ran on electric wires by the Mexborough and Swinton Traction Company into Mexborough and then I'd walk to work from there. Baker and Bessemer had won a big contract to supply South African Railways with axles, wheels and wheel rims for trains. I worked in the wages department. Right from the start, I couldn't see myself staying there for long.

Dave's mum played the piano and she ran a Glee Club entertaining in hospitals and old people's homes. To us at the time, most of the people involved seemed really old and they'd sing songs like 'Jerusalem', but we soon found out a great reason for joining up.

I've always enjoyed a beer and particularly real ale and part of the Glee Club attraction for Dave and I was where the evenings ended. I'd been initiated into proper beer at about eight or nine years old at an Irish wedding held in a school hall where they had a barrel of beer and was told to help myself. That was it for me. I found the taste to my liking and I've continued to enjoy real hoppy ales, as my friends in my local will tell you, but I've never been on stage with a pot belly.

The Glee Club would end every evening with a visit to the pub, so Dave and I joined up, stood at the back and then went for a drink, often entertaining the punters with a few songs from the 30 of us. We'd go by coach to Doncaster. They were fun times. We were in it for the beer, not the girls, as most of them were a lot older, but I met my first real girlfriend I was with for any length of time through the Glees, Mary Kelly. We were together a good year. It was Mary's brother who was in the Glees. He fancied himself as a singer and had brought Mary to where we were singing in Denaby.

Mary was a Catholic girl and I became part of St Alban's Catholic Choir in Denaby after being asked to join by one of the lads who sang in the Glee Club. I'd never gone to church regularly before, but I enjoyed singing so it was natural for me.

Dave and I took on our first proper gig together, as he reminded me when we met up for the first time in 55 years in 2017 at Wentworth Music Festival, as a result of appearing in a talent competition. Dave reminded me that a tenor called Peter Firmani asked whether we had an agent.

That's what made us think about being on the right track and set my professional singing career under way. My uncle Jack was on the committee at the Ivanhoe Working Men's Club in Conisbrough, which is still going strong today, where we performed our first paid gig. I was 17. Dave and I received £2 each for our opening spot of three or four songs that, from memory, included 'All I Have to Do Is Dream', 'Walk Right Back' and maybe 'Peggy Sue'.

The club was packed, as all clubs were in those days. It was a great time to be an entertainer and we were on the same bill as two people who became household names and big stars on television: a Rotherham-born girl singer called Lynne Perrie and Hull-born comedian Norman Collier. Lynne went on to play Ivy Tilsley in *Coronation Street*, as well as Mrs Casper in the film *Kes*, but at the time she was a cabaret singer. I'd met her before when I'd been to a party with Dad where The Tremeloes were among the guests. Her brother is comedian Duggie Brown, a fellow Water Rat and a great friend of Sue and I.

Norman was a big name already and we shared a dressing room with him. He was as crackers off stage as he was on it, and I mean that really affectionately. He was a very funny man and I got the impression he was just being himself all the time. He talked to himself hilariously, it was like he was reading a script. Maybe he was. Years later, I played in his own Norman Collier Golf Classics. Sue and I loved Norman and his wife Lucy dearly.

Dave and I were just pleased to be there. It was just me on guitar and our two voices playing songs made for duos, so the Everly Brothers' hits were just right for us. I was still singing harmony while Dave sang the tune. He had a really good voice and when we met up at Wentworth it wasn't just great to see him, we also gave an impromptu version of 'All I Have to Do Is Dream' backstage, which is now on YouTube.

Opening up the telephone book, closing our eyes and putting a finger on a page was how we became the Grant Brothers. We landed on Grant and that was it. We took the name because we'd auditioned for an agent a short while after our Ivanhoe WMC debut and needed something for him to represent us. He was Slim Farrell and his name hardly fitted the bill as he was about 20 stone. He had quite a few really good acts, including comedian Bobby Knutt. He'd ring and tell us the new dates and pretty soon we were playing every Friday, Saturday and Sunday, with Sundays including lunchtime and evening gigs. We'd play three or four songs and do three spots for each gig, playing all the working men's clubs around Rotherham, Sheffield and Doncaster.

Slim set us on the right track and said we needed parts written for drums, bass and keyboard, so we started using each club's resident musicians, which generally consisted of organ and drums at that time. We became a harmony duo without the guitar, but with more complex material moving more towards the big band songs of Dean Martin and Frank Sinatra.

We must have played hundreds of gigs together as the Grant Brothers and our set lists included fun songs like 'Yellow Bird' recorded by The Mills Brothers, that had the line, 'up high in the banana tree', and 'Well Did You Ever?' performed by Frank and Bing in *High Society*. It suited me because I never thought of myself as a pop singer. I was more a singer of the Sinatra era, but big bands were all but finished. I felt I'd been born twenty years too late.

Ironically, my boss at Baker and Bessemer set me even further along my singing career by using another singer's name that I had no interest in. I'd turned down working for what was still my full-time job one weekend because we were singing. It must have been the straw that broke the camel's back as far as he was concerned, because he called me into his office and said, 'You've got to decide whether you want to be the new Adam Faith or hold down a proper job.' I didn't want to be the old Adam Faith let alone the new one — no disrespect, but I'd have preferred that he'd used a singer I really liked. I was typically Yorkshire in my reply. I just said, 'Well, I think music is my calling, not working in an office.' So I left.

It was a decision that came with its fair share of heartache at times in the mid to late '60s, but it's one I've never regretted.

My second and last proper job was working with British Oxygen Company (BOC) on Bawtry Road in Brinsworth near Rotherham, which was only notable because it's where I met my next girlfriend, Juanita, who worked in the office. She kind of flew away in the end as her father was in the RAF and was re-stationed down in Leicestershire.

My love of big bands and proper singers went way beyond listening on the radio and playing a few songs from that time in the Grant Brothers' sets. I used to travel to Rotherham and Sheffield regularly to listen to any big band nights I could, because although rock 'n' roll and pop were taking over the charts by the early '60s, there were still a lot of local big bands around. There wasn't as much choice of big bands as there was if you wanted pop, but I would go to a pub near Rotherham where they would have a 17-piece band on every week and see the bigger name bands at Sheffield City Hall. I was into bands like the Ted Heath Band and I was buying records by Peggy Lee, Ella Fitzgerald, Frank Sinatra and Nancy Wilson.

Dave and I had a good time together. We'd been schoolmates and singing partners. We'd worn our best teddy boy outfits on stage, but I think his girlfriend was perhaps uncomfortable with the attention we were getting and that we were starting to play further away, so the Grant Brothers came to an end somewhere around 1962-63. It really was great to see Dave again just a couple of years ago and brought back so many happy memories. We always enjoyed singing together.

CHAPTER 3

Tony Christie enters the world with
The Counterbeats circa 1963

When Dave left, I carried on as a solo act with backing from the resident club bands, as we'd had as a duo, but it wasn't long before the manager of one of the top bands on the circuit — The Counterbeats — asked me to join them. I was about 20 and they'd just lost their lead singer Karen Young from Sheffield, who released quite a few records before going on to have a big hit with 'Nobody's Child' in 1969.

By this time, I knew most of the acts on the clubland circuit and I knew that being lead singer of The Counterbeats was a good gig to get, as they were booked two years ahead. I knew their manager already and the rest of the band, all from Doncaster and Sheffield, that included John Cadwell from Maltby on keyboards, the drummer Tommy Le Fevre, who had been resident drummer at the Scala Club in Doncaster, bassist Colin Barstow, and our guitarist, whose name escapes me now, I'm sorry to say. It's one of the problems in getting older and it was over 55 years ago. I know it's no excuse.

The Counterbeats was a very jazzy, classy band and all the players were top musicians. They could have played in any of the bands I've played with since all around the world. I was very happy with it because I could do my big songs and a neat line in impressions that I'd developed, nicking Sammy Davis Jr's act. We were more cabaret than pop.

I wasn't a solo act. I was very much part of the band. That's the way I saw it, but the manager said that because I was doing all the impressions and was the lead singer it should be my name and The

Counterbeats.

That's when Fitzgerald was replaced by Christie. Apparently, Fitzgerald had too many syllables and I needed something snappier and more poppy. I needed a new name.

I was singing full-time by now and we were killing time during the day between gigs. It must have been 1965 because I went to the cinema while we were playing a week around Leicester and the film *Darling* was showing. It starred Laurence Harvey, Dirk Bogarde and Julie Christie, who won an Oscar and a BAFTA for it.

I liked Julie Christie too. I fancied her and the name. Who wouldn't? And that was it, I became Julie Fitzgerald. That didn't work either, so I became Tony Christie — and we became Tony Christie and The Counterbeats.

It might have been the start of Tony Christie, but sadly it was the end of The Counterbeats a short while later. I'm not sure exactly now how the band disbanded, but I remember the bass player getting married and going back to what my old boss called a proper job. We had a good couple of years though and, like all the musicians who have helped me along my way, I'll always be eternally grateful for them being there as part of my journey, but it was time to get right on track — with The Trackers.

CHAPTER 4

Tony Christie and The Trackers enter
the world of recording — 1966

The Trackers was my first real pop band. We played big numbers too, real showstoppers, like 'Jezebel' that had been a big hit for Frankie Laine and that our audience used to go mad about; and 'So Deep Is the Night', that I became known for and was our finale. It's still a popular song among my fans today. Back then, as soon as I started, it went deathly quiet and there was always a cracking ovation at the end. We used to open with 'Stranger in Paradise', Tony Bennett's fabulous hit song, and we would generally play three 20-minute sets, which meant there were no throwaway 'fillers', everything was powerful.

I'd taken over from a singer who was like Roy Orbison in many ways, except he came from Barnsley, and I had to learn all the songs they were playing as well as bringing in some of what I'd played with The Counterbeats, because The Trackers was much more of a pop and rock 'n' roll band. They weren't reading musicians, but they were all fantastic players and sang harmonies too.

We gave the audience what they wanted and there were no egos in the band. We all agreed to do whatever we did, to the best we possibly could and I cannot remember us ever having anything like a serious row or argument. I really enjoyed our way of life. We were always skint, so we took the work wherever it came from, but I had no commitments and was just enjoying the ride that was Tony Christie and The Trackers.

I'd no idea that we were heading anywhere in terms of career, and don't know what we thought might ever happen, because we weren't doing any of our own songs, but we played everywhere in all the big clubland areas of South Yorkshire, the North East, West Midlands, Scotland and the Welsh Valleys, to American bases in Germany.

We always travelled in our van that became known as the Yellow Peril. It may have been a Bedford, I honestly cannot remember, and there's no-one left to ask from the band now. I'm certainly not going to find out through this next chap who comes into our story here.

I love my fans in Germany, who gave me my second big chart career on mainland Europe in the 1980s and 1990s, but I had one incident that shook us all and, for a moment, myself and all the Trackers were scared out of our skins. I could have put other words there.

We were touring air bases in Germany in 1965 and had no idea where we were going, so our agent from Frankfurt had arranged for a driver so that we didn't have to worry about getting anywhere.

I was sitting in the front alongside our driver, with the rest of the band in the back, when, in the course of conversation, he mentioned he had been in Hitler Youth! Well, you can imagine how that might go down with a foreign band on tour in Germany. This was in the '60s, so we were only just over 20 years on from WWII, unlike today when it seems aeons ago, and the lads went into jokey mode.

I'm now just thinking for God's sake stop with the banter as I could see our driver's hands grabbing tighter on the wheel. He'd probably meant to say it to explain that maybe being in Hitler Youth had been the done thing for all young German men at that time, but whatever his reason and however it had come out, the reaction he was receiving from the boys was making him more and more upset. I could see he was getting irate, but nothing could have prepared us for what happened next when he pulled over, opened the glove compartment on my side and pulled out a gun!

We were beside ourselves with fear. They're not the real words either. I'll leave it up to you to come up with how we really felt, but it had all gone too far and that next gig in Germany suddenly seemed a long way away.

Our driver leaped out of the car, went over towards the forest, shot six rounds into a tree, came back, put the gun back in the glove compartment and without saying a word started up the engine and we were back underway.

I have never felt more in danger of losing my life than in those few minutes. It certainly killed the conversation, but thankfully nothing more. We all felt our number had come up and he was going to shoot us. Nobody said a word until we were safely unloaded at the American base.

Sadly, the last of The Trackers passed away just before I started working on this book, and a more wonderful man you could never meet. Mike Ryal was on bass guitar and not just a true gentleman, but my closest friend during my band years of the '60s. We had the same sense of humour, and believe me, sometimes that was needed to get through some of our less illustrious moments.

He went on to become musical director for Cannon and Ball and Marti Caine in their heyday, was always an in-demand session musician, and had his own orchestra. He remained a close friend throughout his wonderful life, that included raising hundreds of thousands of pounds for charity and joined me again when he and I put together another band after The Trackers.

The other Trackers were Harry Croft on guitar, who was the joker, and drummer Barry Wooton, who was always very serious about it all. We rehearsed in Barry's front room. Mike and Harry were from Barnsley and Barry from Doncaster, but the biggest character was our agent, Ernie Ardron. His brother, Wally Ardron, was a professional footballer who had started out with Denaby United near Conisbrough, but who had gone on to play centre forward for Rotherham United either side of WWII and had then played for Nottingham Forest, always banging in lots of goals. He was a famous header of the ball.

Ernie used to trade off his brother's name to get us bookings and tried to be spivvish, but wasn't. His day job was at the steelworks in Rotherham, but he kept us in work and we would play week-long residencies in well-known clubs, like the Greasbrough in Rotherham and Scala in Doncaster, alongside Matt Monro, Moira Anderson and The Deep River Boys. Ronnie Dukes and Ricki Lee were regulars on the South Yorkshire circuit at the time and who we'd also see often. Mike and Barry played for them too.

Another wonderful character and great friend was Ron Shaw, or, to be more accurate, 'the late Ron Shaw', on account of his tendency to be cutting it fine in being on time for travel to gigs. However, there was one time when he was absolutely bang on time. When Ron had married his wife Eileen he'd taken on a 'proper job', but there was a moment after he'd left us when we really needed a roadie. We were heading for a ferry this particular day and spotted Ron. He'd only gone out for a loaf of bread.

We told Ron where we were heading and he came with us, right there and then. Three weeks later we came back. Ron went back to Eileen, who promptly knocked him out! I'm not sure whether he ever bought the loaf of bread.

In 1966, totally out of the blue, I received a phone call at home in Cadeby Avenue from this man with an American accent, who introduced himself as Shel Talmy. I hadn't a clue how he'd got my name or number and I'd never heard of him, but he said he was a record producer and he had a song he wanted me to sing as someone had told him I was a good singer. He asked if he could send me a tape and whether I had a record deal.

I didn't even have a manager, let alone a recording contract. We had Ernie, but that wasn't quite the same thing. Shel Talmy had an amazing track record, working with bands like The Who and The Kinks. He arranged and produced many big hits, including 'You Really Got Me', 'All Day and All of the Night' and 'My Generation'. He sent me 'Life's Too Good to Waste (On Anything but Love Yeah?)', written by singer-songwriter Barbara Ruskin.

I listened to the tape and thought it was a good song. It fitted into the Mod era. My only criticism was that I felt the middle-eight went into a kind of Rolling Stones riff, a bit like the line 'I'm going to tell you how it's going to be', in 'Not Fade Away'. I asked if I could rewrite it, which I did and we rehearsed it at Barry's place before going down to IBC Studios in Portland Place near the BBC studios in London to record it.

It was my first time in a professional studio and we went down in the Yellow Peril, without the aid of any irate, gun-toting drivers, it has to be said. It was easy parking in London in those days and I can't even remember any parking meters, although I suppose there must have been as they started in London in 1958. There's a fact for any of the TV game shows I've appeared on.

We played it for Shel with just the guitar, bass and drums and my vocal and he said it was a bit thin. It wasn't the full, fatter sound he was looking for, so he sent us off for a coffee while he found a few session guys and, half an hour later, there they were: Billy Preston on keyboards, later to become known to some as the fifth Beatle, and who had played with Little Richard, Sam Cooke and Ray Charles; and Jimmy Page, who's the same age as me and was only two years away from forming Led Zeppelin. Billy and Jimmy were the hottest session musicians around, but while they were hot, I remember Jimmy being full of cold.

Jimmy and Billy augmented what we had already put down, backing vocals were added and Shel achieved the fatter sound he was after, I think, although we never spoke again. We were there and back home again the same day and I never remember signing anything along the way. We were back playing another week around the clubs when it was released in the summer of 1966 on the CBS label. I ordered a copy from a local record shop, bought it and that was it.

So far as I know, it never received any real airplay and we didn't get interviewed by any of the radio stations or music press, as we had nobody to promote it for us, no plugger and no management. In that respect, it was pretty much a non-event, but I had my first record release and on the B side was a song I'd written, called 'Just the Two of Us'. It was at least there for posterity — CBS catalogue number 202097.

I was told of a review of 'Life's Too Good to Waste', just recently as the research was being put together for this book, and although it wasn't written at the time, this is what was said: 'This looks like it could well be Tony Christie's first excursion into vinyl and dates to June/July 1966. This is a really great record and should have made some impact way back then, but like so many great records, it just got lost among all the heavyweights of the time.'

It has recently appeared on a compilation album called *Planet Mod* on the Big Beat label and my own *50 Golden Greats* on Wrasse Records. I never sang it live. The song wasn't really what I am or who I wanted to be. It was just one of those things, a good experience meeting fabulous world-class musicians and producers, but the phone never rang, so we went back to our regular workload playing the clubs and what our audience liked and knew. Maybe we were all just caught up with England winning the World Cup — as it was released just as they were reaching the final.

But little did I know how my life was to change the following year — and not through recording or performing, although indirectly that's how my world turned on its head, flipped right over and gave me the greatest feeling I've ever had, regardless of the hit songs.

CHAPTER 5

Sue enters my life

I always call what happened in 1967 my *West Side Story* moment. If you know the film, there's that time when suddenly all the dancers split and you're left with the Romeo and Juliet moment. I used to sing a medley from it that included 'Maria'. For me, you can change it from Maria to Sue with the words, 'and suddenly I've found' and 'say it loud and there's music playing'. I was smitten from the very first time I saw her and have been in love with her ever since. I turned around after we had finished the first two songs and told Mike, 'I think I've just seen the girl I'm going to marry.' She was at the front as we played in a club.

My memory plays tricks and I recall her in a miniskirt, but Sue quickly put me right while we were getting all this together, that she was wearing a maxi dress that night, so I'll let her tell you how she came to be there and what she was wearing. Off you go, Sue.

'I was 18 at the time and working for the Baileys Organisation. Myrna Malinsky was an agent and the booker of huge acts for Baileys, who were a massive name in the '60s and '70s. Myrna was married to Andy Wilson, trombonist with a popular Irish show band called The Witnesses. Myrna wanted to see how good Tony was to book for the Baileys circuit all around the country, but couldn't make it, so she'd asked Andy to go and he'd asked me whether I'd come along as they wanted a female opinion.

'I used to wear minidresses, but that particular night I'd been working and said I'd get changed, but they said to come as I was and that was a cotton maxi dress of summer colours.'

We closed the first half and I thought maybe she'd think I was big-headed or a bit cocky, because I was confident while on stage putting on a show, but more shy off stage. I'm not pushy, never have been, but this time I was so sure of myself.

Fortunately for me, Sue came backstage with The Witnesses, because they wanted to come and meet me and I blagged her telephone number. It took me a week before she'd go out with me. I tried her a few times. She was wary of me because of the reputation performers have and I'd never been short of attention, as many before and after me. The old phrase, 'It's a sweetie shop out there,' was right back then, but I knew Sue was the girl for me and I showed her how committed I was to us. I feel the same today as I felt then, that we were meant to be together. Sue still looks great.

We've had our fair share of highs and lows or ups and downs, as Mr Sinatra would say, but I'd have been lost without her and having Sue alongside me made me more ambitious to be a success in the music business for us and our family.

Sue started travelling with us. She couldn't come along everywhere because of her own job, but we both remember one truly horrendous trip to a club in Merthyr Tydfil in the Welsh Valleys near the Hoover factory. Mike and Barry were in the Yellow Peril, but Sue and I and Harry and his wife Kate were in our car, which at the time was a black Austin Westminster. It was November and we were driving in torrential rain on the old A1 when a stone smashed the windscreen.

There was no company like an Autoglass or quick windscreen repair business that could come out to help and it was freezing. The girls unpacked every item of clothing we could put on, that we had in our cases, and I drove all the way to South Wales, on roads that weren't anywhere near like today, probably over 200 miles with no windscreen. When we arrived it all proved useless. I'd lost my voice through the cold and couldn't even speak let alone sing. My face was frozen and we had to cancel the bookings. It was a disaster for us, but more so for our drummer, Barry, as he'd split up from his wife and needed the cash from the gigs to pay her his maintenance.

One or two clubs were notorious on the clubland circuit. We played this one place in the North East that shall remain nameless, partly for everyone's integrity and also because I haven't a clue which one it was now.

We'd been booked to play two half-hour spots and we'd played the first and went into the club lounge. Ten minutes later, the concert secretary said if we went on straight away he could get bingo on and then we could finish for the night. We said, hold on, that's three spots not two, so he went on stage and told the audience we were refusing to do three spots. They'd paid three-bob to see us too! So there was a riot. We had to make our escape, get the gear and get out. I think two of the band climbed out of the dressing room window.

1967 was also the year I met Tommy Sanderson, not long after Sue and I had got together. He'd heard about me and came to see me and the boys in Wales — his wife Mary May had been a singer with bandleader Henry Hall in the '50s — and he had his own bands, The Tommy Sanderson Sound and The Tommy Sanderson Trio, that played regularly on the BBC Light Programme before Radio 1 or Radio 2 came on the scene that year on 30 September.

Tommy had been involved with Lulu and had connections. He worked at the music publishers Francis, Day and Hunter in London. He said I was too good for the clubs and that I wasn't to work them anymore and that he could get me a record deal, a proper recording contract. I lived with him and Mary May for a while at their apartment in Hampton Court and the first thing Tommy got me was on to radio.

I was singing standards as Tony Christie with the Tommy Sanderson Trio on *Late Night Extra* on the Light Programme and then on *Night Ride,* which started when Radio 2 got under way. *Night Ride* became a long-running, after-midnight programme on the station and was just right for me singing Sinatra, Dean Martin, Tony Bennett, Nat King Cole, all the really great songs I wanted to sing by singers I have always admired. We would record five or six songs for each show. I don't know whatever happened to those recordings, they're probably locked away deep in some dusty archive.

Being in the right place at the right time can all be just good fortune, but there's no doubt Tommy taking me out of the clubs increased my opportunities, because without being in the corridors of the BBC and being broadcast on Radio 2, it's unlikely I'd have seen Des O'Connor, who was the first to give me a spot on TV the following year.

It was tough on the money front though, pulling away from The Trackers, because I had no income. The lads were still doing well as they became Ronnie Dukes and Ricki Lee's band, who at that time were the biggest act in cabaret and were later to make it on to TV and the *Royal Variety Performance.*

Tommy was true to his word and got me my first recording contract with MGM Records and my first release was 'Turn Around', written by wonderful songwriters Les Reed and Barry Mason. Les was the most successful songwriter of the '60s and '70s. With Barry Mason, he wrote 'The Last Waltz', that had gone to No 1 for Engelbert Humperdinck; 'I Pretend' went to No 1 the following year, recorded by Des O'Connor; and 'Love Grows Where My Rosemary Goes', that also went to No 1 in 1970. Les had also written 'Delilah' and 'It's Not Unusual', that did so well for Tom Jones.

It is with great sadness that Les passed away this year. It's an old saying that as you get older, the fewer christenings and the more funerals you attend. Recently, Sue and I have lost some very good friends: Michael Black, who sponsored me in becoming a member of the Grand Order of Water Rats, and brother of award-winning songwriter Don Black; and legendary World Cup-winning goalkeeper, Gordon Banks, who I played golf with many times.

'Turn Around' was much more my kind of song than 'Life's Too Good to Waste'. It was a proper ballad and a proper singer's song. I was at home with it. It failed to chart, but that wasn't anything to do with quality. As sometimes happened in the '60s, two artists had the same release at the same time and Kathy Kirby and I must have split the sales and effectively cancelled each other out of gathering a hit. I received most of the radio airplay, while Kathy was a star of TV and got all the screen time. Either way, it didn't provide me with chart success, but we were getting somewhere this time, as I was getting airplay.

Tommy encouraged me to do more writing as he thought I had a talent for it. I'd go into Francis, Day and Hunter in Charing Cross Road with Tommy, where Les Reed had an office, and remember saying, but I'm not a writer, I'm a singer. Tommy used to tell me that the writing would keep paying when I wasn't singing. As usual, I reminded myself that I was clearly not the sharpest knife in the drawer. Anyhow, I have written quite a lot of songs and once again I wrote the B side, 'When Will I Ever Love Again', so I was learning.

Sue and I decided very quickly that we would love to get married and we were all set in our own minds to get married in November 1967. My dad was a bit concerned that it was all maybe like a whirlwind and put us off from getting married too soon. He said, 'Tony, you don't just marry a girl because she's got great legs.' Well she did and still does have great legs, but what I thought was, why are you looking at my girlfriend's legs? Anyway, we at least took notice of what he'd said, because we'd said that we would leave the wedding to Easter 1968. But we had a good Christmas, if you know what I mean, and that led to us bringing it forward to February.

CHAPTER 6

Sean enters our lives September 2, 1968
and Des O'Connor gives me my first TV appearance

1968 proved to be my most challenging year so far. Life was no longer just about me anymore. I had Sue to think about and we had a baby on the way, our wedding and trying to afford somewhere to live — and at a time when all I had coming in was promises of a future in the music business and a £25-a-week retainer from Tommy, which was by no means enough and occasionally his cheque turned out to be made of rubber. I know he was trying his best, but it just wasn't stacking up right for me at the time. He was putting me up in his place too, so I knew he was trying to help.

I wasn't playing with the band and the only regular work I was getting was the radio broadcasts. I never saw anything from the radio work and Tommy just kept saying it's going to happen. He'd tell me about meetings here or there, but nothing materialised moneywise.

The money might not have been coming in, but the recording continued and my next MGM release, another 45rpm vinyl single, was 'I Don't Want to Hurt You Anymore', arranged and conducted by Tommy and written by me. I wrote the B side too, called 'Say No More'. For someone who didn't regard himself as a writer initially, I'd now written as many songs as I'd recorded of others, but this was the first one where my writing got top billing. It was released in March 1968, just after Sue and I were married and maybe the kindest words that can be said about its success would be that I was somewhat consumed with our wedding to notice it hadn't done anything.

On the positive side, 'I Don't Want to Hurt You Anymore' was to be recorded by a Canadian singer/actor called Robert Goulet, who had appeared as Lancelot in the original Broadway version of *Camelot* and many other stage musicals, as well as a TV adaptation of *Carousel*. He'd had a number of US adult contemporary chart hits and 'I Don't Want to Hurt You Anymore' was used on the flip side of his single 'What a Wonderful World'. It didn't earn me anything except the pride in having one of my own songs sung by someone else. Not bad for a lad living in a flat in Hillsborough.

I understood being in London could be important and was still committed to making things work down there. I thought it might be best if we were to live in the capital permanently, so not long after Sue and I married we began looking for an apartment in Richmond. Sue was about three and a half months pregnant when we stayed a night in a nice little apartment in the basement of a lady's house in London. Sue had caught chickenpox from her younger siblings and found herself getting really hot and uncomfortable. Carrying our first child, being in an unfamiliar place far from home and family, and feeling scared, we went back home.

We hadn't told anyone about Sue being pregnant, as it was still relatively early into the pregnancy and like many couples we'd wanted to keep it to ourselves at first, at least until a certain time, but her dad already knew through her family doctor. These were the days when realism, values and common sense came before being politically correct and her parents' doctor had slipped my father-in-law the word on the quiet because he was worried about her and was a long-time family friend, so when Sue had told him she wasn't well, he'd immediately said for us to come back.

Living in London permanently was over before it had begun. I had no problem with it. I was more concerned with Sue being okay. I was also grateful for both sets of parents for helping us out.

I wanted to be able to provide for us now as a family and because I was releasing records and with Tommy always so positive I continued going down to London to stay over with him, but I was starting to get fed up with it all. The way I looked at it, I was married and wasn't able to look after my wife and our impending arrival.

We had absolutely no money behind us. For the first three months of our married life, we will both be eternally grateful to Sue's sister Angela and husband Keith, who let us live with them before we moved into an apartment — or a flat, if we're being accurate — on Regent's Court, off Penistone Road near the Owlerton greyhound stadium in Hillsborough where we stayed until 1971.

By far the most significant event that occurred for Sue and I in 1968 was the birth of our son Sean on September 2. After the fright Sue and I had both had when she had been feeling poorly down in London, it was for us, like it is for every parent, a wonderful time. To have Sean working with me as my manager today, and having had him drum in my band when he was a teenager, have been proud moments. I'm proud of all our family, from our own children to their spouses and our grandchildren. Family times are always special.

My last MGM recording was released in October 1968, the month after Sean was born, and I guess was quite fitting in a couple of ways. It was 'My Prayer' that The Platters had a big hit with in the '50s. It was a song I'd probably suggested, as it had been a showstopper that I had sung many times with The Trackers, along with 'So Deep Is the Night' and 'Jezebel', which of all the big songs I did at the time I've never actually recorded.

'My Prayer' was produced by Tommy, but was arranged by Johnnie Spence, who went on to be musical director for Tom Jones in Vegas. He was one of the most respected arrangers and conductors in the business, but it appeared I couldn't even buy a hit. It received no promotion and sank without trace. The B side once again was one of my songs, 'I Need You'. Ironically, 'My Prayer' was a hit in the charts again two years later, not for me but for Gerry Monroe from the North East, who had been spotted by Les Reed on Hughie Green's show, *Opportunity Knocks*. Gerry had a Top 10 hit with it in 1970.

Sue and I faced up to some serious problems on the money front in 1968, not least as I'd just been signed up to play across the Bailey Organisation's network through Myrna Malinsky. Tommy had told me I had to say I couldn't honour it. I was never told exactly why, but as

I was to find in the world of professional music, doubtless like many more before and since, whether recording or performing, it is the managers, agents and big companies who always seem to have control.

I kept receiving letters from the Bailey Organisation, threatening to sue me for having not kept to their contract. All this time, Tommy told us not to worry, he was handling matters with the Bailey Organisation through Francis, Day and Hunter, but the letters kept on coming.

One day, we came home to find a notice through the door saying I hadn't turned up for some hearing or other and, as a result, we owed The Bailey Organisation thousands of pounds, plus court charges. We'd only just had yet more help from Sue's dad. I was seriously stressed out by it all.

It was Sue's dad who finally brought me to my senses. He'd been really supportive of my career and still was, but he said, 'This is no good, you're depressed, you're living on promises and you're not working. You'd be best getting your band back together.'

I knew he was right and that's exactly what I did. I had that one last record out on MGM, but otherwise I was back on the road, doing what I've always loved, singing for audiences and bringing in the money. Suddenly I was smiling again, with a beautiful girl as my wife, a newborn son and looking forward to standing on my own two feet moneywise. I'd had some records out and I'd been listened to on the radio, but that's as far as anything had gone for me with Tommy Sanderson. We were broke.

The Trackers never came back, but my good mate Mike (Ryal) was on bass, Johnny Cadwell from Maltby was on keyboards, and on drums we had a fabulous drummer who emigrated to Australia, who once again I'm afraid my memory fails me. My real apologies.

We became Tony Christie and The Penmen. My only regret in getting the book together at this time, particularly for this era of The Trackers and The Penmen, is that Mike is no longer here to help me. He'd have given far more detail for both bands.

It was good to be back out on the road again and we were soon playing everywhere on the working men's club and cabaret circuits, including famous venues of the time that included La Dolce Vita and Night Out in Birmingham. La Dolce Vita had been opened by TV and film star of the time Lance Percival in 1967 and was attracting big names like The Alan Price Set. Around Greater Manchester there were that many working men's clubs, cabaret bars and nightclubs and you could play 52 weeks a year and never play the same place twice. We won the Show Band of the Year title two years running at awards held in the Winter Gardens in Blackpool in 1969 and 1970.

I'm indebted to a post that came on Facebook in the past few years, that showed a bill poster promoting our gig of Sunday 2 February 1969 at Greasborough Social Club, when top billing went to 'the famous TV and radio band The Pedlars'. It's a shame that it wasn't spelled properly as The Peddlers, but there you go. We were next on the bill and I was affectionately titled as 'Yorkshire's Sensational Singing Star' as Tony Christie and The Penmen. To give you an accurate feel for just how full of entertainment these nights were, on the bill were also, 'delightful singing star' Susan Richards; 'appeared on TV with Mike and Bernie Winters', comedian John Paul Jones; and international acrobats The Memares. You can imagine what it was like in the dressing rooms on nights like that.

We played The Wooky Hollow nightclub in Liverpool, where we had a sax player purely known as Lenni with us. I was only reminded of this through the research as Dave Irving, drummer with Sad Café, was at the time playing the same club with a band called Sinbad and that's how Lenni got to play with Sad Café later on.

There was our Dustin Gee moment in Sunderland in the '60s, that could have been with The Trackers or The Penmen. We were staying at Mrs Naseby's place called White Lodge near Roker Beach, where all the acts were put up during their week-long residencies in the clubs. We were all bored during the day and Dustin had this idea of making a giant balloon out of tissue paper, drinking straws and birthday cake candles to produce our own version of a hot air balloon.

It was a night when we were not working. We started it one day and set it off at teatime before our gig the next day. By the time we'd constructed it, the balloon was nearly as large as a small room. We lit all the candles, the kind of little ones you put on birthday cakes, and it looked great. It went quite high and we were all so excited, but then it caught fire and suddenly went whoof! The next day, the *Sunderland Echo* reported the sighting of a UFO on Roker Beach. God bless Dustin. That was the end of our career as balloon engineers.

I also had a much bigger problem in 1969, about six months after Sean had been born, that could have proved the end of any singing ambitions I had. I was working hard, often seven days a week, and often more than one show a day, when I lost my voice. It was a bigger problem than cheques bouncing. At least I'd moved on from that. This was probably one of my worst nightmares. I'd never even thought about not being able to sing.

I'd lost my voice when we'd had to go to Wales with no windscreen, but this was much more serious. I went to see a specialist.

Now, what I haven't told you so far is that by now I was a smoker. I didn't start smoking until I was with The Trackers and my only excuse is that we were playing working men's clubs and when we were in a dressing room between three spots a night we would sit around playing cards, and with the others in the band smoking I eventually joined them. I was smoking when I met Sue — and they were full strength cigarettes, no filter tips.

I went to Harley Street in London and it didn't take long for the consultant, Doctor Chakravati, to diagnose what was happening given that information. I'd damaged my vocal chords and his advice was very simple. He said, did I want to carry on smoking, or did I want to be a singer. So far as I was concerned, singing was what I was put on this earth to do, not smoke. I came out of his practice and still had a packet of Benson & Hedges in my pocket. I'd had one earlier. I gave the rest to the first person who I could see was a smoker on coming out of the consultation.

My first TV break came by chance, but if I hadn't been back on the road singing with The Penmen it wouldn't have happened. Once again, Sue's dad John was responsible for that as I was back playing live.

It was Des O'Connor who gave me just the opportunity and I will always be grateful to him. Des was playing Buttons in the pantomime *Cinderella* at The Birmingham Hippodrome with Jack Douglas from the *Carry On* films, at the same time I was playing at the Baileys Nightclub with The Penmen, which was opposite the theatre. Des had seen us playing after he'd finished for the night.

He came backstage to meet me and said that he wanted to put me on his TV show. It was huge and on a primetime slot on Saturday night. It was probably the biggest show on at the time. I gave him my telephone number, thinking, like you do, that he would never call. But he did and I got my first TV show appearance at the Palladium in *Des O'Connor On Stage* on Saturday 10 May 1969. Mary Hopkin was also on the show. She'd had a massive No 1 with 'Those Were the Days' the previous year. It was terrifying. I sang one song on my own and another with Des. I couldn't afford a new suit for the show, we were so hard up, but it went well and put me in front of millions for the first time.

It wasn't long before I was approached by the man who set me on my way to meet great songwriters, achieve my first chart success, TV shows like *Top of the Pops*, touring throughout the world and No 1 hits, but let's not get carried away just yet. There were plenty more working men's clubs and nightclubs to play, regardless of how generous Des O'Connor had been in giving me my first break. Thanks again, Des!

CHAPTER 7

Harvey Lisberg enters with Mitch Murray
and Peter Callander — circa 1969-1970

We might have been penniless during the Tommy Sanderson era, but at least he'd put me in the right places. I'd now become a record maker, although without a hit, and I'd been on national radio through singing with his band on *Night Ride*. I'd also been to London and experienced what it was like to be around music publishers and in recording studios.

The next man to tell me the same as Tommy had done was the man who actually turned those dreams into possibilities, Harvey Lisberg, who had come to see us at the Winter Gardens in Blackpool in 1970 when we were playing the Clubland Command Performance.

Harvey came backstage and introduced himself, saying that he looked after Peter Noone and Herman's Hermits, who'd had big hits with songs like 'No Milk Today', written by Graham Gouldman. They were also big in the United States. He was also managing Graham and went on to manage 10cc and other bands, Sad Café and Barclay James Harvest. He and another man, who became a great personal friend, Danny Betesh, had joined forces in the '60s and were part owners of Kennedy Street Enterprises in Manchester. They specialise in concert and tour promotion. Harvey had a great track record and I went with him.

Around the end of the Tommy Sanderson era, and the early part of the Harvey Lisberg period, I had not been in a good place. I knew we needed the money. I had been on the verge of quitting the music business completely. Maybe I was never going to quit, but the thoughts were going through my head. Perhaps it was time to quit trying to be

Adam Faith and get a proper job.

There were times, because my band were on a retainer, when I wasn't making enough to pay myself anything once I'd paid them, and sometimes I had to wait until the next gig to make up their wages.

After a gig in the Manchester area, I'd sometimes stay over with a lovely couple, Tommy and Daisy Caldwell, rather than drive over Snake Pass back to Sheffield. They were big fans and from travelling showmen families. Tommy had bingo halls all over the place and he knew I was feeling down. The Bailey Organisation and then the subsequent court case result had really affected me and I was considering anything.

Tommy was fantastic. He listened to me and knowing how I was feeling, he offered to set me up running a bingo hall near Hillsborough in Sheffield, so that I could have some kind of regular income while also carrying on singing. I could have ended up in this business, but decided it wasn't for me. It was good of Tommy to offer.

Harvey organised everything and set me on the road, if not to Amarillo at the time, then definitely the right way to success in this industry that requires a lot of luck combined with a lot of talent, although sometimes today you do wonder whether that's a necessity when you see all these reality series.

If the 1960s had been my apprenticeship, the early part of the 1970s were to be that time when you move from an apprentice's wage to a proper salary. Well it turned out to be far more than that and beyond our wildest dreams. In some ways, looking back, we thought we had won the lottery after having struggled so much for what now seems such a short time in comparison. It didn't feel that way when we had nothing.

1970 provided the impetus for what was to happen in 1971, when my world went crazy, and it was all down to being with Harvey, Danny and Kennedy Street, and of course the prelude to it all with everyone who had been with me along the '60s journey, from Dave and our Grant Brothers act to The Counterbeats, The Trackers and The Penmen. Without any of them, I wouldn't have been able to achieve the success I've enjoyed and keep enjoying today. And Sue, of course, who has been with me every step of the way.

That first year under Harvey's guidance, I performed at two international song festivals on the continent in Belgium (1970) and Yugoslavia (1971); Harvey secured me a record deal with MCA Records; introduced me to the amazing songwriting hitmakers, Mitch Murray and Peter Callander; and I had another flop! I told you it wasn't all straightforward.

Mitch and Peter became my record producers. Peter had been a record plugger before having success as a songwriter and would travel everywhere. Mitch's first big songwriting success had been 'How Do You Do It?' that George Martin wanted The Beatles to record as their debut single, but Gerry and The Pacemakers released it instead, getting to No 1, and they followed up with another of Mitch's, 'I Like It'. Mitch and Peter had hits together for The Tremeloes, Georgie Fame, Cliff Richard and several others. In an interview with *The Times*, I described them as 'the star songwriters of the day', and having them writing songs for me launched my chart career, but as usual not straight away.

Signing with Kennedy Street and Harvey was bringing new experiences all the time and I was now appearing and competing in international song festivals. In 1970, I took part in a song contest in a town called Knokke, a north-eastern seaside resort close to the border with Holland, where I came second to Julio Iglesias. I can't recall the song, although I'm sure it was a Mitch and Peter composition, and Peter and his wife Connie went with us to Knokke where I was representing England.

There used to be a lot of international song festivals and it was another way of getting known. Julio represented Spain that same year in the Eurovision Song Contest, coming in fourth with his song 'Gwendolyne', when Dana won. Hughie Green was there, no doubt talent spotting for *Opportunity Knocks*, while also watching an act that had already appeared on his show. Knokke looked a very rich place and was a popular resort for people in Brussels.

The competition in Knokke lasted a week and was held at the casino on the seafront. Like a lot of song festivals, it had its time and finished a few years later. I was in good company — Engelbert Humperdinck, Matt Monro and Kathy Kirby had all competed previously and Engelbert had won in 1966.

John Wells of the *New Musical Express*, who wrote a fantastic article that appeared on the sleeve of my first LP, said:

'It was as a professional that I first met him (Tony Christie). He was representing Britain at last year's international song contest at Knokke, Belgium and scored a tremendous personal success both for his sense of comedy during the exhausting rehearsals when he kept all the competitors' spirits up, and during his act when he put across a powerfully dramatic performance. And none of us there will ever forget the incredible 'off the cuff' community singing sessions which he led in a local nightclub after the evenings' sessions.'

All I can say John is wow! Those were good times.

June 1970 saw my first MCA release with one of Mitch and Peter's songs, 'God Is On My Side', and all I can say is God wasn't, so far as chart success and radio airplay were concerned. It seemed the strangest of choices. Not really my kind of song at all. I asked Peter what it was all about, and he said it was an anti-war song with both sides believing that God was on their side. I just felt it was a bit of a downer. It wasn't how I'd expected my new recording career to get started.

It was nothing like Mitch and Peter's hit-making machine that had been so successful. Maybe they were looking for something different. It was arranged by Lew Warburton, who was also a conductor and musical director of great repute, and the B side was 'A Thing Called Love', written by Jerry Reed, that later became a Top 10 hit for Johnny Cash.

If I'd been concerned about how a song like 'God Is On My Side' might affect my standing with those who would listen to it, I needn't have worried, as it was banned by the BBC. I can't tell you for definite why, but the Vietnam conflict may have been part of it, as well as the troubles in Northern Ireland. In Belgium, it was released with a different B side, 'Smile a Little Smile', written by Tony Macaulay and Geoff Stephens. It had been a big hit for a British band called The Flying Machine the year previously in the Billboard charts in the US.

My first single on MCA Records might not have been a hit, but the money was at least looking good from the deal Harvey had struck. For the first time in my working life, we had money in the bank, as he had signed what for me was stuff people can only dream of happening to them. I was on an advance that covered the next three years.

The only problem in retrospect was that for some reason I'd been signed to an American contract and that meant anything that was a hit other than in America was only half of the royalties. Since nearly every record I sold was outside of America, that signing cost me a considerable amount over many years.

At the time, I was a singer who just wanted to get on, and like nearly everyone around in those days, I was happy to get a recording contract and guaranteed income. Obviously, the record company knew what they were doing, as they always do.

Having the money coming our way also allowed us to look at moving out of our flat/apartment. We moved the next year. By the autumn of 1970, I was back in the studio working on what would become my first hit song.

This time, the boys — Mitch and Peter — had come up with a winner and I knew it. But I changed their intro — not the words, just the feel.

Song interpretation is my thing, as the title of this book says, that's what I do. When I'm presented with a song, I find my own way of expressing it. That's what my input was to 'Las Vegas' that launched my chart career in 1971 and which I recorded in October 1970.

What I did was to put more soul into it, more fire. It gave it the dramatic start that I felt had been missing from the demo tape.

That's why 'The Lord above made the world for us, but the devil made Las Vegas', has that gospel sounding opener.

Clem Cattini was the drummer on the recording and had played on hundreds of top recordings, including mine. It was recorded at

Chappell Music's studio in New Bond Street, London and was a hit in Belgium in 1970 before it became a hit in the UK. Maybe the Knokke Song Festival had helped as it had been broadcast on TV over there too.

Autumn 1970 must have been a time of even greater celebration too, because the following year it wasn't just hit songs, new LP, TV appearances all around the world, tours, song festivals, new home, new car and an all-round crazy time — it was also a fabulous family time once again with our next arrival!

CHAPTER 8

The UK charts, worldwide hits and
a beautiful girl called Antonia

As far as exciting times go, 1971 must rate as probably the craziest. I was still only 27 at the start of the year and the world was about to open up to me. Everything I'd gone through and that Sue and I had experienced so far was about to change forever — and it started in January when 'Las Vegas' made the charts in the UK.

In those days, unless you were The Beatles, nobody went straight into the charts at No 1, as they do regularly today. Record-buying of singles was a massive business and you had to sell significant numbers to get into the charts at all. 'Las Vegas' was what they call in the trade a slow burner.

I was new. My fame was limited to the clubland scene up until this point. I wasn't known in the south of England and the only real airplay I'd had was limited to insomniacs or night-shift workers and wasn't new material. 'Las Vegas' charted January 1971.

Mitch and Peter had given me a song that felt like a hit when I'd recorded it and it was fantastic to sing. It had given me the opportunity to use the power in my voice, it was new and that meant it was my song.

I was with a record company and promotional team that had proper pluggers. It climbed the charts to No 38 the second week, then 33 the third week and 23 in week 4 on 24 January. George Harrison was by now the No 1 with 'My Sweet Lord', another song I've always loved singing, and Andy Williams was in the charts with another favourite of mine, 'Home Loving Man'. I recorded both for my first ever studio album that was released later in the year.

When 'Las Vegas' stalled in week 5, going down three places to No 26, it seemed as though that was going to be as good as it was going to get. It had been a fabulous adventure. The song was getting played regularly on the radio across all stations, whether BBC Radio 1 or 2 or Radio Luxembourg, Radio Caroline — the big stations of the day — and everything was looking good.

The big TV programme to get on to was *Top of the Pops* and I made my debut on the programme that aired on 4 February. On the show were Elton John, who was in the charts with 'Your Song', Cliff Richard, The Supremes and The Tremeloes, who I used to see regularly on the circuit. An appearance on the chart show was the Holy Grail to success and always caused a lift in sales. I can't tell you what it did to the number of copies bought in the next few days, but when the chart came out for 7 February it was at No 21 and stayed in the charts for another three weeks afterwards.

'Las Vegas' didn't just do well in the UK. It was in the charts throughout the world, launching me in Australia, New Zealand and South Africa, where it reached even higher. It charted in Holland and Germany and all around Europe. My TV shows weren't limited to the UK either. Suddenly I was flying everywhere. Germany, Austria, Switzerland, Belgium and Holland have always been particularly good to me and I was flown over by the record company or the TV show to sing it on so many shows.

The B side changed dependent on which country it was released. Largely, it had been one of my big stage show songs, 'So Deep Is the Night', that was written by Chopin, but in some it was a song called 'Let Me Be Turned to Stone', also written by Mitch and Peter.

Having regular radio airplay and TV appearances shot everything through the roof and the offers of work started coming in from everywhere. It was phenomenal what just one hit song could do.

I was now playing the cabaret and nightclub circuit, performing six nights a week at the same venue in cabaret, whether in London, Birmingham, Manchester, Newcastle or Glasgow, but there was one element of it all that was a little uncomfortable.

Harvey had said I should forget the band, that I was no longer Tony Christie and The Penmen and that I was now a solo act and a chart act appearing on TV and in demand.

His words were that I wasn't a group singer. I should have a bigger band, which became a 10-piece with a horn section that included French horns, trumpets and trombones, as I liked that big band sound, but the band wouldn't be billed as anything other than my band and needed players who would go anywhere, anytime, because that's what professional session musicians do. And all of this was on the strength of 'Las Vegas'.

I carried on for a while with The Penmen. We were friends and we had existing bookings on the clubland circuit that we honoured at the agreed rates, so I was working for old money for a while. But I was also being booked all over the place by now on serious money and needed session guys who could come in and do a job anywhere in the world and it just wouldn't have been feasible with The Penmen. Mike was always great about it all. He knew how things worked and he was never out of work himself throughout his wonderful career.

Sue, Sean, 'the bump' and I moved into our first house, a nice three-bedroomed detached, about three years old with a car port, in Norton Lees in Sheffield, not long before our impending arrival. It cost £5,750 and because we hadn't any history with a bank, Sue's dad John (Ashley) signed as guarantor to help us out getting our first mortgage.

John was a good businessman and together with Sue's mum, Irene, they made a great team. He also told Harvey he wanted 1 per cent of Tony Christie. He was shrewd.

The advance Harvey had struck was serious money and, combined with the accumulation of live work and TV appearances, the figures were starting to stack up, but Sue's dad wasn't one for letting me get carried away. Harvey was surprised we'd only bought what he felt was a small house, but to us it was far more than we'd ever had before, and after the flat it was a palace.

We had a journalist come over from Germany, not long after we had moved in, who described me as 'living in this modest little house'.

I think he'd anticipated something much larger for someone who was in the charts and on television. If he'd come a month or two before, heaven help what he'd have written about our flat.

If we'd felt elated about how well 'Las Vegas' had done and what it had brought about, it was nothing compared to my second chart success. It all started when these two amazing men, Mitch and Peter, caught a train to come and see me, full of themselves that they had my next hit in the bag.

Strawberry Studios in Stockport near Manchester has legendary status in the world of pop music, with 10cc, Neil Sedaka, Paul McCartney and a host of other big names recorded there. Harvey had Graham Gouldman in his songwriting stable and he had joined Eric Stewart as a partner in the studio. They went on with Kevin Godley and Lol Creme to create 10cc.

The studio's name had come in honour of The Beatles' 'Strawberry Fields Forever'. I was recording songs there as demos for my first LP, when Mitch and Peter came in with this little cassette player. They'd caught the train to play me this song because they'd just written it, wanted me to hear it and get it recorded as a follow-up to 'Las Vegas' as quickly as I could. 'We want you to record it because we've written it for you and we think it's got hit written all over it,' they said.

My musicians were all classy, jazz musos, who played things absolutely spot on and weren't into pop music — and to hear the cassette with Mitch on piano playing with three fingers and using one on bass, while going parp-parp for the trumpet and trombone sounds with his mouth, I could see they were smirking as musos do, but I just knew it was a smash, a massive hit, and that's how 'I Did What I Did for Maria' came about. The rest of the guys in the studio were thinking, 'Really?!' But I just knew. It was a great hook, a fantastic song which allowed me once again to tell the story with terrific feeling.

Mitch and Peter booked a three-hour session at Chappell Studios in London for as soon as I had a day available. It was recorded on a four-track mix with the choir, orchestra and band all mixed on three tracks leaving one clean track for me. Lew Warburton was arranger again and gave it that great sound. The boys were just so finicky about everything. If I changed one note, Mitch would say, 'Can you do that again, to the tune I wrote?' and Peter would say, 'I can't hear the lyric properly, try and make that lyric stand out again.'

After about 20 takes, my voice started getting hoarse and I was becoming concerned about it as I had a show that night. I was working a week in cabaret in Manchester, had come down on the train in the morning and was due back on stage at 10pm. They said, 'That's the sound.'

I think they used to make me sing and sing until my voice had that huskiness, they loved that. They also wanted my voice as powerful as possible and always, of course, on the money. I remember telling them, when I'd achieved what they wanted, 'Yes, and I've got to work tonight.'

'I Did What I Did for Maria' was released in April with another Mitch and Peter song on the B side, 'Give Me Your Love Again', which had its own life played as a Northern Soul record at places like the iconic Wigan Casino, The Twisted Wheel in Manchester, Mojo Club in Sheffield, Blackpool Mecca, Winter Gardens in Cleethorpes and The Golden Torch in Stoke-on-Trent.

I was to revisit the Northern Soul scene again in more recent times with my album *Now's the Time!* But let's get back to 'I Did What I Did for Maria'.

This time it wasn't so much of a slow burner, but it still took a few weeks before it gave me my first Top 10 hit. In June, it reached No 2 in the official chart, and in some other UK charts it was my first No 1, but again it was another worldwide hit and went Top 10 in at least six countries. It was relentless at the time. The phone was now constantly ringing, offering me work, and I wasn't turning any of it down. When you've been as poor as we had been, you take the work wherever it comes — and now it was also coming as serious money.

It first hit the charts on 2 May when it came in at No 47, but then it made 34, 24 and 17 in the following weeks at a time when 'Knock Three Times' by Tony Orlando and Dawn was holding down the No 1 spot. Once you were a new entry on the Top 20, you were pretty much guaranteed an appearance on *Top of the Pops* and mine came that week.

I didn't appear in the studio this time, it was a promo clip, and others who appeared were Neil Diamond, Stevie Wonder, the Hollies, Peter Noone, another of Harvey's acts, and the other Christie — Lou, from the US. I was either performing for a European TV station at the time, as it was simultaneously hitting the charts all around the world, or was at home because Sue was close to giving birth.

Promotional videos were just starting around at that time and I filmed one as a cowboy. I remember walking down the street on a set that might have been used for a Western movie. Maybe at Elstree Studios? And another take, where I was on a horse, but I'd never been on one apart from maybe a donkey on Skegness beach, let alone ridden one.

The cowboy clip was used for *Top of the Pops* on 27 May and again on *The Golden Shot* hosted by Bob Monkhouse with Anne Aston on 30 May. I know this because Sue was in hospital watching the video, having gone into false labour just a couple of days before our life was to be transformed once again with a baby girl. Sue remembers watching it in hospital and saying that it looked like I was really hanging on to the reins in fear for my life! She wasn't wrong.

Those two TV appearances must have helped because when the chart was revealed, as it always was between 5pm while 7pm every Sunday, 'I Did What I Did for Maria' was No 8 — my first Top 10 hit. And the following week things were going to get better in all ways.

Antonia was born on 13 June. Sue says I was always ill when she was in labour, maybe it was just worry. We now had Sean at just over 2 years 9 months old and our beautiful daughter. I couldn't have been happier. A fabulous family, new house, a second worldwide chart hit and more work than I could ever have dreamed. Putting all that to one side though, 13 June was a very special day for all of us. Sue and I were thrilled.

The previous week's chart had seen me move into the Top 10,

probably aided by my *Top of the Pops* appearance on 27 May, but my *Golden Shot* appearance hadn't been until around 4.40pm on Sunday 30 May, by which time there had been no time for people to go out and buy the record to count for that week's chart, and the shops were also all shut on a Sunday. This meant all the sales that were generated as a result of my first national TV show appearance other than *Top of the Pops* would count towards the following week's chart on Sunday 6 June.

The Golden Shot was massively popular and regularly pulled in around 16 million viewers at that time, even more than *Top of the Pops* and arguably more my audience. The combined effect, of appearing on them both and another week of sales since I was on screen, propelled me from No 8 to No 2 that same Sunday 30 May, with just *Knock Three Times* left in front of me.

They talk a lot about tweets and twitters today. Well, what stopped 'I Did What I Did for Maria' from getting to No 1 was more of a different kind of bird sound. Typical, really, that I should be denied by noises the creatures I care about so much make, but it was Middle of the Road's 'Chirpy Chirpy Cheep Cheep' that took over from Tony Orlando and Dawn at the top. The following week I was beneath both songs at No 3. Middle of the Road had reached the Top 20 in the week I'd made No 2, getting them on *Top of the Pops* and from there they zoomed up to No 1. I got back to No 2 the following week as 'Knock Three Times' went down the chart — and then I stayed in the Top 10 a further two weeks at No 6 and No 7.

But hold on just one second, because, as well as the official chart, there were also other charts and I made No 1 in the UK in both the *NME* and the *Sunday Mirror*. I received a telephone call while working at Wooky Hollow in Liverpool telling me the record had gone to No 1.

The celebrations started and I didn't get back home until 8 o'clock the next morning, when my sound man dropped me at home where Sue's mum was waiting to tell me Sue had been taken to Nether Edge maternity hospital. The paparazzi were outside when I got there and were asking if it was a girl, were we going to call her Maria. We called her Antonia Maria.

We'd added to our family with a gorgeous baby girl and I'd made it to the top of the charts. Life couldn't be any better and Yorkshire's national newspaper, the *Yorkshire Post*, reported my chart success like this:

"I Did What I Did for Maria' has now sold more than 500,000 copies. It is No 1 in the British Hit Parade and South Africa. It's also in the charts in Switzerland, Belgium, Germany, Holland and consolidates the breakthrough Christie made in January with 'Vegas' after 10 years of slogging around less glamorous clubs of Yorkshire, the North East and Wales. The former wages clerk of Conisbrough is appreciative and pleased, yes, but says he doesn't feel like dancing through the streets. He has a touch of the Joe Lampton's (Room at the Top) about him, a singer who is at least finding room at the top in show business. He's a seasoned professional rather than a pop butterfly. He says: 'The big difference 'Maria' will make is in the single date engagements, 14 shows a week, finishing the night wet through and dashing out into the cold night air to move on to the next venue. Only four weeks ago I was playing two dance halls a night in Ireland, some 80 miles apart. When that was over and 'Maria' became a hit I hoped that was the last of that kind of thing.' Tony went on to say: 'I'm a singer of standards rather than a raver', and says he admires Tony Bennett.

'I don't want all this adulation from screaming girls and middle aged women. It's not for real. When you're a sexy superstar you're watching the lines of your face and smallness of your hips, that's not for me.' Christie says his next single will be his most important and could clinch his success. 'It will probably be another Mitch Murray and Peter Callendar song,' he said. This week he's topping the bill at Batley Variety Club.'

I'd had a fantastic run in the official chart. Two weeks at No 2, six weeks in the Top 10, nine weeks in the Top 20 and 17 weeks consecutively in the Top 50 from 2 May to 22 August. I'd even had a brush with fame! I appeared on the *Basil Brush Show* with Basil and 'Mr Derek' actor Derek Fowlds on 11 July, which may have gone down well with Sean at the time and certainly wouldn't have done the record any harm, as we stayed at No 18 on the strength of it for a second week.

It had become my first No 1 in the UK and New Zealand, No 2 in South Africa and Ireland, No 3 in Australia and Switzerland and No 4 in Germany.

There are plenty of videos of me singing 'I Did What I Did for Maria' available on YouTube, mostly in front of a TV audience, but there's one that has had over 2,600,000 views of me dressed in a red silk shirt from Brown's Boutique in London. It cost me 90 quid. A lot of money in 1971. I'd never paid anything like that before, and since we were only just earning the money, both Sue and I had our sensible heads on, but this was a big song and it deserved the best we could give it.

The video has proven even more popular than the record and is me with permed hair wearing the said red silk shirt with yellow trousers. We'd also bought a brown fringed jacket that I wore with a darker brown shirt and is shown on one of the other videos, but it is the one with the red shirt that gets all of the comments — and they're not because of the shirt.

The brown fringed jacket and brown shirt made their appearance on a European TV show with what is meant to look like some gallows in the background ready for my execution, as the story unfolds in the song with the words, 'Sunrise, this is the last day I'll ever see', and a chap with a Spanish looking hat, maybe it was for a Spanish TV company, ready as executioner.

At the end of June, I was also back on with my second major song festival work, this time in Split, a city of Yugoslavia that is today Croatia's second largest. It was a beautiful city, again another seaside resort, but this time on the much warmer Adriatic Sea.

The Split '71 International Festival of Pop Music took place from 30 June to 3 July. The festival had been set up to include a Yugoslavian section and a European section. In the Yugoslavian song class, there would be 18 songs all sung in their native language and by Yugoslavian singers, but then also sung in English by international singers like me and on this occasion Vince Hill. He and I became great friends. It was a great contest for me as I was voted Best Singer at the Festival.

It was here I also sang 'Have You Ever Been to Georgia?' written by Graham Gouldman, that was a release by The Peddlers. I'd recorded it for my first LP that was due to be released that same month of July.

In the end, 'Lamento' came second in the contest and one writer reported that I looked a little disappointed. Well, you don't go all those miles not to win, do you? But it was a great song and personally I felt it was a lot better than the one that did win. 'Lamento' took the Silver Coat of Arms award. I enjoyed the song festivals as they were different from the other work I was doing, and they saw me travelling around the world and getting better known — and there were more to come.

By July 1971, I was becoming established as a singer with hits and, returning from Split, it was time for the launch of my first LP, that in the official charts is recorded as being titled *I Did What I Did for Maria*, but was actually never given a title other than my name. It featured 12 songs, including both the hits, and in all, six of Mitch and Peter's songs, including 'Walk Like a Panther', but not the one that provided me with another Top 10 hit in the '90s. There was even one of mine, 'What Do You Do'.

John Wells of the *NME* gave a tremendous write-up on the back sleeve. He wrote: *'If you live north of The Wash you'll know all about Tony Christie. He gets top billing playing the highly competitive night-club circuit and such is his popularity that it's more often than not to packed audiences. The Northerners have discovered him and know when they are on to a good thing! South of The Wash he's not yet been fully accepted and most know him mainly as the singer whose record 'Las Vegas' was latched on to by the more enterprising disc-jockeys and played non-stop on BBC radio. There were instant comparisons made between him and Tom Jones (which can't be bad) though to me he can out-sing all his British contemporaries and proves it on this album.'*

I don't know where you are now, John, but wherever you are, thank you!

The LP was released under the title *Las Vegas* in at least Germany and New Zealand with a different cover pic. It stayed in the charts in Australia for nine weeks.

I had bought a Ford Mustang like Steve McQueen drove in the film *Bullitt*, but I only had it two weeks because it was left-hand drive and for me to overtake anything, particularly lorries, would put Sue in danger.

CHAPTER 9

When the day was dawning in 1971

It was staggering, after six years of recording songs with no success to suddenly finding I was being played all around the world was a fabulous feeling. I was receiving phone calls as regular as clockwork telling me which countries 'I Did What I Did for Maria' had charted in lately. It all led to opening up even more different places to play and an Australia and New Zealand tour was in the process of being planned for later in the year. The only thing we didn't have was the follow-up single.

Mitch and Peter didn't have the next hit for me at the time, but Harvey was over in America, probably when 'I Did What I Did for Maria' was riding high over in the UK. He was in New York on business, looking for songs and he approached Don Kirshner of Aldon Music who was known as The Man with the Golden Ear because he had a stable of writers in the famed Brill Building in Manhattan that were all household names, such as Carole King, Gerry Goffin, Neil Diamond, Burt Bacharach, Hal David and Neil Sedaka.

Harvey was in search of a gem, a song that would continue the success I'd had and when Neil (Sedaka) played him 'Is This the Way to Amarillo?' Harvey knew he'd found my third consecutive hit, not just any hit, but it turned out, as we've all found out, to have almost supernatural powers coming back alive many years later, but always a perennial favourite.

Harvey had taken my recordings and played him 'Las Vegas' and 'I Did What I Did for Maria' and asked whether he had any he was working on or had finished that would suit me. Neil played him a few and the last song was 'Amarillo'. Harvey said, 'Why didn't you play that song first?' and Neil said, 'Because it's not finished, we can't think of the lyrics that will go in place of the Sha-La-La La-La-La-La-La section.' But Harvey said, 'That's the hit, the catchy part. It doesn't need anything else.'

To be absolutely accurate, 'Amarillo' was written by Neil Sedaka and his regular writing partner, Howard Greenfield. They'd written most of Neil's hit songs when he'd first burst on the scene, like 'Calendar Girl', 'Happy Birthday Sweet Sixteen' and 'Breaking Up Is Hard to Do', that reached No 1 in the Billboard chart.

When it had originally been written it was going to be called 'Is This the Way to Pensacola?' — a city in Florida. Neil also told me much later, when Sue and I saw him in concert at the Royal Albert Hall, that the tune to the first line, 'When the day is dawning', originally came from The Archies' hit song, 'Sugar Sugar'.

Neil is reported to have explained Harvey's visit and 'Amarillo' like this in an interview from 2009: 'It was originally a rough demo on cassette. Tony Christie's manager came to see me saying he had a new singer who sounded a bit like Tom Jones. I played him it and he liked it immediately.'

Harvey brought back two songs from Neil. The other was 'Solitaire'. I've always loved that song and it's still a favourite of mine today. I wanted 'Solitaire' as the follow-up to 'Amarillo', as I felt it would have been my fourth big hit in a row, but MCA wouldn't put it out, saying it was a ballad and that I was known for up tempo songs.

I put it on my next LP instead and then Andy Williams released it and took it to No 4 in the UK in 1974 and The Carpenters had a Top 20 Billboard hit with it in 1975. Ah well, you can't win them all, as they say, and 'Amarillo' has proved itself for me over and over again.

Mitch and Peter heard it as soon as Harvey came back from the States and said I had to drop whatever I was doing at the time and get into the studio before anybody else got hold of the song. They knew it was gold dust. They have written me many fantastic songs, but credit to them — they knew just how good this was.

Recording of 'Amarillo' took place in the familiar surroundings of

Chappell Music, once again with the same team of Lew Warburton arranging and the boys Mitch and Peter as producers — and the record was released on 15 October in the UK. We'd gone from doing what I did for Maria to Marie who waited for me. And for once this was not a song about death, the devil, gambling and retribution. It really was exactly what it still is now, probably the ultimate feel-good song.

But first time around in the UK, it didn't perform as well as in the rest of Europe, Australia and New Zealand. In Germany, Sweden and Denmark it went to No 1 and the following year went to No 1 for two weeks in June in Spain. In Australia, it reached No 10, South Africa No 6 and in New Zealand No 2, just beaten to the top spot by John Lennon with 'Imagine'. If I was going to lose out to anyone, then you couldn't get better than The Beatles. I played a medley of their hits with my band at the V Festival after 'Amarillo' had its resurgence in 2005 and we often played Beatles songs with The Trackers and The Penmen.

You could hear 'Amarillo' being played everywhere. I was flying around doing TV in between my cabaret circuit venues and once again I was back on *Top of the Pops*. This time, I was sporting some large shades for my appearance. It wasn't that I had changed my image. My baby Antonia had caught me across the eye with her fingernail, causing a bleed and it was really red and sore. It was suggested that I wore dark glasses to hide it. One of the film crew loaned me his.

It wasn't as big a UK hit as 'Maria' because it was the summer hit in Spain and this was the time of the British tourist invasion over there due to cheaper flights and accommodation. I was on *Top of the Pops* twice and a third time when it was used as the chart rundown song. The record peaked at No 18.

You can still see and hear the *Top of the Pops* performance thanks to YouTube, but if it flummoxes you a bit, it's because the same was used on Germany's equivalent pop music show called *Disco* with Ilja Richter presenting the show. The video is what is sometimes now called a mash-up of the two shows, so that it looks like I'm performing for the German audience. One of the other giveaways is that the *Top of the Pops* backing singers, The Ladybirds, are featured in the foreground.

In retrospect, 'Amarillo' performed very well in the UK because it stayed in the charts for all of the last three weeks before Christmas and the one afterwards and these were the biggest buying weeks of the year for records, as people who wouldn't normally buy during the rest of the year went out and bought for everyone and everybody.

The Book of Golden Discs, that catalogued all the records that had sold a million, recorded 'Is This the Way to Amarillo?' having reached that figure and the gold disc being awarded. It records the record being No 1 in Germany, Spain, Austria, Belgium, Switzerland and Sweden and Top 20 in six other countries.

I had an absolutely fantastic band with me wherever I played. Mike was on bass and Dave Hassell on drums, who became my first musical director. Dave is world-class, as anyone will tell you, and he has played with everybody, has appeared on every music TV show and still nurtures talent today through various universities. Dennis Kelly and later Vinny Parker were on keyboards, with Richie Close on piano. Phil Chapman on saxophone became musical director after Dave — and another world-class drummer, Eric Delaney, joined me. Mel Dean took over as guitarist and musical director in 1974 and was with me right through to 1985.

Australia and New Zealand were beckoning, in addition to the multitude of other gigs back home that were coming in, along with continual appearances on television in Europe. The first tour of Australia and New Zealand came in the period somewhere between recording 'Amarillo' and appearing on *Top of the Pops* and, early in 1972, I was on my way to tour South Africa. That first flight to Australia took over 42 hours with Pan-Am. I found out later I was on the equivalent of the old UK milk train, landing at, it seemed, every destination possible along the way. First landing in Frankfurt. We must have landed six times on the way. From that time on, I've always booked one-stop hauls.

Although it was never released as a single in the UK, 'Have You

Ever Been to Georgia' was released over there before 'Amarillo' because I was touring. New Zealand and Australia had really taken to me and, at the end of 1971, I was in the Top 10 most successful recording artists on the chart that year, in great company with the likes of Paul McCartney, George Harrison, Creedence Clearwater Revival and Neil Diamond.

Back then, I never did much talking during my shows and I never saw myself as a sex symbol, even though having success does give you a bit more confidence in yourself on stage. First and foremost, though, I always let the singing do my talking. My view is people have paid to hear me sing. It's a bit different today. Sometimes now people like to hear about your life.

One thing was for sure, once I'd been poor and struggled, I was determined I would take every scrap of work that came my way. 1971 had changed my life completely.

CHAPTER 10

Reno, Varna, Tokyo — I was down every Avenue and Alleyway in 1972

'Amarillo' was still rolling along after Christmas and into the New Year, with TV appearances sending me on yet more air miles — hitting No 1 in Sweden in March for 4 weeks and Spain later that year, kept Harvey and the boys busy at Kennedy Street. My exploits at song festivals on mainland Europe hadn't gone unnoticed either, which led to a summer visit to Bulgaria and a winter journey to Japan for more during 1972.

After the South Africa tour early in the year, Sue and I were settling into a life of regular, constant work, with me jetting off here, there and everywhere, while she looked after Sean and Antonia at home. But it wouldn't be too long before we would move to a larger, grander affair, more in keeping with what the German reporter had anticipated.

On my way back from Australia and South Africa, I'd received a message asking me to stop off in Hamburg because 'Amarillo' was No 1 and they wanted to give me a Gold disc. I wasn't going to stop them. My first award as a recording artist.

Harvey brought Neil (Sedaka) over from the States, following the success of 'Amarillo', to record new songs at Strawberry Studios in Stockport. I think his idea was that by having Neil over here he might get first playing of another stand-out number for me as a follow-up single. Neil put together a whole album while he was here in just a fortnight, backed by all four members of 10cc. The subsequent LP, called *Solitaire,* was released in 1972. I sang 'God Bless Joanna' on my next LP that he'd released on his LP *Emergence* in 1971.

Mitch and Peter had my next single release ready and 'Don't Go

Down to Reno' added even further to my growing reputation on mainland Europe, reaching the Top 10 in both Switzerland and Germany, peaking at No 6 and No 5 respectively. It also made the Top 20 in Belgium, peaking at No 17, and in New Zealand it reached No 8 during a 12-week run.

I've always enjoyed sports, like cycling, golf and following football and I've kept myself in good shape. Around this time, I was running, playing some golf and squash. Well I might have been trying to make sure I looked good, but in one way it all went wrong one day when I had my nose broken playing squash. It's a good job I didn't have another *Top of the Pops* appearance at the time. After having used shades for 'Amarillo', I may have had to wear one of those head masks footballers wear today when they've had their nose broken.

In May 1972, Sue fell ill while she was staying in Castelldefels near Barcelona in northern Spain. It was a holiday, but I had flown to Yugoslavia with Derek Rawden, my tour manager. Derek's wife Maureen had been with Sue, but had to fly home because she'd had a serious reaction to many mosquito bites and had suffered blood poisoning. Fortunately, Sue had the fridge well stocked in the suite and Sean, at just three and a half years old, was trying his best to look after his sister Antonia, feeding her crisps and other food and milk. He was telling the hotel staff that his mummy was poorly, but the maids wouldn't go in as they thought the room was possessed.

After two days, Sue managed to get out of bed, go downstairs and speak to the staff. The management were not surprised their staff would not enter the suite, as we were then told that just a week or two previously the actor George Sanders had died of a cardiac arrest two days after a barbiturate overdose. He left behind three suicide notes.

My next major date was 6 June and another new country for me to visit, this time with Sue. We headed for the coast once again, this time to Bulgaria. Another fabulous destination. A resort called Sunny Beach on the shores of the Black Sea.

The Golden Orpheus was both an international song contest and a Bulgarian song contest, a bit like the one in Split I'd competed in the previous year, but this time I wasn't competing. I was the headline act to the whole show, performing a 10-song set, including all my hits. It was a great experience. The BBC had sent out a film crew and a Bulgarian TV station was also there. Dave Berry, who had a big hit with 'The Crying Game', competed for the UK.

Unbeknown to me at the time, and even until about forty years later, the whole competition and my performance had been recorded and put out as a double LP in Russia and eastern European countries. I'd treated it as being rather like any of the regular TV appearances. You can now pick up copies of the album or listen to it on YouTube where my performance is there in its entirety. My part of the album is called *Recital at the Festival The Golden Orpheus*.

We're actually lucky to be alive because Sue and I may not have been here to tell the tale. We only found out what happened the next morning!

We'd gone down for breakfast and I'd said to Sue, 'Can you smell smoke?' I just put it down to the chefs having a bad start to the day and having burned the toast or bacon or whatever. It's then that we found out one of the TV cameramen had fallen asleep while smoking a cigarette on the first floor and had set fire to the bed.

The whole hotel had been evacuated, apart from Sue and I. We were on the top floor. When the hotel management called out our names, my band said we were present because they thought we'd gone to a party and knew there was a curfew and we could have been in trouble. Since there had been a 10.30pm curfew, we'd decided not to go, so we were in our room while everyone else had been evacuated and that could have been the end of us.

We enjoyed our time at Sunny Beach.

Bulgaria was a communist state at the time and Sue and I had a conversation with a taxi driver one night who spoke perfect English, and in the course of conversation told us he was a professor. We asked why he was driving a taxi if he was so well qualified and he explained that he had spoken out against the country's politics.

We also had a young girl acting as our guide when we visited the capital, Sofia. I asked her why all the beautiful churches were locked and boarded up. She was evasive. She didn't want to talk about the country's communist state and moved the conversation to a more positive theme. The one thing she did tell us, was that she and her fiancé had to pass certain exams to gain permission to marry the following year.

In those days, you couldn't take any foreign currency out of the country, so as we left we gave what money we had remaining. She said, 'This will help us with our wedding and more.'

Meanwhile, back home, I'd started recording songs for my second LP, *With Loving Feeling*, when the boys turned up again with a new song. Mitch and Peter hadn't come up with a completed song, they'd just put together the hook they had at the time — no verses, just the chorus. They were working on it for a new TV series starring Robert Vaughn and Nyree Dawn Porter, and during a break from the album recording asked whether I could go into the studio next door and record a demo for Lew Grade. It was his ITC Entertainment production company who were making the show and its first episode was broadcast on 29 September. It was called *The Protectors*, created by Gerry Anderson, who made the marionette series *Thunderbirds*.

The band I recorded the demo with were CCS, who had legendary musicians like Alexis Korner and Herbie Flowers in their line-up and had scored a couple of big chart hits themselves, with 'Tap Turns On the Water' and their instrumental version of Led Zeppelin's 'Whole Lotta Love', that became the *Top of the Pops* theme tune for a long while. We just recorded the hook Mitch and Peter had written and they took it straight to Lew Grade who loved it. He told them to get the rest of the song written and said, 'Whoever is singing it here, I want that voice.' They came back with the full song, we recorded it and that was another channel opened up for me — songs for TV shows and films.

There are a lot of my fans who prefer 'Avenues and Alleyways' to anything I've ever recorded. It has been used in films too and was another chart record to add to my growing collection.

I went out to Madrid to record a version in Spanish and the studio producer told me I had a pure Castilian accent. The TV series was renamed in Spanish *Los Protectores* and I sang 'Avenidas Y Paseos'. I'd never spoken a word of the language, but got through it by pronouncing it all phonetically. I also sang a Spanish version of the B side, 'Nunca Fui Nino', which was another of Mitch and Peter's songs, 'I Never Was a Child', and recorded 'Don't Go Down to Reno' as 'No Vayas a Reno'.

My dad was proud, as he studied Spanish, holidayed there almost every year and spoke with a pure Spanish accent — what we would call, in the UK, the equivalent of perfect BBC English. In Spain, he would correct the locals when they used their regional dialect. Mum wasn't impressed.

While I was about to have 'Avenues and Alleyways' played for weeks on end as the theme tune, I was also back on the road in the UK playing the cabaret circuit and made a second appearance on *The Golden Shot* with Bob Monkhouse on Sunday 3 September, and two of the biggest shows on mainland Europe — including *Starparade*, hosted by Rainer Holbe on 26 October, that the James Last Orchestra featured on before they began launching their own successful albums; and Germany's version of *Top of the Pops*, called *Musikladen*.

On *Starparade*, I sang 'Avenues and Alleyways' and 'Don't Go Down to Reno' while walking across a huge stage of various levels in a cabaret dinner suit and, in retrospect, with one of the biggest bow ties on the planet. But on *Musikladen*, I clearly went for something younger-looking. If you catch the shirt on YouTube, just be prepared! All I'm saying is that it was of its time, I think.

Singing in Spanish, appearing in Germany, touring in South Africa, guest vocalist in Bulgaria — where next in 1972? This time it was Japan and the World Popular Song Festival held at the world famous Budokan arena in the beautiful gardens of Kitanomaru Park in Chiyoda, Tokyo. This was where The Beatles were the first rock group to play after it had originally been built to host the judo competitions at the 1964 Olympics. Appropriate again for Sue and I because we were now into another martial art — karate.

I sang a big ballad, 'What Becomes of My World?', another song written by Neil (Sedaka) and gave it the treatment, the full works and received a couple of awards for vocal performance and composition, but it was another British act that won the overall title. They were a vocal group called Capricorn and they won with a song called 'Feeling'. It was a song of that era, very much in the New Seekers style.

It's funny who you'd run into at these international festivals. The Budokan is where I met two boys and two girls who were performing as simply Bjorn and Benny and Two Girls. Bjorn and Benny had already had a big chart hit in Japan. They were in the next dressing room to me. We talked. They knew my records as I'd done well in Sweden. Nice people and very hard-working. They'd been releasing records as long as I had. Within the next 18 months, they had won the Eurovision Song Contest, as Abba, with 'Waterloo'. The rest, as they say, is pop music history.

1972 was still the big cabaret club era. It would carry on being that way for only about five or six years more before it started its downward spiral and meant singers like me had to find regular work elsewhere. But right now it was still big business with packed clubs, wonderfully colourful entertainers, whether singers, bands or comedians. In some ways it was a crackers era. The period from 1968– 1975 was particularly full of eccentrics and although I wouldn't have wanted to live the lives of some of the stars I still loved listening to their stories.

It was also a time when some club owners had their own standards of dress sense for people coming into their clubs and we found ourselves on the wrong end of it one night.

I was playing the really popular Talk of the North on Liverpool Road in Eccles, Manchester. The club had a fabulous following and under its owner, Joe Pullen, it was attracting all the big names. It had been a cinema and then The Majestic Club, before Joe and Fred Talbot had turned around its fortunes in the '60s by booking top acts.

Joe was a stickler for tradition and had his rules that ladies were not to wear trousers and men had to wear a shirt, tie and jacket. I don't think he was necessarily the only club owner to enforce this rule and he would certainly not get away with it in today's world, but that was his ruling.

We turned up with Sue wearing a fabulous-looking black trouser suit with rhinestones down the sides. She looked a million dollars, so far as I was concerned, and was looking great after recently giving birth to Antonia. We were all set for a great evening with me top of the bill and family with us too, but Sue was told she wasn't allowed in.

If we'd all been there just on a night out we would have walked out, but because I was due on stage and the band were all there we held the upper hand and Sue's dad put it to Joe like this: 'If she doesn't go in, her husband doesn't go on.' Joe politely gave in.

A fabulous era, the '70s, and a smashing one for Sue and I. We had a brilliant time and for us as a family it was going to get even better.

CHAPTER 11

Time for new avenues at home and abroad in 1973 and 1974

TV appearances came thick and fast during January 1973, firstly with me singing 'Avenues and Alleyways' on Granada TV's *Lift-Off with Ayshea*. Ayshea Brough was also to represent the UK in Tokyo in 1975, as I had earlier. Within a fortnight, I was back on *The Golden Shot* again with Bob; and at the end of the month, I was on the screens as part of Vince Hill's *They Sold a Million* series, with Dusty Springfield also featured.

My second LP, *With Loving Feeling,* released in February 1973, fared much better in the UK charts than my debut LP. Mitch and Peter writing together contributed three of the twelve songs, but both also wrote an individual song each. Mitch wrote 'Life Without You', while Peter had collaborated with Geoff Stephens on 'Daddy Don't You Walk So Fast', which had reached No 1 in Australia and No 4 in the US Billboard charts for Wayne Newton.

I finally had 'Solitaire' on one of my records, as I'd hoped, and another Sedaka/Greenfield song, 'God Bless Joanna'. The rest simply added to the songwriters' hall of fame on the record, with Phil Spector, Barry Mann and Cynthia Weil's 'You've Lost That Loving Feeling'; Gerry Goffin, Carole King, Jerry Leiber and Mike Stoller's 'On Broadway'; and Burt Bacharach and Hal David's 'A House Is Not a Home'. If you'd have added Lennon and McCartney, and Simon and Garfunkel, you'd have nearly encompassed all the great songwriting combinations of the '60s. It was my most successful album in the '70s.

During that same month, 'Avenues and Alleyways' made it into the Top 40 in the UK, reaching No 37, but once again New Zealand was to give me my fourth consecutive Top 10 hit when it had reached No 4 in January — and it did well in Australia too, leading to another tour of both countries during the year, but times were already by now changing on the charts with 'glam rock' taking over. The Sweet were No 1 with 'Blockbuster'. They'd also appeared on *The Golden Shot* with me in January.

In March, I was a guest along with the popular group White Plains on the children's show *Crackerjack*, filmed live at the BBC Television Theatre, now known as Shepherd's Bush Empire.

We moved to our new house in Endcliffe Grove Avenue, near Endcliffe Park, to the south west of Sheffield. The house was called Somersby. At the time, I thought it was pretentious, but I was wrong. It was an 8-bedroomed house, something more in line with what the German reporter had alluded.

I'd settled into a life of recording, cabaret and nightclubs in the UK and touring abroad, combined with the TV work — and at home I kept fit through running, cycling, squash and karate, that both Sue and I had taken up.

I reached blue belt. Sue was an orange belt. And would you believe it, I had my nose broken again! This time from a roundhouse kick.

At Endcliffe, our house had a large cellar space and we had set it up as a gym and a bar, with a wine cellar. I prided myself on having a well-stocked wine cellar. I had bought six cases each of vintage 1964 and 1966 Chateau Lafitte and Mouton Rothschild and an 1871 vintage port that had been kept in a barrel for 100 years and bottled in 1971. Sean, at just 10 years old, and his friend JJ, had opened a couple of the bottles with their penknives and had drunk most of the contents of one of them. They were ill afterwards and Kath our housekeeper said she thought it was something they had eaten, but they were giggling and Anne the nanny said, 'They're not ill, they're drunk!'

Weight has never been a problem for me. I'm slight in build and was always about 10 and a half stone. I'm only around 11 stone today as I've tried to keep myself in shape. In the '70s, I'd often be running around Endcliffe Park and the rest of the area burning away any excess.

My other sport was golf. When we were killing time during the day, I'd play with the rest of the band. We'd find a course and hire some clubs, but in the early '70s I joined Lees Hall Golf Club and acquired a 12 handicap. I've knocked around that kind of figure pretty much throughout my playing career. The course is to the south of Sheffield, over 100 years old and is challenging with fantastic views of the city. I'd often play with friends who were mainly business people who had shops. Geoff Frost was one of the group I'd play with, a real character who had a carpet shop. He had carpeted our very first flat.

Our group became known as The Fiddlers and we'd go to other courses, rather like pub golf societies arrange to visit new venues. The kind of thing where you all end up putting a fiver in and the winner on the day takes the pot, but then has to get the round in at the 19th afterwards. I've been very fortunate to have had three holes-in-one over the years and my first came at Lees Hall on a medal day one Saturday in the '70s. There was a tee for the next hole just above the green and the players waiting to start there watched it go in and shouted! I was elated as you might imagine. Some golfers have played all their lives and never had one.

When you have a hole-in-one on a course it is customary to buy everyone in the bar a drink when you've completed your round, which I happily did.

I used to play an iron from the tee most of the time. When I'd started, I'd played a 3-wood off the tee because I couldn't get the hang of a driver, but then moved mostly to a 3-iron which served me well hitting the ball with draw to give extra distance. I've outdriven a 2-handicap player who was using a driver. I gave away my driver to a good friend. The best round I ever played was to 3 over, at Southend Golf Club, where I think the head of British golf played at the time. Golf became my escape. More later.

Bruce Forsyth was a very serious golfer and I once played a four-ball with him. As much as he enjoyed a joke, when he was on the course he meant business. I'd taken him to a couple of courses,

Lindrick Golf Club in South Yorkshire and Abbeydale Golf Club.

I found Bruce wonderful company off the course, but a little intense on it. Some grammar school boys saw him on the putting green and stuck their chins out, making the typical remarks you'd expect — 'Good game, good game' — and Bruce was, let's just say, not very complimentary to them. His words were along the lines of go forth and multiply.

TV Specials were nothing new to Bruce, but they were to me and I hosted my own TV programme on Wednesday 1 August 1973 as part of the *Music My Way* series. Amazing how things had gone in two and a half years. Back in 1970, 'God Is On My Side' banned and just another flop, now my own BBC1 show. Vicky Leandros had her own show in the series the week before and we were to work together in Europe many years later. Sometimes I could have pinched myself thinking this couldn't be real. But that doesn't mean everything falls your way.

People in the music business generally have experiences of 'the one that got away', whether it was an act they should have signed or a song they missed out on. I had that in 1973. Geoff Stephens had written massive hits for The Hollies, Cliff Richard, Herman's Hermits and had landed a No 1 in the US with 'Winchester Cathedral'.

Geoff had mentioned he'd written a song for me and I recorded it, but somehow The Drifters had got hold of it, released 'Like Sister and Brother', and it became their third consecutive Top 10 hit in the UK. Strangely, years later, I was talking with The Drifters and they said how much they liked my version.

The Lovers was a popular TV show written by the legendary Jack Rosenthal in the early '70s, starring the late Richard Beckinsale (*Porridge* and *Rising Damp*) who died so young at 31 in 1979, and Paula Wilcox (*Man About the House*) who married Nelson Riddle Jr. You'll see the significance of mentioning this much later. *The Lovers* was one of those sitcoms that was very sweet and innocent compared to today and there was a film that followed the TV series. I sang the theme song 'Love and Rainy Weather', written, once again, by Mitch and Peter.

The film was released in 1973 and we were at the opening night. The song was released as a single in May, but didn't reach the UK chart Top 40, though it became another hit for me in New Zealand where it reached No 8 later in the year in September, around the time when I was touring, and was followed by another hit over there, 'You Just Don't Have the Magic Anymore', that reached No 14 in November and was a hit in Australia the following year.

It was around now that I met Bill Tidy, who is one of the most famous cartoonists in the UK, with his work in *Private Eye* and the *Daily Mirror*. He lived in Southport and I was playing Southport Theatre. I went in a nice little pub across the road from the theatre that had been recommended. It had everything on draught, which I really enjoy. I met Bill there, who lived around the corner and we had a drink together. We've remained in touch and a little later we both had another friend in common.

John Junkin was a great friend. He'd appeared in The Beatles' first film, *A Hard Day's Night*, as well as many other films and TV programmes. He was an accomplished scriptwriter, actor and performer. Sue and I had met him when we were on a cruise holiday with Sue's parents and her sister on a ship called *The Arcadia*. We got chatting, made a good friendship on board and ended up giving him a lift home to Hampstead.

His apartment was on the top floor. Cameron McIntyre and his wife Coke were in the ground floor apartment. Their son Michael was born a couple of years later. We saw Michael as a toddler when we visited John in years to follow. I wonder whatever happened to him?

John used to do warm-up for Bob Monkhouse's TV shows and at the time we became friends he was writing comedy routines with another of my mates, Barry Cryer, also a Yorkshire lad. John had his own afternoon show on TV called *Junkin*. I was John's best man when he married Jenny in 1977 and Sue and I are godparents to their daughter, Annabel.

The Talk of the Town was the cabaret nightclub to play in London during the '70s and I was fortunate enough to be booked there twice — firstly for two weeks in February 1974 and then for three weeks in 1975. Comedian and impressionist, Mike Yarwood, was next up after me, followed by the New Seekers. The Talk of the Town had been the magnificent Matcham-designed Hippodrome Theatre and when it reopened, as a casino and nightclub under the Hippodrome name in 2012, I was honoured to be the first act invited to set it going once again.

After one of the shows in my first run at Talk of the Town, I had comedian Harry Worth come backstage in my dressing room. He was a big TV star with his own shows. Everyone from back then must remember what he did, lifting his leg and arm by the side of a shop window which, through its reflection on the TV screen, looked as though he was jumping in the air.

Harry was from Hoyland Common near Barnsley, and I said, 'You're from Barnsley, aren't you?' My question took him by surprise and flummoxed him even more when I said I was from Conisbrough. We were both from the same kind of area. That's when he said, 'Don't be stupid, you're American, aren't you?' He laughed his head off and left.

While touring and cruising were adding to my globetrotting exploits, 1974 was also significant in my recording career for being the first and only time I've had two studio albums released in the same year — *From America with Love* and *It's Good to Be Me* — and I even recorded my 'live' album at the end of the year, so all in all it was probably my busiest recording period and it brought one of my best-loved songs, 'Happy Birthday Baby'.

From America with Love was, as you might imagine, recorded in the US. Sue and I were over in the States for two months. For three weeks, Angela, Sue's sister, brought Sean and Antonia over. Keith, Angela's husband, stayed at our home with their girls and held the fort. At one time during the '70s, Sue and I began considering perhaps living there.

The album was produced by Snuff Garrett, or to give him his real name, Thomas Leslie 'Snuff' Garrett. He'd produced hits for Sonny and Cher, Brenda Lee and later went on to producing Nancy Sinatra. This was the first album I'd ever recorded without Mitch and Peter being in charge of production, so it was new territory for me, but singing is singing wherever you are and I thoroughly enjoyed being out there and especially having time with Sue, Angela and the children.

We stayed at the Beverley Hilton in Los Angeles. The car park was at roughly the same level as our suite and I'd leap over our balcony to its roof and run around there to keep in shape.

We were there a few weeks while I put the vocals down for the album and in that time we also managed to visit Universal Studios in Hollywood, and Disneyland with Sean, Antonia and Angela.

Disneyland was great and we were given the VIP treatment, as MCA Records was part of the organisation. They were building the set for *Jaws* at the time. The film came out the following year.

The opening song on *From America with Love* was 'Words (Are Impossible)', that had been a Top 20 UK hit for an Italian singer called Drupi, and was one of three songs from the LP that also appeared on my *Best of Tony Christie* LP in 1976. There are a number of country music hits, including 'The Most Beautiful Girl', that Charlie Rich charted with, and 'Tequila Sunrise' by The Eagles, as well as 'Drift Away', which had been a massive hit for soul singer Dobie Gray. I've always liked country music and with a producer like Snuff Garrett, who was known for the genre, I was in good hands.

Three singles were released from the LP, but only two of them in the UK. The first was 'A Lover's Question', another country music hit by Clyde McPhatter in the '50s and written by Brook Benton and Jimmy Williams. It made No 11 over in New Zealand, but 'Happy Birthday Baby', released later that year, went to No 7 there and in Australia the following year it peaked at No 1 in the Sydney chart. But of all my '70s hits, it stayed on the chart for the longest period of 38 weeks.

It just shows what having good songwriters can do for you. I'd been blessed with being given great songs by amazing writers like

Mitch, Peter and Neil to gather my big hits of 1971, and now I had this one from Barry Mason and Roger Greenaway. Barry had written some of the biggest hits of the '60s, most often in partnership with Les Reed, and had Engelbert's 'The Last Waltz' and Tom Jones's 'Delilah' already in his locker.

'Happy Birthday Baby' was also so close to being my first UK chart hit for a year and a half and was on the breakers list for what has been recorded as an astonishing 11 weeks without quite making it to the Top 40. It certainly never stopped it being one of my most requested songs from fans and audiences wherever I've performed.

My other LP released in 1974 was *It's Good to Be Me*, produced by Mitch and Peter with Lew Warburton handling all arrangements — the team that had been with me throughout the past three years. 'Love and Rainy Weather' was included. Mitch and Peter contributed two others, 'If You Stay Too Long in Oklahoma' and 'A Year and a Wife and a Kid Ago'. The opening song was 'If It Feels Good — Do It', written by Mike Vale and recorded by Northern Soul singer Della Reese in the early '70s, that I reprised when playing V Festival in 2005.

It's an album filled once again with songs by great songwriters. I wrote the title track to the LP *It's Good to Be Me* with Peter (Callander).

Clubland was still going strong in 1974 and it was to lead to several special moments for me, including an appearance the following year on the TV programme that publicised working men's clubs like no other had done before. I was playing the nightclub and cabaret circuit, the top clubland venues, travelling abroad on tour and making regular TV appearances on the continent, doing what I've always tried to do, keep working.

In 1969, I'd won a Clubland award in Bolton and in 1974 I received the Male Vocalist of the Year award at Blighty's in Farnworth near Bolton. Awards are very nice to receive and I've been honoured that people have thought so much about me to cast votes and say such kind words about a lad who came from humble beginnings in South Yorkshire. This same year, I also played over in Jersey, and believe me, I saw some sights over there, whether it was the entertainers or the club owner who disappeared on benders for two or three days. Like I said, the '70s were a crazy yet wonderful time.

1974 came to a glorious close for me when I recorded my third album in a year! It wasn't released until 1975, but was recorded at the fantastic Fiesta nightclub in Sheffield, that had been opened in 1970 by Teesside brothers Keith and Jim Lipthorpe and had been compared to 'more like a trip to Vegas'.

It was billed as the biggest nightclub in Europe at the time, with seating for 1300, and The Jackson 5, Stevie Wonder, Ella Fitzgerald all played it. Being my adopted home city, and where I'd performed so many times, the Fiesta was like coming home each time I played there and I'm sure it will have been the same for my good friend Marti Caine, whose TV show I had the pleasure of appearing on. I know how much she and I both loved playing our home city.

The album was recorded over two nights and used the same travelling studio and engineers as the Rolling Stones. I found out one of the engineers came from Bradford, but he spoke with what I thought was a posh accent. When I said that's not a Bradford accent, he replied he'd learned to speak properly as a boy by listening to talk shows on the BBC. I did what I do. Sang my heart out as I do every night and had the wonderful Andy Wardhaugh to thank as musical director. The album was produced by Peter Sullivan, who had worked with Tom Jones and Engelbert.

It was the first album to feature all the chart hits and includes my crowd-pleasing big numbers, 'Ol' Man River', 'If It Feels Good — Do It', 'MacArthur Park', 'Didn't We', the 'West Side Story Medley', 'So Deep Is the Night' and 'Hey Jude'. I even got a laugh out of introducing 'So Deep' … as written by Frederic Chopin and Burt Bacharach, but the bigger laugh was when I announced that to my knowledge the earliest known recording of this was in 1876 by Jimmy Young.

Listening back now, the album really captures that spirit of the '70s, high energy, rousing band and the audience that have always been very special to me in Sheffield. It had become my home in the '60s, where I met Sue and will hold a special place in my heart forever. It still brings back those days now, amazingly over 40 years ago. Where does the time go?

Sadly, the Fiesta didn't last long. Union troubles caused it to close in 1976. I played it again around that time. It came back to life under new ownership, but closed for the last time in 1980. I've heard some say it mirrored Sheffield, which was buzzing with industry and full employment in 1970, but by the end of the decade the steel and coal industries, which had been the reason for its buzz, were on the wane. It also mirrored what was going on with clubland and my UK career towards the late '70s.

1974 had brought some fantastic moments and memories — recording in the States, recording at home in the UK, the Talk of the Town, the live album at the Fiesta and UK TV appearances on the BBC's *Music with Martell*, Yorkshire TV's *Stars on Sunday* and BBC's *They Sold a Million*, hosted by Vince Hill — but they were nothing compared to the emotions I would experience the following year. Didn't we almost have it all? Well, we were to find out through ups and downs that brought about the most fantastic 'up' of all.

CHAPTER 12

Whatever may come, whatever may be
As long as there's you, it's so good to be me
And then we were five in 75 —
after a bit of wheeltapping and shunting

1975 started well and it was Bernard Manning who introduced me on the ITV show set in Granada studios, but under the fictitious working men's club *The Wheeltappers and Shunters*. I'd played at Bernard's Embassy Club in Manchester several times, it was pretty famous in the north of England and because I used to finish there around 10.30pm, we would double-up on the night with another club in the area at the top of Oxford Road, where we played downstairs, and apart from Matt Monro, I was the only performer to play a fortnight there.

Now this next bit shows just how naïve I was back then. When I used to go on stage at this club, there was an eating area just to one side and after about three or four nights I asked the maitre d' about why the same women seemed to be sat there each night with different men. He just looked at me as though I were some halfwit. He was probably right.

Wheeltappers was filmed in what looked like a typical old club with Colin Crompton acting up the concert chairman's role and Bernard as compere introducing the 'turns' from near the bar with pints flowing and frothing. The audience was made up of men and women who were regular clubland people.

'He's done all the big clubs and now he's doing all the little clubs, he's our very own northern superstar,' were Bernard's words as I arrived on stage sporting a bright red jacket and open collared shirt, not as far open as the album cover to *It's Good to Be Me*. I loved the signs they had up in the studio, typical of the old clubs. There was one that said: 'No bad language on ladies' nights.' I sang 'Avenues and Alleyways', 'Amarillo' and 'Ol' Man River', and like many of these programmes you can still find my performance on YouTube, as well as on the videos released of the series. The programme was broadcast in March 1975.

New Zealand and Australia were beckoning once again and this was the time when Mel Dean joined me as musical director. Mel's a superb musician and still a great friend. We had a fantastic time on the 1975 tour listening to *The Goon Show* and even playing ludo — hardly rock 'n' roll, I know, but it kept us going.

We wanted to tape the *Goon Show* LPs because the BBC in New Zealand had loaned them to us and we borrowed a reel-to-reel, spending all night recording. We met Spike Milligan's best friend, from his army days, Gunner Harry Edgington, in Wellington. He had come to see my concert and came backstage to see me. The next night we had a free day, so I invited Harry to join Mel Dean and I for dinner because I was interested to find out more about Spike. Spike wrote a song for me with George Martin, The Beatles producer.

Our Australian tours were usually around Sydney and we'd play clubs there that were 5 storeys high with casinos. We played the club where Warren Mitchell was famously at the time paid-off for swearing whilst in his character Alf Garnett from *Till Death Us Do Part*.

While we were out in New Zealand, MCA took the opportunity to release another record to tie in with the tour. They chose 'Words (Vado Via)' from my *From America with Love* album, with the flip side being 'Gifts', written by Alan O'Day.

The 'Live' album from Sheffield Fiesta was released at the end of May and reached No 33 in the UK charts. Those who were there, when we were recording over the two nights, still talk about it and hold the record dear to their hearts. I think it stands up well after over 44 years.

The New Zealand tour was difficult for me, as Sue had miscarried while I was away. We had always thought we would like to have three children, and while she had lost the baby at just nine weeks into pregnancy and was brave about what had happened, saying it wasn't a big thing, we were both obviously disappointed.

When Sue was advised by her gynaecologist not to try for any more children, due to her past health problems, he had also asked whether we had thought of adoption. We had always wanted to adopt and we thought by having two naturally born children we wouldn't stand a chance.

This was also around the time when Operation Babylift was taking place, evacuating children from South Vietnam.

Sue's gynaecologist had told her he was on the board of governors at Sheffield Adoption Society and that while he had no influence over decisions regarding adoptions, he could and would give her and her family a good reference, because he knew us and that we would give any baby or child a good home.

Things didn't start to happen straight away. Everything with adoption rightly takes time, going through all the appropriate processes and ensuring you are the right and fitting parents.

Eight months after we had been approved, we received a phone call from the Adoption Society telling us we had a baby girl who had been born on 20 August 1975. We were all absolutely thrilled. We had to wait five and a half weeks before we could see her. Immediately we saw Sarah, we fell in love with her and couldn't wait to take her home that day. Sean and Antonia were so proud of their new baby sister. Our family was complete.

However, within two days of having Sarah at home, Sue recognised that Sarah had a problem. Sue noticed a lump in her groin that came out when she cried and then disappeared. Fearing this was a hernia, Sue and I took Sarah to our doctor who couldn't find the swelling. Subsequently, after five visits to the doctor, Sue and I took Sarah to the children's hospital in Sheffield. We were particularly concerned, as the adoption had not officially gone through and we didn't think we would be able to sign for an operation, which we thought she needed.

We were seen immediately by a junior doctor. When we told her the symptoms, she pressed gently on the lower side of Sarah's tummy and out popped the hernia. The doctor said we were so right to bring her straight away and asked when she'd had her last feed. Sue had only just fed her because our doctor had said to do so.

Sarah was taken straight to the ward and her little legs were elevated to reduce the hernia and save her life. When it was safe to do so, Sarah was operated on and had her hernia repaired. She was so tiny that she was then put into an incubator for 24 hours.

I didn't like leaving Sue and Sarah. I was appearing at the Fiesta nightclub in Sheffield that night, but when I went on stage I had no voice and had to cancel the show, something I never do. Fortunately, Sarah recovered and came home a few days later.

As the official adoption date was approaching, Sue was becoming anxious because Sarah wouldn't officially be our baby daughter until the final adoption papers had been signed. A friend of Sue's mentioned that a well-known clairvoyant Yvonne Clapperton, who lived and still lives in Sheffield, might be worth seeing. We talked about it and agreed to see her. We thought it might help.

What Yvonne was able to tell us was amazing. Yvonne said on her first reading that we had three children, but that one was passed over and not very long ago, but she also said we were looking after a third child, a little girl.

Sometimes it's hard to accept that others can see things the rest of us cannot and I certainly have no explanation of why, but Yvonne was right and provided us with much needed positivity just when we needed it. She said this baby we were looking after would be with us forever. She also asked if there had been anything wrong with Sarah's legs and we told her what had happened. Yvonne said, 'She will always be strong and able to cope with what life throws at her,' and that she saw problems with her legs, but not to worry.

Thank God we didn't know just how bad things were going to get for our little girl, who was fine until six weeks before her third birthday when Sue noticed Sarah's knee was swollen and becoming more so by the day. This time we went straight to the hospital. They couldn't find what was the cause, but asked us to return the following week. During this time, the knee had become inflamed and very stiff and sore. We were referred to a paediatrician, who in turn referred us to a rheumatologist. Sarah was diagnosed, on her third birthday, with Still's disease, a juvenile form of rheumatoid arthritis. Yvonne was right. Our little girl from then on and throughout her life has been strong in mind and spirit, but not in health. She has always defied anyone who tells her things cannot be done. As a teenager, she was told that she may never have children because of other health problems and medication, yet now she has the most wonderful boy, Isaac. In the Bible, Isaac was son of Sarah.

Through Sarah's childhood, she missed quite a substantial amount of her education because she was either in hospital or at home poorly, but she always said that when she grew up she wanted to be a teacher and became a teacher in primary schools. Before she was 30, she became a head teacher, until she had to retire at 42 years old because of ill health. However, Sarah never lets the grass grow under her feet, and is now a parish councillor, governor to two schools and the local party planner! She's always the last one to leave.

Antonia always wanted to travel and took up a position in the Foreign Office.

Antonia spent her 21st birthday on Copacabana Beach and with friends took part in the magnificent Rio Festival. Antonia made many friends and one of them was Ivani, a Brazilian girl, who had a French boyfriend called Stephane. Ivani and Stephane later married in Paris. By this time, Antonia had a posting in Paris and went to the wedding. There she met her future husband Raphael, who was Stephane's cousin.

How ironic. Antonia, an English girl working in Paris, would marry Raphael, a French boy working in London. And they now live in Belgium with their three lovely children. Since living in Belgium, Antonia has been studying and is now a qualified specialist teacher and assessor of dyslexia and literacy.

Sean and Lisa were school sweethearts and were destined to be together always, but it took 17 years for them to finally 'tie the knot'. Lisa works for British Airways and had always wanted to marry at the Grande Roche in the Paarl valley in the wine region of Cape Town, South Africa. She had flown there many times over the years with BA. They had their dream wedding in a tiny chapel at the Grand Roche on Valentine's Day in 2002. Their names and marriage date is on the chapel door. By this time they had two little boys, Joby and Caius who were so proud to be page boys for their mummy and daddy. They were dressed as little drummer boys and looked so adorable. Their family was to be complete on New Year's Day 2006 when their daughter Deià was born. We were all delighted and it was a great start to our new year.

We have always had a belief. We go to church and we believe in one God, but it is our belief in people helping others through sending good thoughts, praying for others and acting as guardian angels that is strong. I wouldn't want anyone to think we don't also have our feet on the ground and that we think clearly and logically about problems, but we also believe in the power of positive thoughts and it has worked for me, particularly with one instance in more recent times.

Sue and I have both been extremely lucky to have come from strong family backgrounds.

We have always been very close with Sue's sisters, Angela and Jackie, and their husbands Keith and Peter. We'd enjoyed wonderful holidays together. Angela and Keith's daughters, Jackie, known as little Jackie, and Samantha, were born around the same period as Sean and Antonia, so were almost like brothers and sisters.

Jackie and Peter's son Carl was born later, but they were all very fond of their little cousin. Sue and I are godparents to them all. Tragically, Samantha, Sammy to us all, died far too early in life at just 37 years of age, and we were all heartbroken; but little Jackie has done amazingly well. She lost both her eyes due to retina blastoma when she was a baby and has carved out a really great career for herself working for Guide Dogs for the Blind. Carl is now a successful record producer with Bullet for My Valentine and many others.

I'd fancied a barge holiday on the Norfolk Broads. It was something I was to do on TV in more recent years on a celebrity programme, but back then it just didn't happen for me. We had booked and were going with Angela, Keith and their children, but then I was offered a three-week run at the Talk of the Town again. I couldn't turn it down.

I gave the barge holiday away to my golf mate Geoff Frost, who came back and told me it was the best holiday he'd ever had!

My second run at the Talk of the Town was just brilliant though and it gave the opportunity to sell more copies of the *Live* album which continued selling well over a long period. My old pal Vince Hill took over from me and The Platters followed him. It really was the place to play in London.

Our beautiful daughter Sarah was born halfway through my run at the Talk of the Town.

When the adoption was finalised, with Sarah three and a half months old, there was a bit of last-minute panic in getting a heel test done, the necessary papers that needed signing by Dr Gordon and a rush to get to the judge on time, but we did and Judge Pickles told us Sarah was ours, nobody could take her away from us and that she was a very lucky girl. I think we were the lucky ones.

I know sometimes I might not look it, but I do get very emotional. I did cry and at that moment we all did. Sue, me, everyone. Tears of joy and happiness.

I was playing in Manchester all that week and I'd been coming back home to Sheffield every night before going across via Snake Pass or Woodhead Pass, dependent on the weather.

That day we celebrated with lunch at Johnny's Italian Restaurant on Ecclesall Road and when they found out why we were there and in such high spirits we were inundated with bottles of champagne. It was a fantastic afternoon and I was grateful I had a driver.

It is the first and only time I have ever gone on stage with a drink in me. We were at a nightclub not far from Bernard Manning's

Embassy. Mike Ryal said it was the funniest thing he'd ever seen. Someone threw a request on stage and every time I bent down to get it I kept kicking it forward. I said, 'Good evening ladies and gentlemen,' after every song and the club owner was looking at Mike in an odd way. I'm sure he was wondering what the hell was going on.

Mike was great. He picked up the bit of paper with the request on it and then mentioned to the owner that the adoption had gone through earlier that day and that Sarah was officially our daughter. He also mentioned the copious amount of champagne. The club owner was wonderful. He got on the mic and told everybody my news and the audience roared.

'Christie is so professional, but it really was hilarious,' Mike said later. I was so embarrassed and would never have dreamed of going on stage drunk either before or since, but I had been given such a great gift, the gift of a daughter and I was Sarah's dad. Emotional attachment, relief from stress, call it whatever you like. It was a great feeling — and the owner even bought Sarah a beautiful red and white dress.

You could say 1975 was a great year for us. A few really emotional moments, but certainly things turned out right family-wise, touring, recordings and big-name venues. The hits? Well, you can't have everything all the time, but even that was to come good again near the end of the year.

'Easy to Love' had been an October release as a single, with the flip side 'Now My World Is Yours'. Both songs were produced and arranged by Jeff Wayne, who went on to release his musical version of HG Wells's *War of the Worlds*.

I was just starting to think that the charts in the UK were beyond me again, when a Geoff Stephens and Barry Mason song came my way. Another songwriter, Tony Macaulay, once told Barry if it had a happier ending it might have done even better. 'Drive Safely Darlin'' was released in December and I appeared on *Top of the Pops* again, this time hosted by Noel Edmonds, in January 1976. It reached No 35 in the UK and also charted in Australia and in New Zealand, where it gave me my ninth Top 20 hit, reaching No 17. Geoff and Barry also wrote the flip side 'Sweet Summer Souvenirs', but if getting another hit was to be the start of the year there was again a lot more to come in 1976 and 1977.

spike milligan

9 Orme Court,
LONDON. W.2.

15th May, 1978
(Dictated 12/5/78).

Tony Christie Esq.,
3 Endcliffe Grove Avenue,
SHEFFIELD. S10. 3EJ.

Dear Tony,

Delighted you liked the tune and the words, but would
like to change the melody and the lyrics; great change
all the lyrics and the tune, and change the singer.
Sorry you are down with the dreaded grollicks of the
throat, but remember my dear lad, it only happens all
the time.
I have asked Norma, my Manager, to clear it with George
Martin, but you don't have to, once a number has been
published anyone can record it.
I have just come from the Ivor Novello Awards, and Snow
Goose was one of the nominations, alas we lost to Cavatina
which won the prize.
Never mind, next year I am going to enter God Save the
Queen with Arab lyrics, it's bound to win.

As ever,

Spike

Spike Milligan.

CHAPTER 13

A Song that wasn't quite for Europe,
a musical set in Argentina,
and a jump suit that became a one-summer wonder

One of the greatest privileges I've had as a singer is to compete at song festivals all around the world, from Yugoslavia and Belgium to Japan and Bulgaria, so when the opportunity came to sing a new composition by the songwriting duo of Geoff Stephens and Tony Macaulay, well it had to be done.

I was knocked out that I'd been chosen to sing 'Queen of the Mardi Gras' in A Song for Europe, that was recorded live at the Royal Albert Hall for the BBC, with Michael Aspel hosting the show on Wednesday 25 February. I'd been quoted in the press as saying I thought it had just the right beat and the sort of catchy number which could very well win Europop, as I referred to it, and that it was tailor-made for the contest, a hit song that the postman whistles.

We all thought it was a winner until we went down to rehearsals and on came Brotherhood of Man with 'Save Your Kisses for Me' and their great routine. I just looked at Frank Ifield, who was one of the twelve acts. We raised our eyebrows because we knew there and then who was going to win.

The voting system was down to 14 regional panels, each with 12 jury members picked from the general public, so in effect while 12.6 million watched the programme the selection of the song to represent the UK was down to 168 people. Sounds crazy, but this was before telephone voting and they still came up with the right decision because the right song won. It was Eurovision.

'Queen of the Mardi Gras' came in third with 129 points and I gave it everything I had with my five backing singers and my white suit, but it wasn't a walkover for Brotherhood of Man, as a band called Co-Co finished just two points behind them. They later went on to represent the UK in 1978 and had Cheryl Baker with them, who worked with me at one time and went on to win with Bucks Fizz.

Frank didn't fair very well at all, but was very gracious. 'Queen of the Mardi Gras' was released a month later with the flip side another Stephens and Macaulay song, 'Wall of Silence'.

It was around now that Sean, now about 8 years old, left his grandfather stunned with a calculation he was trying to get straight in his head. It went something like this and was all about conception. Sue's dad's club had a kids' disco night on a Wednesday.

Sean and Samantha, Sue's sister Angela's daughter, were having a conversation in the back seat of the car as their grandfather was driving them home after the kids' disco. Sean was trying to work out when he had been conceived and was wondering about why, since he was born in September, his mum and dad had married in the February previously.

Sean had asked Samantha when her mum and dad had got married and Samantha said, 'Oh, I think I was premature like you, Sean.' Their grandfather, who was listening to this conversation, nearly drove off the road!

The International Pop Proms was a show broadcast by Granada on the ITV network and saw me singing 'Las Vegas' on TV in the UK for the first time in a while under the direction of Les Reed, who has sadly passed away during the writing of this book, as the conductor, and was held at the King's Hall in Belle Vue, Manchester in April '76.

But it was my TV appearance with Marti Caine on her show, *Nobody Does It Like Marti*, that I remember far better because, firstly, she was brilliant as always, and secondly, we appeared a few times on the same bill in the '60s, so we knew each other and got on great. She had a fabulous voice as well as being very funny and it is tragic she left us so early at only 50 years of age. We sang a duet of Cat Stevens' 'Wild World'. Marti was a fantastic talent.

I'd also just seen the release of what was to be my last studio album with MCA Records, *I'm Not in Love*, featuring the fantastic 10cc classic. I'd recorded the album during October 1975 and January 1976 and it was produced by Geoff Stephens.

'Like Sister and Brother', that Geoff said he'd written for me, also appears on the album, along with 'Queen of the Mardi Gras' and 'Drive Safely Darlin''. It's a lovely album chock-full of great songs like 'Love Hurts', 'Feelings' and 'The Way We Were'. It was recorded at Nova Sound Recording Studios in London.

'On This Night of a Thousand Stars' brought about another string to my bow in 1976, when I took a role in the original cast recording of *Evita*. I'd been approached by these two young men who were really nice and struck me at the time as typical public schoolboys. They'd just had a massive success with *Jesus Christ Superstar* and the story of Eva Peron was their next venture.

They had come to see me at a show in Cleethorpes on the Lincolnshire coast. They explained what it was about and that my role would be Agustin Magaldi, a well-known singer of the time in the 1930s and known as 'the sentimental voice of Buenos Aires'. Magaldi was to bring Eva Duarte, as she was then called, to the Argentinean capital.

I was invited to Andrew Lloyd Webber's beautiful home in Knightsbridge where he played me the song. Tim and Andrew called each other by their last names, which is what gave the impression of public school, with Andrew saying things like, 'Rice has written a good lyric for this one,' and Tim saying similar about 'Lloyd Webber'.

I stayed in a hotel for a couple of days while the recording took place at the famous Olympic Studios in London, where the Rolling Stones, Led Zeppelin, The Beatles and Jimi Hendrix had all recorded. It was a musical, and very different to anything I'd done before. It seemed a bit all over the place, because as I was recording my parts, as I sing on four of the songs on that original album, Andrew and Tim were still auditioning for the rest of the parts. I saw Colm Wilkinson come in. He played Che on the album and is a fantastic Irish tenor. He is better known now for playing Jean Valjean in *Les Miserables* in the West End and on Broadway.

While 'On This Night of a Thousand Stars' is the song most who bought the album will remember me for, I also sang 'Eva, Beware of the City'; joined Che, Eva and others on 'Goodnight and Thank You'; and the 'Charity Concert' track.

The original show first went on to the West End stage in 1978 and I was offered the role, but I was booked up two years ahead, had another Australia tour coming up and my band would have been out of work. I finally made it to the stage in the West End many years later in something completely different.

The album *Evita* was released in November 1976 and reached No 4 in the charts in 1977, with 'On This Night of a Thousand Stars' released in January 1977. On the flip side was 'Bewitched, Bothered and Bewildered', written by Richard Rodgers and Lorenz Hart.

The Best of Tony Christie became my second Top 30 album, staying in the charts for a four-week run in November 1976, aimed at the Christmas market. Harvey wrote the sleeve notes extolling my 'magnificent vocal strength and lyrical interpretation.' Thanks Harvey.

1977 signalled the start of a change in music when punk came in with The Sex Pistols and The Stranglers and many others.

I was one of the more fortunate, as at least I'd had hit records and my bookings were stacked well in advance, but this was the year when my contract with MCA came to an end, leaving me without a record deal by the end of the year.

Three singles were released during the year. In April, 'Smile a Little Smile for Me', that had previously appeared on my very first album and was backed by 'It's Good to Be Me', came out presumably to have something around to promote on TV as I appeared on Thames TV's ITV networked *The Little and Large Telly Show*, alongside other guest stars Mud and Dana on my birthday, April 25. I'd already appeared with the Nolan Sisters on Vince Hill's *Musical Time Machine*

Above: My first centrefold for *Playgirl* magazine.

Right: An old family photo with one of my relatives holding the squeeze box that I still have at home.

Below right: Our family home in Montague Avenue, Conisbrough.

Below: My mum and dad Paddy and Iris Fitzgerald. What a handsome couple. Circa 1950s.

Proudly taking my
first car for a spin.

The Wrong Trousers.
My brother Neal and I.

The annual street day out from Conisbrough in the charabanc. Far right: My mum Iris,
with her hands on the shoulders of my brother Neal and myself. Summer 1952. In our
best tweed jackets.

A rare shot of The Trackers, circa 1965. L to R: Mike Ryal on bass guitar, Me, Barry Wooton on drums.

My new bride and I in Spain. Our first holiday together.

Sue and I looking pensive with our darling god-daughter Jackie. She was christened in the hospital chapel the day before a major operation. Thankfully, she is still with us. Sue was 4 months pregnant with Sean.

Sue and I with our little boy Sean in Spain, circa 1971.

T.C. live. 1971.
(Alamy)

Single cover for
'I Did What I Did
for Maria', 1972.
(Alamy)

Receiving a Gold Disc from Lulu for in excess of 1 million worldwide sales of 'Amarillo', which was Number 1 in a number of European countries, August 1972. (Alamy)

Me with the manager of Kennings Motor Company in Sheffield in the early '70s taking delivery of my new Roller!

Breakfast at nanny Irene and grandpa John's house. Very '70s kitchen.

Our house Somersby, Endcliffe Grove Avenue, Sheffield. We later added a two-storey extension to the right of the building.

Left: Disneyland LA with captain Sean and little Antonia. A day off during the recording of my *From America With Love* album. 1974.

Below left: On the practice putting green at Lees Hall Golf Club, Sheffield, circa 1975.

Below right: Karate lesson in Dublin, 1976.

L to R: Dorothy Soloman, Robin Boyle, Lene Zavaroni, Brian Willey, Jackie Trent, Paul Brodie, Charles Beardsall, Me, Tony Hatch, Alyn Ainsworth. Berlin Airport, 1976.

Sean, Antonia and little Sarah, 1978.

My little Sarah in the dress the owner of Blighties Club bought her on our big day!

My gorgeous family.

Sue and I in Las Vegas at The Grand just before it burnt to the ground.

Above: Enjoying a drink with John Ashley my father-in-law and John Junkin who we had just met on board the *Arcadia*.

Left: John and Jenny Junkin with our god-daughter Annabel.

Performing live in 1976.
(Alamy)

On *Hits Europa*, June 26th,
1978. (Alamy)

Our house in Streetly, Sutton Coldfield. I loved this house.

Sue and I (note the moustache) with Anne and Ashley Jackson the artist at the Jumbo Chinese Restaurant in Leeds on Easter Sunday, 11th April 1982. It was our favourite haunt on many Sundays when we lived in Sheffield.

Fun memories with Peter and Jackie at a pyjama party in the mid-80s in Sutton Coldfield.

Strawberry Studios, 1980s.
(Alamy)

Sharing a beer
with my dad,
Christmas 1987.

Beautiful evening
on the MS *Europa*.
Sue says, 'Very
'80s dress.'

A wonderful
evening with our
great friends
Jenny and John
Junkin.

Having a laugh with Sheffield's funniest comedian and actor Bobby Knutt.

Myself and good old mate Bill Tarmey, actor/singer extraordinaire.

Janette Krankie in Australia — sorry Ian, think she's found a replacement.

Above: Howard Keel Golf Classic Dinner – see who you can spot.

Left: Singing with my hero Howard Keel.

Below left: Sue and I with the magnificent Howard Keel. Fond memories of him and his lovely wife Judy.

Below right: With Vic Damone in Howard Keel's suite. A great evening.

on the BBC on February 1.

Summer seasons hadn't been something I'd been used to, but Harvey thought it was a good idea, perhaps latching on to the TV shows that were being shown in the summer at coastal resorts so, on July 18 and for a seven-week run, except for two weeks in August, I headlined twice-nightly at The Pier in Cleethorpes with Cannon and Ball as my support act. Guys 'n' Dolls took over from me for the fortnight because that's when I headlined at Bridlington Spa in East Yorkshire. I followed Mike Yarwood's fortnight and Ken Dodd followed me.

One thing I vowed never again was to wear a jumpsuit on stage. They must have been all the rage for entertainers and pop stars around then and I'd chosen to wear one, but it soon went once I'd finished. It was just too much for a guy like me.

I'd had one moment when I'd been watching television in my dressing room and suddenly heard my band playing my opening number. I dashed down two flights of stairs and ran on to the stage with my zip open all down the back of my suit. I went on stage and Mike (Ryal) had to come to my rescue and zip me up after the opening song.

The second single of the year was 'Stolen Love', written by three people I can't unfortunately tell you anything about (Seals, Bryant and Williams) and on the flip was 'First Love, Best Love', written by Berni Flint. It was my only single to be produced by Mike Berry and Hal Shaper, with Laurie Holloway as arranger, who was musical director for Michael Parkinson's shows and *Strictly Come Dancing*, and was released in late July.

I was running around everywhere, playing Blighty's Nightclub in Farnworth to help raise money for a surgical unit, with Stu Francis on the bill; to headlining Jollee's in Stoke-on-Trent with fellow South Yorkshireman and sadly missed great entertainer, Bobby Knutt; and then another time with the great Paul Shane, who went on to become a big TV star in *Hi-de-Hi!* There were week-long stints at The Troubadour Club in Cardiff and in others throughout the UK, but the days of two-week residencies in nightclubs were coming to an end.

My final single release with MCA Records was another change for me. For the first time, I was to release a record as a duet and with a lady with a tremendous blues voice. Dana Gillespie had played the original Mary Magdalene on stage in the West End in *Jesus Christ Superstar* and I think we first came together around the time I was singing as Magaldi in *Evita*. The single that was released in November 1977 was called 'Magdalena' and is billed as Tony Christie featuring Dana Gillespie. I recall singing the song with her on the BBC's *Pebble Mill at One* show in Birmingham.

Perhaps someone at MCA thought I was destined for a career in musicals at that stage, because the flip side was a song from the Andrew Lloyd Webber and Alan Ayckbourn production, *By Jeeves*. The song was 'Half a Moment'. And that was it. I was out of contract with MCA.

CHAPTER 14

It was to be a Sweet September

Although the '70s were coming to a close, I was still keeping busy on TV and in the nightclubs and we were still living the dream with a new Rolls Royce every year and my TON10 number plate. We'd earned enough to send our children to good schools and loved our house, our neighbours, family and friends in Sheffield. I was keeping fit running a couple of miles up the hill back to ours and around the nearby park when I was at home, playing golf with my friends and enjoying my real ale beers. I'm a proper CAMRA man when it comes to beer and enjoy a pint or two with the lads down at my local to this day, with one of my favourites being Timothy Taylor's Landlord. Always a good pint.

My TV work was varied in 1978, including BBC's *Cabaret Showtime* with American singer-songwriter Diane Solomon in June, followed by two Granada TV programmes for ITV. The first of those was *Juke Box Saturday Night*, that looked back to popular songs of the War Years in July; and then Paul Daniels' *Blackpool Bonanza*, that was broadcast on 20 August, another great entertainer now sadly lost.

This was a return to the lavish TV sets with huge stages that I was to feature in for many years on mainland Europe and came about because we were in Norcalympia in the Norbreck Castle. It sounds great and it looks great now looking back at my part in the show, which took up nearly seven minutes with my rendition of 'Macarthur Park' and 'Didn't We'. Two fabulous songs written by Jimmy Webb and both recorded by Richard Harris. It also featured my new look of the curly perm. Well, it was 'in' then you know.

The arrangement was absolutely superb by Les Reed; and with

Derek Hilton as musical director and the Pop Proms Orchestra, you just couldn't go wrong. I even appeared with the three Elvis impressionists who had been appearing in *Elvis — The Musical* at the Astoria Theatre in London and were to go on and win several awards. PJ Proby was supposed to do the gig, but couldn't be there, so I closed the show singing 'Blue Suede Shoes' with Shakin' Stevens, Tim Whitnall and Bogdan Kominowski.

1979/1980 were extraordinary years in many ways. I was in varying ways disappointed, surprised, worried, distressed and elated, all at different times. And it was to see another chapter begin in my recording career when I met with songwriter and producer Graham Sacher.

My disappointment during this time was in the royalty income for my records with MCA. They were telling me they hadn't recouped their investment, but I couldn't believe it. I was very disillusioned, particularly when it looked as though others were earning a lot of money off just one hit. I'd had records in the charts around the world and wasn't getting anything back. Yes, we'd had good money in terms of the contract, but I felt there should have been more than we had received based on the sales we had been told. It turned out the contract I'd had with MCA had been an American contract, which meant anything sold outside of America earned me half. Just about every record I sold was elsewhere!

I wasn't an accountant and I never will be, but in this game, like many more artists before me, it seems it's the record companies that always win. Having said all that, this isn't about crying over spilt milk now, it's just stating where I was at the time. I have absolutely no regrets about what happened thanks to Harvey, who got me that recording contract. I know there are many more entertainers out there who will never get the opportunity I received, so this is just me telling you how I felt in 1979.

The other downbeat side was that cabaret-style clubs were now closing with increasing regularity.

Disco and punk or new wave music had changed everything. Glitzy dancefloors of discotheques, like those shown in the film *Saturday Night Fever*, and kids with green hair and chains through their mouths were into 'new' music. It led to the work being more spasmodic, with perhaps one night in Wales and the next in Scotland. That might be okay when you are touring the UK, playing sell-out 1200-seat theatres, but when you're entertaining a couple of hundred, and by now sometimes far less, it is tough on the body and mind as well as the wallet and bank balance, I can assure you, regardless of how many hits you've had or haven't had.

Worry came in the form of a phone call from Sean's housemaster at Shiplake. He'd fractured his spine playing rugby at 11 years old, although he hadn't known at the time. His housemaster had asked whether we knew of anything troubling Sean because he was constantly asking for paracetamol and saying he was experiencing headaches. We talked with him over the Christmas holidays and he said it was his back that hurt when he sat. He'd fractured his spine playing for his rugby colours and ended up having what we were told was a very complicated spine operation.

Sean had to have a bone graft and has two large screws holding his vertebrae together. It was a long healing process and he was in a body brace for months. Thank God all is well now.

Elation came in several ways. I was presented with the Male Vocalist of the Year award at the *Club Mirror* National Club Acts Awards of 1979/80, held at the Lakeside Country Club in Frimley Green, Surrey. Check this out for the others who received awards: Paul Daniels, Freddie Starr, Patti Boulaye, The Rockin' Berries and Faith Brown. All fantastic entertainers.

Surprise came with my first European continent-only hit record, 'Sweet September', which was recorded and released in late 1979 and became a big hit right across Europe, reaching No 7 in Switzerland, No 16 in Germany and No 13 in Austria in early 1980. I had a new TV career, this time much more in Europe than at home and a new look, albeit still with the curly perm when I appeared on the show *Starparade* with the songs, 'What a Little Love' and then 'Sweet

September'. Gone was the showing of the hairy chest and in its place was a suit with sparkly tie and scarf.

'Sweet September' has remained one of my most enduringly popular songs in Europe and was written by Belgian and English songwriters BM Heinz and Phil Francis, who was a member of a Belgian pop group called Octopus. It has a Greek feel to it and fits perfectly for what Europeans refer to as Schlager music, songs that you can clap along with on the beat. It's the kind of music that brings a smile to everyone's face on the continent and it is a joy to continue singing it today. I became known in the Schlager music genre.

'Sweet September' was my first release for RCA Victor but, like all of my new solo recordings for the next 20 years, only on mainland Europe. I'd hooked up with English songwriter and producer Graham Sacher in 1979. Graham wrote some lovely songs for me, including 'Mexico City' and 'Ladies' Man'.

We first met when I was booked for a corporate event at a big hotel near Heathrow Airport. Graham was there with another popular singer, Malcolm Roberts, whose song 'Love Is All' had been a big hit in the late '60s. Malcolm introduced me to Graham when they came back stage, as he was recording with him. Graham said he'd always wanted to meet me and as a record producer and songwriter he'd like to work together.

I had the new record deal with RCA and Graham had the rights to this wonderful song 'Sweet September', that was my first mainland Europe only hit. It was a great start and gave me new opportunities with TV, which as we all know makes the difference when you're trying to sell records. One of the backing singers on the song was Cheryl Baker, who I'd met while competing in A Song for Europe.

The only stipulation I ever made about performing on mainland Europe was I wouldn't sing in anything other than my native language, not because I couldn't have tried, but because I was told the minute you do that you destroy your reputation as an international artist, unless you do it on the very odd occasion, like I had done in studio with 'Avenues and Alleyways' and 'Don't Go Down to Reno' in Spanish.

'Sweet September' was backed on the flip with one of Graham's songs, 'I'm Not Chained to You', and he also wrote the flip side to the follow-up single which charted in Germany again, but just outside the Top 50, with 'Train to Yesterday', written by German Schlager music songwriting duo, Robert Puschmann and Friedrich Dorff. In the course of writing this book, it has come to light it was played on a TV programme called *Foreign Stars* in the Soviet Union. I was going further and further east! Graham's B side was 'Summer in the Sun'.

'Mexico City' was the third single release and this time Graham wrote both the A and B sides, with 'What a Little Love Can Do' on the flip, that I sang on the *Hit Parade* TV show. It wasn't a chart hit, but that's probably because it appeared on my first all-German/European LP release for RCA Victor, *Ladies' Man*, which really was a success, charting 12 May 1980 and staying in the charts for nine weeks.

Ladies' Man included six of Graham's songs and two of mine, 'Devil in Me' and 'Once More from the Top'. The album was also released across Scandinavia on the Polydor label and in Holland on CNR. On the LP cover, it looks as though I've taken up smoking again as I'm holding a cigar. I think my tie could have been better organised. It was good to be back in the charts and on the TV. The following year, I was honoured with Die Goldene Europa from the German radio's Saarlaendischer Rundfunk for outstanding performance in show business.

While the hits in the UK were now seemingly in the past, I certainly hadn't been forgotten by TV at home and I once again had my own show as part of HTV's nationally networked *The Entertainers* series on Saturday 7 June 1980.

My distress around this time? Now, let's just get this right, not just distress, but my devastation came from something Sue and my brother-in-law Peter found hilarious. Now at this point, it's worth recalling my love of birds here and how my grandfather used to tell me all about them. It's something that has never left me.

I had a bird called Timmy, that one of my mates from my local, the Nottingham House pub on Whitham Road, had rescued. He was a cross between a goldfinch and a canary. I was heading off to Germany for another TV appearance one morning and went to say good morning to my pet Timmy and he just swung round from top to bottom while still attached to his perch. He was dead, and in not quite the words of *Monty Python*'s famous dead parrot sketch, I found the only reason he had still been upright when I had seen him was that he had been glued there!

Sue is still crying with laughter now while I recount this tale, but I was truly devastated. She and Peter tell me they did it because they didn't want me going away feeling bad, but I'm not so sure. Peter, who is from Chesterfield, and was staying with us, had stuck Timmy's claws to the sandpaper on the perch! I've never been into swinging birds of any variety!

I was always coming home with birds and animals and usually from my mates in the pub. One time, I arrived back with a giant rabbit called Rhoda, that I'd taken on because my chum Peter, who was a lorry driver, said his wife had told him he couldn't have it anymore. Sue thought it was so big it looked more like a wallaby. Sadly, Rhoda met a fateful end one night due to a fox.

Although those two events were distressful, they were nothing in comparison to the stress that was about to come my way in 1981. The year that nearly broke us.

CHAPTER 15

The end of Endcliffe and my time in Sheffield

If you turned on your TV in Germany or the UK in 1981 and saw me either singing my Schlager songs for my European fans — including 'Summer Wine', written by Graham, that didn't chart, but was a nice song, backed with 'I'm Coming Home', written by Graham and I, or performing with Marti Caine again on her BBC show *Marti* in March, or my hits on Granada's *The Video Entertainers* for ITV — you'd probably think nothing other than there he is again. But it was to be a tough time.

In March 1981, I'd also performed at the Egyptian Embassy in London before Princess Alexandra and Mrs Sadat for charity, on behalf of Egyptian handicapped children, and as a result plans were afoot for an Egyptian tour the following year in 1982, yet behind the scenes I was having the most troubling times of my career since the late '60s.

I'd been getting twitchy about the way in which the nightclub scene was going. I was also no longer having hits in the UK. Everything was moving on and I was beginning to panic.

Out of desperation, I went into what was to prove a disaster from day one until the end of it — and by then, we were in up to our necks.

Thinking about it logically, I had felt maybe it was time to try something, invest in a business that would bring in some more cash. I didn't want to work in a new set up, just be a partner that would perhaps even allow me to ease up a little on being away from home, as I still seemed to be forever touring and running around from country to country. I felt having another enterprise might be a good backstop, perhaps enabling me to say no to some of the gigs I was accepting and spend time with Sue and the children. It was a living nightmare for about a year and almost bled us dry.

I went into business with Mike Doughty, a good friend who was landlord of my local, the aforementioned Nottingham House, or 'Notty House', as it was known. We had known each other a while and I put money into a club at the back of the south stand at Sheffield Wednesday's Hillsborough ground that had previously been known as the Ozzie Owl Club.

We called it Christie's, but before it even opened things started going wrong. Sue hated it from the beginning — the club itself (not the football club), the décor. It just wasn't what we should have gone into. It was meant to be a restaurant and disco, not a place where I would perform.

The day we were going to open we found out it needed a new dancefloor that was going to cost tens of thousands. It needed re-strengthening as the cement was crumbling and we didn't have enough capital to do it. We sunk in even more to get the place open as disco was all the rage, but now we were already seriously under pressure. I already wanted to get out, but we seemed too far in.

There are some who remember it fondly these days on websites — and others who don't. I can't say our experience of Christie's was anything other than of it being one of the worst times of our lives. People just didn't seem to want it to exist. We lost the music licence, as there had been complaints about noise and whatever else was happening as people were leaving.

It certainly wasn't what I had envisaged when we'd gone into it and it never took off. I'd go down to be there when I wasn't working elsewhere; and Sue worked behind the bar at times when we were short-staffed. I was never comfortable there and felt stupid that we were in danger of losing everything.

I sold whatever I could to stave off bankruptcy, because as well as the debts through Christie's there was also outstanding tax where I'd thought I was up to date. I checked in a decent-sized life insurance policy, cars, personalised number plate and the house, basically whatever I could sell. I've made a lot of mistakes in my life, but this was by far the biggest.

Looking back now, I'm glad it went down. It gave me a huge kick up the backside and made me concentrate wholly on my real career.

My accountant had a sense of humour about it all. He suggested I go bankrupt and sing under my wife's maiden name! I forgave him for that, but otherwise you could have been listening to Sue Ashley for the past 37 years! I think he meant just the last name, but I could have been the original Boy Named Sue.

I was given 18 months to pay off the tax, as I'd been able to pay some of it immediately.

We sold the house to Rick Savage of the Sheffield rock group Def Leppard, who went on to sell multi-millions of albums in the States, and we left Sheffield. We just had to get away and we moved to a really lovely house in Streetly, Sutton Coldfield.

I had been working while we had Christie's. It wasn't as though I'd taken any kind of back seat, it was just that what I had planned for us to make money had cost us nearly everything we had. It was time to get everything paid off, paid up and back straight. Once I'd got my head back around everything, I took every scrap of work I could take. I told my agents, just get me the work, I don't care where it is or what it is.

I was back to playing places I hadn't played since the '60s, of those that were left, because clubs were still on their way downhill. And I was back to performing six or seven nights a week, but I was determined never to get us into that same situation again. I've always been a workaholic and this was definitely the time to be one.

On the one hand, I was going up to Butlin's in Ayr on the Scottish coast every Thursday, and on the other, I was in the air to Australia, New Zealand, the Middle East, Germany and Scandinavia.

Christie's may have been my ultimate bad experience, but it taught me a very big lesson. I'm a singer and certainly not a businessman.

CHAPTER 16

Light at the end of the tunnel,
putting a light in your window
and a new drummer!

'Four weeks in Australia; two weeks on the *Sea Princess* between Sydney and Singapore, two weeks in Singapore and four weeks in Scotland, stopping only for three days during which he is giving a concert at London's Royal Festival Hall,' was one of the quotes from journalist Ann Busby in a newspaper in what must have been 1982.

I'd been quoted as saying, 'I've got to work myself to death for a couple of years to try and get back what I've lost. I'm busier now than I've ever been. Luckily I've still got my voice. I learned a lot from Christie's — stick to what you know best. It's thrown me back into the business. I neglected my real business during the Christie's saga. I turned down tours and spent a lot of time in Sheffield trying to make a go of the club. I'm not bitter, I've got over all the worry. There isn't much call for my sort of work in England. It's abroad where all the work and the money is. I like England and it would be a shame to uproot my family but if the right offer came along I would have to say yes and live abroad, I'm afraid.'

It's amazing how that last part eventually came true ten years later, but back then it was all about performing anywhere and everywhere — and it still brought about fantastic opportunities.

Derek Franks became my agent in the early '80s and it's he and his wife Debbie who looked after me so well with bookings all around the world for many years. His Derek Franks Organisation business looked after artists like Gerry and the Pacemakers, Gilbert O'Sullivan,

Alan Price, Vince Hill, Buddy Greco and one I introduced to Derek — Al Martino — having met him on tour.

Derek would contact me while I was on tour in Australia and say, 'Whilst you're there, can you pop over to New Zealand for another two weeks,' as though it was just like going to a local corner shop. I'd be away sometimes between six to twelve weeks with my faithful musical director Mel Dean. Another time on a six-week, Australian tour, he'd say, 'Can you get on the *QE2* and they'll take you to Singapore?'

When I told Derek that I hadn't seen Sue for six weeks and I wanted to go home, he rang back and said, 'They will fly her out to Sydney,' which they did. So, we went on part of the *QE2*'s Round the World trip. I performed two shows on board and part of the rider was they had to fly Sue out.

Since then we've had some fabulous cruises, especially on the German cruise liners, such as the MS *Europa*, where they have as many staff as there are passengers and everything is 5-star plus. We have seen places we would never have seen, from South America to Russia.

On that first *QE2* sailing, I had another weird experience. I'd been used to fans getting in first at my shows and coming to the front, wanting to be close, and on-board ship there was a rush, or at least as rushed as they could manage, of older people wanting to be on the front row.

Unfortunately, due, I hope, to their age and nothing more, they would all then fall asleep. It was very odd. People behind them were having a blast, enjoying the show and this lot were all in la-la land. I had a word with the stage manager about it when I came off and he said that I shouldn't worry because the previous week Frankie Vaughan had been on and had come off crying, thinking he'd lost his touch.

I met Al Martino around this time too. He used to take blackout curtains wherever he went and always cooked his own food on a little stove he took everywhere, along with his own pots and pans. He cooked scrambled eggs for breakfast for Sue and I one time while we were in a hotel in Switzerland. By then I'd introduced him to Derek and he would look after him on tour.

During the tail end of 1981 and into early 1982, I had another hit in Germany, this time with 'Put a Light in Your Window', written by Tony Hiller and Paul Curtis, which was backed with the B side 'Paradise', the first collaboration to be released between Graham Sacher and I. It reached No 32. Four of Paul's songs have won the UK's Song for Europe contest, including The Shadows' 'Let Me Be the One', that finished in second place in Eurovision 1975, so he had European pedigree.

'Put a Light in Your Window' was followed up with another single in 1982 that, although it didn't chart, holds fond memories. It was called 'Long Gone' and was written by myself and my good mate John Junkin. The B side had 'Time' written by Graham and I.

Paul Curtis became part of the songwriting team for a very short while with me and Graham and the next single was 'Me and Marie', written by the other two. I wrote the B side with Graham, 'Caribbean Nights'. There must have been something getting into my brain about 'Me and Marie', because I remember saying to Sue something rather uncomplimentary about the song. I asked her to tell Graham I wasn't happy with it. I wanted him to find some new songs because I wasn't going to sing this **** anymore. His reaction was that songs like 'Me and Marie' were what the European audience wanted. I didn't think so about that one and its lack of success possibly tells its own story.

My second album with RCA was *Time and Tears*, released in 1982 and featuring all the songs from the four singles and four more including another that John (Junkin) and I wrote together, 'Another Lonely Day'. Graham wrote some lovely songs at the start. We had some decent hits that had plenty of airplay around Europe, but towards the end of our recordings together, I just felt the magic of those early hits was gone.

'Ti Voglier Mi Amore (I Want You My Love)', written by Graham and I, was a further single release on RCA Victor with a combined Sacher-Curtis-Christie song, 'Higher on Your Love' on the flip, but there were two more albums that also saw the light of day in 1983 and both produced by Graham. I'd stay with him in Surbiton while we were writing, and Paul would be there too. It was a team effort on the writing side.

The two RCA Victor albums released that year were *As Long as I Have You*, which showcased what we had written as a three; and the other was a country music album of standards, including 'Rhinestone Cowboy', 'Ruby Don't Take Your Love to Town', 'Blue Bayou', 'Lucille', 'Jambalaya', 'I Recall a Gypsy Woman' and 'I can't Stop Loving You'. It was a joy to make as I've always loved country music and had included others, such as 'The Most Beautiful Girl', 'Tequila Sunrise' and 'Stained Glass Blue', on *From America with Love* in 1974. I recorded it in Strawberry Studios, the first time I'd released what I'd recorded there.

1983 was also the year I performed at the Royal Festival Hall with legendary arranger and conductor Billy May and the BBC Radio Orchestra for BBC Radio 2. Billy was a trumpet player with the Glenn Miller Orchestra during the war years and when he formed his own band for studio work he recorded with all my heroes, Sinatra, Peggy Lee, Nat King Cole and Ella. It was an honour to sing under his direction and with the fabulous Kenny Baker on trumpet.

By now my life was getting back on track again, our life was much better without the hassle of the club to worry about.

We had moved in 1982 and I was back having fun on the golf course, doing pretty well in Celebrity Pro-Am days, and flying light aircraft whenever time gave me the opportunity. I'd gained my private pilot's licence during the mid-70s and regularly flew a two-seater Cessna 150 with the registration GBBC1. I flew once a week for a while.

I'd taken up flying having chatted with a chap who was a member of my golf club in Sheffield and used to fly from Doncaster out over Sheffield. I'd take Sean and Antonia up for a spin. Sue flew up to see me one time in the North East when there had been a rail strike. A friend brought her. I don't think she enjoyed the flight very much.

My licence had arrived the day before we flew out for a New Zealand tour and I was offered the opportunity to fly a Cessna 172 to Wellington's main airport — not, I hasten to add, from the UK! Just a local flight in New Zealand, but great fun.

Back on terra firma, our move to Foley Road East in Streetly was ideal. We were nearer the kids' schools and I loved the house and the area. I'd known about the area through my friend Peter the lorry driver, who had given me the big rabbit and the bird in Notty House. Years before we moved, he had given me directions of how to get to Wales one time using a different route.

That's when I'd seen and fallen in love with the place. We couldn't just buy it outright, as we may have been able to before the Christie's debacle, so we took out a mortgage like everybody else and it was great. The kids were growing up and the work was coming in through Derek and Debra thick and fast. Sean was now a teenager and, I've got to tell you, an impressive drummer.

Scan was 16 in 1984 and joined the band around that time. We'd known he would be a musician right from the start. We'd had musicians in and out of our three homes in Sheffield and he would be up with them from being four to five months old.

Antonia would sneak in too. She remembers it well. 'It was one of our secrets from Mum,' she said, as I've been writing. 'We knew we shouldn't have been up, really, but we would watch snooker on television with Dad while the band had some of Mum's casserole.'

Sue would pretty much be running a continuous pan of stew for when I arrived home with band members at any time of day from the late '60s through the '70s and '80s. We were usually getting in at the early hours of the morning, having travelled back from the shows and Sue used to call Sean and Antonia the 'Daddy's home' radar, because they both seemed to instinctively know when I'd arrive, they would wake up accordingly.

Like any child with rhythm and wanting to play drums we had to take the cutlery away from Sean in restaurants, but he'd taken lessons and at 12–13 years old he was playing in the school's bands. His headmaster had told us not to worry about his studies, as he was a great musician and they didn't want to lose him. He was holding the bands together.

I was about to play a six-week run with my band at The Palace Casino on the Isle of Man and my drummer couldn't make it because his mum was terminally ill. Sean said he knew everything and to let him play. I had no problem at all with Sean's ability, the only problem was he was in hospital at the time, not the best way to apply for a job under the circumstances. He'd been a passenger in a car accident that had left him with a dislocated leg and damaged arteries. It had been serious, but he was on the mend. We checked with the consultant, who explained that if he stayed off the leg he should be okay. Sean joined the band and played from then on, until Sue and I made our move to Spain. It was another proud moment for me, my son playing in my band. You can't buy that kind of joy.

CHAPTER 17

Jerry Toger takes over as manager —
I meet Dusty Bin
The Bradford City Fire —
and our reason for leaving the UK

I've followed football since I was a kid and, as we all know, two massive tragedies occurred at English grounds during the '80s, where 152 people lost their lives purely through attending matches. The first of those was 11 May 1985, when at the end of a fantastic season that had already seen Bradford City promoted, a fire in the stadium at Valley Parade was the cause of 54 Bradford City fans and 2 Lincoln City fans losing their lives. It was a day their families, friends and fellow supporters will never forget and such a tragic day for everyone.

I joined a host of singers, actors, TV personalities and others, who recorded 'You'll Never Walk Alone', as a charity record to aid the families who had lost loved ones in the disaster that I know will never leave them. Ours was only a small effort in comparison to the agony and despair many have faced for the past 30-plus years, but I hope it helped in some way through the recording. Gerry Marsden had decided to do it and he starts the song, with me next and then the Nolan Sisters, before the whole choir, who were called The Crowd. We appeared on *Top of the Pops* and the record went to No 1 on June 1, 1985.

Four years later at Hillsborough football ground, at the Liverpool v Nottingham Forest FA Cup semi-final, 96 Liverpool fans were to lose their lives due to overcrowding in the Leppings Lane stand. Court cases still carry on to this day. I truly feel for everyone who lost their lives; and their families who still live with the disaster every day. I guess I played an even smaller part in helping than with The Crowd, as I was involved in a concert at Sheffield City Hall to raise aid for the families and those who had been injured.

On a much lighter note, Cynthia Payne, who became known as Madam Cyn, attended that night. She came backstage. At the time, she had been standing for election in the General Election with what she called the Payne and Pleasure Party. She gave me her autograph on her election flyer and signed it: 'To Tony, thank you for all your past custom.' We had it on our fridge for years.

In July 1985, now no longer with a record company deal, I had a single released by the same company that had been responsible for the record by The Crowd. It was the song 'The Wind Beneath My Wings' on their A.1 Records label, but again the best part of that recording was for me the B side, again another Christie/Junkin song, 'Dancing in the Shadows', where I am credited for the first time as producer. John and I were always great mates and so were Jenny and Sue.

Clubland may well have been struggling, but I was still finding work in between my cruise ship work and tours set up by Derek and Debra. Once again, I was honoured as Male Vocalist of the Year in the *Club Mirror* National Club Acts Awards for 1985/86, held for the first time in the north of England at the Quaffers Club in Bredbury near Stockport. Bernard Manning was compering and comedian of the year was Michael Barrymore.

In July 1986, I made what was now a rare appearance on a UK TV show, when I sang 'Rainy Night in Georgia' on the game show *3–2–1*, hosted by Ted Rogers, including his sidekick Dusty Bin, at Yorkshire Television studios in Leeds. I'd just flown back in from another Australian tour and wore a white suit performing the song and then delivering the cryptic clue to the contestants. I enjoy cryptic crosswords, but I don't know whether I'd have worked out any of the *3–2–1* clues.

On the Australian tour, I'd also met up with Ian and Janette Krankie and Petula Clark. The Krankies had finished their tour and I had finished mine. Petula was taking over from me at the same venue in Tweed Heads. We decided to go to a restaurant on the wharf to celebrate and have some good seafood and a few 'drinks'. It was a really good night and we had a lot of laughs and a lot of drinks.

My career in Germany and the rest of Europe had taken another turn in the mid-80s too, when a gentleman called Jerry Toger from Munich first became my agent for work over there and then became my manager. It was around 1986 that my work on the continent, Ireland, Australia and New Zealand began taking over even more from the UK club work.

Jerry was the man who began my next great period of chart success, but it wasn't to come instantly. First, he organised a new record deal with Polydor and in 1986 I had a new record release, the single 'Keep On Dancin'', written by Glen Focus, Freddie Manders and me. It was backed with 'Strangers', written by myself, Freddie and M Recilas. Record releases get you back on TV and 'Keep on Dancin'' did the job.

The follow-up single was 'Battle of Wounded Pride' in 1987, written by Geoff Stephens and John Carter with the B side being 'Memories', written by the same collaboration team as 'Strangers'. Neither single gave me a hit, but they gave me renewed exposure and that was to pay off two years later when I met the man who was to give my career its biggest boost since Harvey put me with Mitch, Peter and Neil Sedaka.

1989 was a turning point. It had all been going so well with the Swing into Spring UK theatre tour, which I'd undertaken with Vince Hill, Patti Gold and the big band sound of the Squadronaires. We'd played everywhere, including the London Palladium, each night performing a three-and-a-half-hour show of US chart hits and more besides.

I then suffered from two serious incidents of being ripped off by not getting paid for a week in Wales, where the promoter 'did a runner' with the takings, and another who didn't pay me for playing a week's work in the reopening of the Wakefield Theatre Club, that had played host to some of the world's best during the '60s and '70s, had then become The Pussycat Club and had reverted back to its original name. The owner didn't just rip me off, but other artists as well.

Those incidents were enough for Sue and I to decide that the time had perhaps come for us to leave the UK and head for Spain. I'd been filming for a Dutch TV show on the island of Aruba in the southern Caribbean with Helen Shapiro and Dutch singer, Albert West.

It was Sue's friend Anna Devine from Streetly who introduced us to Mojacar in Spain around that time as she had bought a villa. We fell in love with its very rustic appearance on the coast, having been there for a short spell in August 1989 and on our third day put down a deposit on a holiday villa.

It still took a while before we left, for what seemed like for good, but by 1991, aside from coming back for family events and occasional UK bookings, that was to be it for us for the next 15 years — and my career had gone stellar once again, thanks to four amazing people.

CHAPTER 18

Enter Jack White — Welcome to My Music

Jack White, Jerry Toger, Fritz Rau and Max Schautzer changed everything for me from 1990. Sue and I had finally made the decision to leave the UK and we were in the process of selling our house in Sutton Coldfield. I was ready to relax, play golf in the sun and take things easier.

I had carried on playing theatres and clubs back home, despite the rip-off merchants of 1989, but home was now just above Mojacar Playa on the Costa De Almeria in south-east Spain. The town's whitewashed housing is built in to a rocky hillside that leads down to the beaches from Europe's only desert and when we were there the population was well under today's 6000.

Our plan was to rent for six months and build on a small plot of 3000 square metres we had bought, in all about three-quarters of an acre on the hill overlooking the Playa, but we never got the building licence, the land was turned rustic, which meant we could not build on it, but we had found that we loved where we rented so we stayed there throughout our time in those warmer climes where the sun always shines. We still own the land today.

Mojacar in 1990 was nothing like the size it has grown. It is an ancient village and had no streetlights, no pavements or supermarkets. It was just raw and superbly sparse when we first moved there. This was the time before it started becoming really popular. It's an hour from Almeria and is now known as the Spanish Riviera. It's one hour away from Murcia and two hours from Alicante.

In the 15 years we were there, we made great friends and thoroughly enjoyed the lifestyle. Our kids were adults, or close to being, so when we left Sutton Coldfield, Sarah was at 6th form and staying with friends, Antonia was working at the British Consulate in Brazil, and by now, Sean and his then partner, now wife, Lisa, had a place in Walsall. He was in a band with Donal and Tony Rogers at that time. Tony went on to play with the chart band The Charlatans and is still with them.

Jerry Toger had told me that Jack White, probably at that time the most famous music producer in Germany, wanted to meet because he wanted me to take over from David Hasselhoff as his main male recording artist.

Jack had played professional football in the '60s for PSV Eindhoven in Holland. He'd changed his name from Horst Nussbaum, which literally translated means nut tree, when he began producing English-speaking singers in the '80s after cutting his teeth on the German market.

He had produced pop stars like Laura Branigan and Jermaine Jackson and had written several hits too. He worked with Engelbert and David Hasselhoff and was now keen to work with me. He had found out I was free from a recording contract.

We met in Munich. The meeting went well. He asked if I fancied doing something a bit different, real Schlager music that would suit the European market and it suited me fine. Jerry arranged the recording contract with BMG Ariola and so I started on another amazing chapter.

The next year was one of the most fantastic times of my life as a recording artist. My first single release was 'Kiss in the Night', written by Jack and Charles Blackwell, who was the lyricist. He'd worked with the legendary Joe Meek and had been producer and arranger for songs by Tom Jones, Engelbert, PJ Proby and Kathy Kirby. Charles had also written the 1962 No 1 single 'Come Outside' for Mike Sarne and Wendy Richards and he'd co-written with Jack for The Hoff.

Some of the songs I'd sung while being with Graham Sacher had been regarded as Schlager music too, but this time it was full-on in that genre and opened up a whole new world. It was great to be recording again, but even better this time than either with RCA Victor or Polydor, because my records were being bought by tens and hundreds of thousands. It all kicked off with 'Kiss in the Night', that went straight into the German charts having first hit them in July 1990 and stayed on the chart for much of the rest of the year.

'Kiss in the Night' also brought about my first appearance as a guest on the phenomenally successful *Wetten, dass..?* TV show, hosted by Thomas Gottschalk, that was broadcast throughout Europe. The other celebrity performers included Placido Domingo and Tina Turner. I appeared on the show again when Phil Collins was a guest.

I was also on a big TV charity show in Berlin with many other world-famous actors, singers and comedians. I was called to the stage from my dressing room. I came out, turned down this long corridor to be met by dozens of photographers happily snapping away. I thought to myself, my God, I didn't realise I was so famous. Then they started making hand signals to me to move sideways. What I didn't know was that the maestro Luciano Pavarotti had left his dressing room and was walking behind me!

I'd played great venues in the UK, like the London Palladium, the Royal Albert Hall and the Royal Festival Hall, but now I was playing arenas, 7500-seater venues, huge TV shows broadcast throughout Europe — and that was down to another true gentleman who became a good friend, Fritz Rau.

Fritz was a German music promoter and once again it was Jerry who introduced him. Fritz ran one of the biggest agencies for artist tours across Germany and Central Europe, putting on the best shows. He even brought Sinatra over to Hamburg, just before Frank passed away in 1998, and I finally had the chance to see my hero live in concert. I'd always been busy previously when he'd toured. He'd been to Germany a few times during the '90s and not only were we going to see him, we were also going to meet him backstage before the show, but the Christie jinx struck!

Sue and I have missed out on seeing a number of other stars at various times, not through our ill health, but the people we were due to see. It's as though they know the Christies must be on their way, quick, let's not appear! But on this occasion, Fritz had arranged for us to meet Sinatra backstage.

I was looking forward to meeting him in the flesh, but our plans were scuppered when we encountered a protest march while in our taxi on the way to see him.

By the time we got there, having ditched the taxi, and Sue having completed the last mile in high heels as quickly as she could, it was all in vain. We'd just missed him. He'd taken the car to the stage. He was in the wings waiting to go on when we arrived and was flying straight from the venue to the Connaught Hotel in London, where he always stayed when in Europe.

Unfortunately, the Frank Sinatra I'd grown up listening to was now 82, had all sorts of health problems and had trouble remembering his intros and lyrics. When you're standing watching a legend, your hero, forgetting intros, coming in at the wrong times for his own hit songs, it is very sad, but we still loved seeing him perform.

I'd have loved to have seen him in his prime. This turned out to be his last show away from the States. He managed a couple more back there before he passed away a few weeks later. An amazing performer and, hell, what a voice! A real song interpreter.

Single releases followed in quick succession in 1990 and 1991, leading to what was to become my biggest-selling album ever, until a certain little happening in 2005.

The CD singles had become the calling card for the TV companies and radio stations. 'Come with Me to Paradise' charted in Austria and Germany. In Germany, it was my biggest hit single during the '90s, but the important thing was airplay and appearing on the major TV programmes — and Central Europe really liked me. Thankfully, they still do.

Sean continues receiving fan mail every day. I'd become more famous in Germany, Austria, Switzerland and the rest of Central Europe than I was back home in the UK, and the respect and adoration I received was, and still is today, very special to me.

Max Schautzer had one of the biggest shows on TV. He was the mainland Europe version of Terry Wogan in the UK and regularly had me on his always large and impressive shows. He's Austrian-born and became one of the leading radio and TV presenters in Germany. His was a big family show and all the major stars appeared. Each show was held in an open air theme park every Sunday morning during the summer. Max lives in Kitzbuhel and Cologne with his gorgeous wife, Gundel.

Max and Gundel became great family friends and the four of us were all together one night after I'd played in the Beethovenhalle Concert Hall in Bonn. Max had invited us for an after-show supper and we arrived at the restaurant about 10.30pm where there was a massive fish tank with a giant lobster inside.

When we left there was no giant lobster in the tank. Sue was mortified! She and Gundel had been talking to it as we'd entered, like it was a pet — and then we had eaten it!

Germany, Austria, Switzerland, Holland, Belgium, are all still great to me. It appears if you're liked there, then you are liked and supported forever and I'm immensely grateful for all the love and affection mainland Europe has given me over the years. They all became just as much my home countries for travelling and friendship in the 1990s as the UK and Spain.

I know it's a very British way of saying it, but everything really is very well organised in Germany. The people look after you and everything is done to make you feel comfortable. I loved my time in the spotlight there, where I was often described as immaculately dressed and 'the gentleman of the music business'. I had a German TV company, ZDF, come over to the UK earlier this year to interview Sue and I on my birthday.

We took them to see our beautiful cathedral in Lichfield, where our grandsons, Joby and Caius, had been choristers. They were very impressed with our city and we had a wonderful day with Manny and the crew.

1991 was the year of the phenomenally successful *Welcome to My Music*, an album that sold over 450,000 copies alone in Germany where it went double platinum, and it also became my first release anywhere but in Europe for a long time, as it also sold well in South Africa. Jack clearly had the golden touch. It reached No 7 in the German charts and remained in the charts for 30 weeks and the following year *Welcome to My Music 2* charted, staying for 13 weeks.

Welcome to My Music 2 incorporates 'Las Vegas' and 'Avenues and Alleyways', along with another selection of songs by Jack, with lyrics from a team of writers including Charles Blackwell, Fred Jay, Barry Mason, Jerry Rix, Norbert Hammerschmidt and Kurt Hertha. There are other songs and the most notable of those for me was the inclusion of another Christie/Junkin song, 'It Happened in Sevilla'. The albums and singles were all recorded at Smash Tonstudio, Paradise Studios and DI Musikstudio in Munich and Jack's Place in Berlin.

My third album with Jack was *In Love Again*, released in 1993 and followed a similar format using two of my previous well-known songs, 'Don't Go Down to Reno' and 'Solitaire', alongside another host of songs by Jack with his stable of songwriters. I contributed two of my own — 'Sweet Angel in Blue' and 'My Little Latin Lover' written with Jack.

Jerry and Fritz organised some fantastic tours. There was a sell-out 35-venue concert tour in early 1992, followed by another 35-show sell-out at the start of 1993. The 1995 tour started with 33 venues and saw an extension of 13 dates in both Germany and Austria. I couldn't go wrong and my songs from that time, such as 'Kiss in the Night' and 'Come with Me to Paradise', are now massive hits on YouTube. Both tours were brilliantly produced by Stefan Reich.

There were TV appearances all the time in the 1990–1995 period and while all of them were big shows, perhaps the most bizarre was singing 'Come with Me to Paradise' with a dancing pig. The presenter was wearing a sparkly blue top hat as well.

The last album Jack White produced was *Calypso and Rum* in 1994. It's particularly notable for me because I was involved in writing every song. The title track was released as a CD single, along with

'Moon Over Napoli' and 'Dreaming of Natalie', which has also proved a really big hit on YouTube.

Sadly, the recording business, being what it sometimes can be, ended up somewhat acrimoniously with Jack as it had also with Graham, but let's not linger on the whys and wherefores. Our partnership in the first half of the '90s was certainly one that worked very well and our final CD single release was another song we had written between us, 'We're Gonna Stay Together', a duet with Greek/German singer Vicky Leandros, who supported me on tour. Vicky was in the charts in the UK in the early '70s too. Her husband was a baron and looked after us well when we visited their place. He knew how to enjoy a drink.

The *Calypso and Rum* tour was a real highlight. The audiences loved the hits from the '70s, but they also really loved all of my Schlager songs, 'Sweet September', 'Calypso and Rum', 'Moonlight and Roses', and the others from the *Welcome to My Music* albums. By the mid '90s, I had an extensive catalogue of songs to choose from, whether aimed originally at the UK, World or Central European tastes, and my fans loved them all.

My band were all great players, top musicians generally based around Hamburg and when we were getting ready for a tour, I'd be rehearsing with them for about 3–4 days. I like Hamburg because there's always plenty going on. It's a busy city on the Elbe River and very cosmopolitan. Everyone seems to speak English too, which helps.

At the beginning of 1996, I signed to Intercord, one of Germany's major record companies based in Stuttgart. Two years earlier, they had been taken over by EMI Records. My first album on Intercord was *This is Your Day*, recorded at Chameleon Studios in Hamburg, and included the CD single 'Mona Lisa's Smile', that had been particularly well received, as Jerry had announced, on Radio Jacaranda Stereo, the most important radio station in Pretoria. Another CD single, 'Never', followed in 1996.

I now had a new songwriting partner, Engelbert Simons, who I'd worked with previously while with Jack.

Udo Jürgens, who had won the Eurovision Song Contest for Austria in 1966 with 'Merci, Cherie', was an excellent Austrian composer and singer-songwriter, who sold over 100 million records. He'd written the title track to the album *This is Your Day* for his daughter's birthday. I changed it to a wedding song, writing a new lyric in English. My good friend Don Black was going to do it, but was very gracious in letting me write it the way I felt it would work.

Engelbert Simons contributed towards several of the songs on *This is Your Day*, including the most successful song from the album, 'Oh Mi Amor', that has had over 500,000 hits on YouTube. Engelbert had written for many leading artists all around the world.

The era away from Jack White also brought about the release of *This is Your Day* in Australia, New Zealand, South Africa, Thailand and Denmark, with a tour in 1997 that would include Denmark as well as Germany and Austria. Suddenly, I was back being promoted by a record company all around the world.

CHAPTER 19

Come with me to our 15 years in Paradise

W hen we first moved to Spain, I just thought this was it, this was
where we would probably be for the rest of our lives. England
seemed to have forgotten about me and time had moved on. I still went
back for the occasional appearance on TV or the odd concert and I'd
play in celebrity golf days, but that was pretty much where it all started
and ended in terms of my music in the UK.

We left the UK to live in Spain on 12 December 1991 and we were
looking forward to having all of the family out with us for Christmas.
I called Antonia to make arrangements for her flight from Brazil and
she told me the ambassador couldn't give her the week off that she
would have needed. We were all really upset because we hadn't seen
Antonia for months.

I asked Sue what she would like for Christmas and she said she
just wanted all her babies home, no other presents. I had to do
something about it. I called Antonia and she said she now had
clearance to come over. I didn't tell Sue as I felt this would be the best
present ever. I organised Antonia's flights using our friends Pat and
Edna's phone and Sue was totally unaware.

On Christmas Eve, Gill Bradley, Keith's wife, at Badger's Bar in
Mojacar, took Sue out for a little last-minute Christmas shopping so
that I could pick up Antonia from the airport without Sue knowing.
When Sue and Gill came back, I was sitting at the bar, but how strange,
the radio was on playing Frank Sinatra singing 'I'll Be Home for
Christmas'. I looked at Sue and we both started crying, but my tears
were happy tears.

Gill went into the kitchen and called Sue to come in. She pointed to the corner where our beautiful daughter Antonia was standing. At first, this didn't register with Sue, even though she was looking straight at her. Then Antonia said, 'Don't I get a hug?' with a big smile on her face. Sue just screamed in delight and the whole Playa must have heard! It really was a wonderful Christmas. We were all together.

It was to be another 18 months until we saw Antonia again.

Sue and I were on the MS *Europa* on a South American cruise. We were docking in Belem in Brazil on the Amazon delta. Antonia flew in to meet us for the day from Brasilia. That day, I had been offered a big TV show in Germany. I had to leave the ship in Belem, so I had a couple of days to spare. Antonia said, 'Don't fly there straight away, Daddy, come and stay with me in my apartment for a couple of days in Brasilia.' She wanted to take me to her favourite restaurant where she said, 'They treat me like I'm one of the family.'

It was a very busy night at the restaurant and the service was unusually slow and the waiters were not so friendly. They were bouncing our drinks and plates on the table. We didn't notice so much at first because we were so happy being together. We were holding hands across the table and hugging and kissing. Antonia was puzzled by their unusual unfriendliness. When the owner came in, she got up from the table and asked if he would like to come over and meet her dad. He smiled, threw his arms up in the air and called, 'Es Papa! Es Papa!' again and again. All the waiters then came round and gave us all a great big hug.

Sue and I loved the life out in the sunshine and I joined a local golf club. It was only a 9-hole course up in the hills and I soon made several good mates. Golf had always been my escape and out in Spain it was ideal. Every fortnight, we would go to Almeria and play one of the courses around there. They were all superbly well maintained and manicured. The Costa De Almeria has now become one of the most popular golfing destinations in Spain with championship courses and many ex-pats retire out there specifically for the golf. They were designing and opening new courses all the time during our time.

I'd played in quite a few celebrity golf tournaments before we moved to Spain and had done pretty well, winning one or two. I was a member of the Variety Club Golf Society. I'd won at Frank Carson's golf day in Northern Ireland and at Les Dawson's at Royal Lytham St Anne's. The tournament at Lytham was very special.

The legendary Yorkshire cricketer, Freddie Trueman, won by a long way that day with a team of four. Fiery Fred was born in Stainton near Maltby, less than 5 miles from where I was born. Les invited me back to his private club afterwards. I was gobsmacked and also so proud he'd invited me. It was a small gentleman's club, nothing seedy.

When I went to Les's house to meet his then first wife, Meg, I looked at all the celebrities' cars parked outside. They included Bentleys, Rollers (including mine) and Mercs. 'It looks like it's a Mafia gathering,' said Les. Well, of course, I had met Al Martino, who was a great friend and had appeared in *The Godfather* movies.

In September 1990, I had played in a golf tournament with film stars Howard Keel, Jack Lemmon and Johnny Mathis. We all stayed in a hotel in Manchester that night for the dinner and the evening. It was part of what had grown to be the Howard Keel Golf Classic, organised by the great ex-footballer, Willie Morgan, and his gorgeous wife, Kay.

Howard was a very tall man who enjoyed his whisky and, as Sue describes him, 'A beautiful specimen and an amazon of a man.' That night, we were all called out of the hotel at 3 or 4 in the morning because the fire alarm went off. Everyone congregated in the car park and Howard came down in very Hollywood style, sporting dressing gown, cowboy boots and a large glass of single malt.

And then there was my double, my doppelganger, Vic Damone, who'd had million-selling records with 'Again' and 'You're Breaking My Heart' in 1949, and 'On the Street Where You Live' in 1956. His real name was Vito Farinola. He must have been ageing well, or maybe it was me ageing not so well, because people kept getting us mixed up on the course. He was 62, I was 47. He was married to actress Diahann Carroll at the time, one of his five marriages.

I'd been booked elsewhere that evening, so I wasn't there until later and the way it turned out, Sue was sitting next to Vic at the dinner. That kind of exacerbated the problem. Now that he and Sue were together it really did look to others as though he was me.

Eddie Large came up to Vic, thinking he was me and said, 'How are you then, you old bugger, everything all right?' That was when Vic said, 'Who is this Tony Christie?' and Sue just said, 'He's my husband.'

The Howard Keel Classic became an annual event, run for a long time by former Manchester United and Burnley winger, Willie Morgan. When Howard died, Don Felder of The Eagles took over for a while before I began hosting it. Don was a cracking golfer. We raised funds for the NSPCC and Christie cancer hospital in Withington, Manchester.

I've been very fortunate through the celebrity golf world to have had the opportunity to play with some wonderful players on world-famous courses. I've played at St Andrew's, The Belfry and Gleneagles, and once coupled Australian Greg Norman who won The Open twice. I know why The Open is often played at links courses, as I've always found them more challenging than the rest.

Out in Spain, I also played in Toni Dalli's golf tournaments. Tony was a great Italian singer who had come to Yorkshire when he was younger, had been talent-spotted and ended up playing Vegas and having his own American TV show. He had opened a restaurant in Marbella, which is where the Dickie Henderson Classic was also held. Although he's now retired, his sons now run four restaurants in Marbella and Malaga. Sue's sister Jackie and husband Peter had bought a place in Marbella and would come and watch the golf with Sue. I also received invitations to play in Tenerife.

Living and playing in Mojacar certainly improved my game and there were times when I was playing at least three days per week. It's also where I had the other two of my three holes-in-one. I'd regularly be on the course for around 7am and would then meet Sue for lunch afterwards.

Among my golfing buddies made up of ex-pats, was Keith Bradley, who played right back for Aston Villa for many years and set up the

Badgers Golf Society. Keith and his wife Gill had moved to Mojacar after his football career ended and they had just opened Badgers Bar before we arrived. Things were a lot different then. Apart from Badgers near the Hotel Indalo, there was Los Amigos and another place called The Winking Frog. There were great Spanish bars and restaurants, like Fernando's, Tito's, El Cid and Felipe's, that we regularly patronised.

I fondly remember Keith's karaoke nights. He kept us all entertained.

Our daughter Sarah and her husband Martin held their wedding blessing on the beach at Felipe's with the local vicar conducting the service. It was perfect. Felipe's put on a magnificent 5-course banquet. Sarah and Martin chose Mojacar for their blessing because it was there where they first met. It was a holiday romance that lasted.

We loved the food in Mojacar, particularly the sea bass cooked in sea salt and all the shellfish.

Our routine, if I wasn't playing golf or working away, was to pop down to Felipe's and have a cortado and take in the day's newspapers. I'd set my mind to the cryptic crosswords. Lunchtimes were the beach bars at Mojacar Playa or up in the hills.

We weren't ones for going into the bars in the evening, but often our lunches would turn into full afternoon party sessions, as everyone gradually came together in the sun, eating tapas and drinking wine.

One of our favourite restaurants was Novecento, which is now called Ochociento, on Mojacar Playa and I received probably one of the warmest receptions ever when we first walked in. It was, and still is, run by an Italian called Marco and serves fantastic pizza. He'd been trained as a chef in Germany and as soon as we walked in he said, 'I know who you are. I have all your records.'

I also developed into a useful bowls player, playing once a week, so much so that I was selected to play for Mojacar in the Spanish Regional Championships, but a big TV slot came up in Germany just when the championships were to be played, so Badger (Keith) took my place. And they won!

If my work in Germany was for a reasonable length of time, Sue would come, but if it was basically a fly-in and fly-out same day or within a night or two, I'd more often than not go on my own.

Sometimes I'd take the eight-hour drive up to Barcelona to get a flight; or drive a much shorter distance down to Almeria airport where I'd fly to Madrid and stop over there to catch the flight to Germany. One day's job would take three days overall, but I wasn't complaining. It was work and it wasn't as though I had retired. I was writing, performing, appearing, and the German cruises I was booked on were absolutely top dollar in every way. The tours were always high-class affairs.

It really was a glorious time and the friends we made then are still good friends today. It would have been nice having all our family around too, but they were all growing up and doing their own thing — and they came out for holidays. Lisa, Sean's wife, was out regularly with Joby and Caius, and Sarah came when she could. It was more difficult for Antonia because she lived further away.

Bryan Adams used to go to Mojacar before he became world-famous. Our friend, Betsy, recalled chatting with him in Felipe's one day when he was a lot younger. He'd said, 'Look for me on TV, I've quite a lot going on.'

Betsy Lees and her husband, Arthur, were the first couple we met at The Winking Frog, which was sometimes called simply The Frog and was owned by Bob the Frog. Betsy introduced us to everyone. She was a wonderful party person, very sociable and used to appear as a voluptuous maid in the Hammer House of Horror movies, as she was a make-up artist at Elstree Studios. She had a beauty school in Stourbridge. They'd moved out to Mojacar on the advice of Arthur's consultant, as he suffered from chronic asthma and needed to be where he would benefit from the weather.

We travelled the world while we lived in Spain and the cruise liners became our working holidays where everything was laid on. These were full of people who wanted to enjoy themselves and hear my songs. We met Werner and Marlene Schoder on many of the cruises. They practically lived on the MS *Europa* and took two suites on board.

Werner has invited us to stay in Germany many times, telling us that our house is there ready for us whenever we go. He lives in Herrngarten near the Rhine. Sadly, Marlene passed away recently. We had lovely times with them both.

'Kiss in the Night' was always a big hit with my German and Austrian fans on the cruises and I'd have my musical director and quality European musicians. My band members for my concerts around 1992–1995 included Billy King (arrangements, keyboards, guitars), Madeleine Lang (backing vocals and percussion), Rolf Köhler (bass), Nick Oosterhuis (keyboards) and Detlef Wiedeke (guitar). On the cruises, I'd work with my main band and with the excellent musicians they had on board.

Our friends, Pat Coyle and Edna Foden, loved our boxer Max and took care of him and our house when we were away. Patsy and Sammy Skelton would do the same when Pat and Edna couldn't. Max would be spoilt rotten by them all. I sometimes think he had a better social life than us.

We also had the irrepressible Maggie Moyle, who cleaned for us and was fantastic at ironing my shirts. She used to come round and sing all the Irish rebel songs. We certainly couldn't have done the travelling we managed together without any of them.

When it rains for a while in England, I have to say my mind drifts back to those days in Mojacar and all those lovely times we had — and, of course, the golf. Strangely though, the one time I recall going to one of the local festivals it rained all day. It was such a shame for the Spanish girls who were called Baccara, who were headlining and had that big hit with 'Yes Sir, I Can Boogie'.

I returned to England from time to time, but because I hadn't been on TV or radio or in the media spotlight in the UK for such a long period, there were some who wondered whether I was still alive. Apparently, according to Piccadilly Radio, sometime in the '90s I'd been pronounced dead. One of our friends rang them and said they'd just had dinner with Sue and I in Spain and I looked quite well. I've been around in the business long enough to know that's how it goes and didn't take it too hard.

If only they could have Googled me in the '90s, they'd have known just how my career had looked after me in Europe and how established I was — and then Sue's sister, Angela, rang with news I couldn't have expected in a million years and a song that Sean said I should record. It all happened in 1998.

CHAPTER 20

Time to prowl back into the UK charts after 23 years

A few years later, I couldn't be found, although I had been spotted one time, when someone tried to track me down. Mobile phones still had a long way to go in 1998 and smartphones were a good decade away too, so the tried and trusted means of putting a story in a newspaper was the way chosen.

Jarvis Cocker from the band Pulp had written this song, and DJ Parrot, of The All Seeing I, had contacted the *Sheffield Telegraph* to see whether anyone could find me, as they wanted me to sing it. Sue's sister, Angela, rang one day, saying there was a guy who wanted to speak to me. I asked his name and she told me that it was Jarvis Cocker. I said give him my number.

The story in the newspaper had been reported like this: '*Sheffield band The All Seeing I are hoping to put together one of the more bizarre musical connections of modern times: themselves and Sheffield's big-voiced balladeer Tony Christie. But they are having difficulty tracking him down. DJ Parrot wants Christie to sing on the album they are currently recording for London Records. 'We have all been long-term admirers,' says Parrot. 'Partly it is because he is from Sheffield but also because we feel that his style of singing would fit in with what we are doing. We think there could be some interesting results. Jarvis Cocker of Pulp has also said he will write some lyrics. Christie, who left Sheffield some time ago, is believed to be living and working in Spain. Ironically he was recently spotted by music business agent Johnnie Peller on Ecclesall Road. Anybody who knows how Tony can be contacted should contact…*'

I received a phone call saying Jarvis Cocker had written a song called 'Walk Like a Panther', that he wanted me to do. I'd had a song with the same title on my first album, written by Mitch and Peter, but this was completely different. I said to send a copy of the demo to Sean because he knew more about what was happening in England and then Sean sent it over to me. When I first heard it with Jarvis singing on it, I thought what a strange song and wasn't sure. That was my first reaction and it just shows how wrong you can be — or at least how wrong I can be.

Sean talked me into it and, like I said, he knows better than me about music in England. He just said do it, what had I got to lose? It was quirky, different and someone had written it with me in mind, bothered so much to get in touch with me and had a proven track record in writing hit songs. In retrospect, it was Mitch and Peter all over again in a completely different vein, 28 years on from when I'd first met them.

I came over, recorded it, found out somewhere along the way that Jarvis had liked the title of the song from that first album so much that's why he'd used it, but I still wasn't convinced. I'd fitted it in with being on tour in Germany and hopped back over to rejoin my band the next day. I thought little more about it.

I'm from England and you always want to be successful in your home country. A few weeks later, 17 January 1999 to be exact, I was successful in the charts once again. Sean rang to tell me that song I wasn't sure of was being played every hour on Radio 1. I was never a Radio 1 artist in my first time around in the UK, always very Radio 2. Then he told me it had gone straight into the charts at No 10.

I flew back to perform 'Walk Like a Panther', on *Top of the Pops* for the first time since 'Drive Safely Darlin'' in 1976, then flew straight back out to continue my tour in Germany. And for the record, the writing credits weren't just Jarvis, but also included Richard Barratt (DJ Parrot), Jason Buckle and Dean Honer from The All Seeing I. Amazing boys, just amazing. I thank you all so much.

The song is all about Sheffield and how times had changed for people who live there and performers who have had others stealing their limelight. Jarvis writes really well: *'A halfwit in a leotard stands on my stage; the standards have fallen, my value has dropped, but don't shed a tear.'* He's original, of that there's no doubt, and used to drink in the same pub as me in the Notty House. Maybe it was the Yorkshire bitter that brought us together, both in his lyrics and the beer. Either way, 'Walk Like a Panther' has become one of the favourites in my set both in the UK and in Europe. I sometimes do a long version of it and the fans love it.

Even the *NME* were on my side, as they were to be again ten years later when I released an album that many consider to be my best yet. They said of 'Walk Like a Panther': *'People just don't write songs like this anymore. It has the vocal gravitas of a man, a common man, defiant in his invective against his lot, his shitty neighbourhood. It is brave, impassioned and chuffin' catchy.'*

We made a tremendously fun video of the song filmed in Castle Market in Sheffield, which has now gone. It closed in 2013. It features loads of Sheffield people from the market and those who were just there on the day, normal people all mimicking panthers. It's had over a third of a million hits. The All Seeing I had wanted me to do a full album with them and maybe I missed an opportunity there, as nothing else happened in England after it. I went back to Germany and then to Spain. It had been another great little journey. Unexpected, but fun and I'd bagged another hit in the process. Back to work, back to the golf and back to the sun.

And anyway, we had another special event to attend in July 1999 when Antonia married Raphael in Anjou in the Loire Valley. They'd met at a wedding in Paris and she'd said the same kind of thing as I had said when I'd first seen Sue, that she had met the man she thought she would marry.

CHAPTER 21

The World before the second coming of Amarillo

Family has always been important. Whether with my mum and dad, granddad, uncles, aunt and brother Neil, or having Dad's Irish family around singing songs. Sue's parents and family too. We're a strong unit. Family has been everything to Sue and I. A special mention here for Neal in filling some gaps and providing photographs from long ago. Thanks, Neal.

Mojacar was a wonderful place for Sean and Lisa to bring Joby and Caius; and Antonia and her husband Raphael, who is from Bordeaux, to bring Paddy and Thais. We had moved back to England by the time Lisa gave birth to Deià; Sarah, who married Martin, had given birth to Isaac; and Antonia gave birth to Louis. We love them all dearly and see them as regularly as we can.

We didn't know it at the time, of course, but after 'Walk Like a Panther' had been a hit, we only had another three years before a TV comedy series would change our lives and bring us back home.

My last CD single release in Germany came in 1998, just prior to 'Walk Like a Panther', and the title was prophetic: 'Never Say Auf Wiedersehen'. It was another of the ballads I'd become known for and again saw me on the big TV programmes, yet it couldn't have been in sharper contrast to my *Top of the Pops* appearance around the same time, nor the video we'd shot in Sheffield.

My last album release for Intercord, but now officially on the EMI label, was *Time for Love* in 1998, which included 'Never Say Auf Wiedersehen', written by Nick Munro of Hamburg.

There have been all kinds of compilations — some I've been made aware of, some I've never seen, but there are others that were new recordings that were thoroughly enjoyable to record and not just another package of songs repackaged.

There's the *Great Hollywood Movie Songs* album with the Stuttgart Radio Orchestra in Germany, conducted by Klaus Wagenleiter and released in 1999 when I was with Jerry Toger.

I spent a week in Stuttgart recording all the songs; and *Weihnachten mit Tony Christie*, again with the Stuttgart Radio Orchestra, became my Christmas album released in 2001; with *World Hits and Love Songs* released in 2002. And then a CD single release on the Voice label of a song by myself and Graham Sacher, 'Baby Come Back'.

TV work was still going strong with appearances on the popular ZDF programme, *Lustige Musikanten*, and NDR1 programme, *Welle Nord*, for Northern Germany, filmed in Hamburg in 2001. There's a rather enthusiastic orchestra playing 'Don't Go Down to Reno', and a cliff edge video of me singing 'The Eyes of a Woman in Love' in 2002.

The legendary Dieter Thomas Heck is a man who deserves special mention too. He was known as the presenter of the ZDF *Hitparade* programme I appeared on countless times during the 1980s and 1990s. Dieter presented it just before I started having my hits with 'Vegas' and 'I Did What I Did for Maria', until he finished in 1984. He went on to present big family shows where I was a regular guest and a gala for German Cancer Aid called Melodien für Millionen. And then there's Stefan Reich, who was the producer for my big German tours in the '90s.

I was happy enough. My family were all in good health. Work was good. Tours, festivals, recordings and cruise ships. The UK Top 10 hit, 'Walk Like a Panther', had been a nice little extra that I hadn't expected, but there were no other plans. Golf, work, family — that was the way it was meant to be, surely?

On 8 August 2002, my world was about to spin like a record again!

CHAPTER 22

Rising like a phoenix with a No1 single and No1 album

We all know what happened in 2005. Or at least everyone thinks they do.

Here's the Tony Christie version of what happened and how what started with the simple use of 'Is This the Way to Amarillo?' for about a minute or so in the second series of the TV programme, *Phoenix Nights*, written by Neil Fitzmaurice, Dave Spikey and Peter Kay, brought Sue and I back to England, reignited my UK career and gave me more opportunities than I had ever dreamed possible.

Since then, I've had so many career highs, as well as one fairly horrendous time that I'll recount when we get there, but to get to play the Royal Albert Hall, Glastonbury, the V Festival; to release an album critically-acclaimed by the British music press; to appear on stage in the West End. These are things I'd thought were way beyond me back at the turn of the new millennium.

I'm grateful for all that has come my way and while the use of the song, when the characters Max and Paddy (Peter Kay and Paddy McGuinness) are driving the Asian Elders minibus, was the catalyst to all of this, it is my son Sean I really have to thank for his forethought, tenacity and determination. It was he who saw the chance to make something more out of what hadn't been anything other than a brief, fun part of a telly show.

I'll tell this with the help of Sean, because there were a few interesting twists and turns along the way, and I'm not meaning poor old Ronnie Corbett falling off the treadmill when I talk about funny turns.

The period from that first transmission of *Phoenix Nights* series 2 on August 8 in 2002, to the re-release of 'Amarillo' in 2005 for Comic Relief, was getting on for being nearly three years, and yet everyone probably assumes the media surge just took off straight away. In reality, it took quite a time and involved Sean in a lot of meetings, discussions and a few hiccups, not of his making.

Sean was a big fan of *Phoenix Nights* and I'd seen it too. I'd thought it was hilarious, but never thought any more about it than that. For anyone who has ever worked in clubland and somehow bypassed the series, it was a really fun take on the small working men's club circuit I played years ago and pictures them as they were around that time in 2002, with an owner trying his best to keep things going. Clubs, even though they are no longer what they were when I started, still have a part to play in the community. They still have their place and Dave Spikey's role as compere was incredibly funny. It is also important to remember that there are many clubs that are still going strong, despite the way life has moved on.

Possibly not a lot of people will remember, but just before 'Amarillo' was played, in the same scene, Max and Paddy were also singing along and trying to get the elders to join in with Dennis Waterman's 'I Could Be So Good for You', the *Minder* series theme tune, that had featured him and George Cole, but that hadn't caught the public's imagination as much as 'Amarillo'. Suddenly, it was getting played everywhere. It was being requested by a whole new generation that had never heard it before, who saw it for what it has always been — a real feel-good party song. Apparently, Peter Kay went on to use 'Amarillo' in all his shows on tour.

Sean saw 'Amarillo' being played on *Phoenix Nights* as a real honour and felt really proud for me that this record, which hadn't been played much on the radio for years, was now getting its second life.

Years earlier, Yvonne Clapperton had predicted one of my songs would become an even bigger hit second time around. We weren't anywhere near there yet, in terms of how my world was going to change. Right again, Yvonne!

This time around, the airplay 'Amarillo' was getting gave Sean the impetus to see where it would all lead. I'll let Sean take over for this next part, as he can tell it better than I can. He did all the work. Over to you, Sean.

Back in early 2004, I'd started organising a UK tour with the help of a Scottish promoter I'd been put in touch with called David Halford. The tour would run through Oct–Nov, around about 20 days. When looking for promo opportunities, I approached what was then the biggest daytime ITV TV show, This Morning, *hosted by Richard & Judy. The celebrity booker I spoke with was keen to have TC on the show until she asked me when his new album was due to be released. I said there was no new album, just the tour. At that time the show's policy was that the guest should be plugging a product, a book or album, etc. They told me it wasn't enough for him to appear on the show with just a tour to promote.*

This is when I decided to contact Paul Spraggon of SSB Solicitors. Paul had acted for my band Job when we were signing our management and record deal. The guys and I hit it off with him straight away. If anyone knew the best route to getting a new record deal for TC, it would be Paul. He's one of the most loved and respected music lawyers in the business and we remain close to this day.

Paul and I met up, and as it was a glorious sunny day we decided to go around the corner and sit outside at a cafe on Kensington High Street. I began to tell him about my dad and the predicament we were in, not having a new album to plug which would open more doors to promote the upcoming tour. Paul wasn't aware my dad was Tony Christie at the time, so I had to backtrack a little. At this point, I feel I have to mention Chris Weller, Paul's amazing PA, because she always looked after my dad and I from this time onwards, and made sure Paul, whose diary was always stupidly busy, made time for us. Chris and her husband Andy remain close friends of TC and the family.

So, after Paul's initial surprise, and after a little family history and banter, I asked him what I should do and who I should approach label-wise. He said I needed to see Brian Berg at UMTV because my dad's original contract was signed to MCA in LA and that Universal now owned his catalogue. Brian was 'The King' of the TV-advertised compilation album. Paul then said, "The problem is, Berg is a very busy man and it will probably take you weeks to get a meeting." Paul gave me Brian's details and off I went back up to Lichfield to email Liz Clarke, Brian's PA. As it happened, I didn't have to wait weeks for a meeting, I got a reply within hours asking me to come down to Universal the next day and meet Brian, David Rose (Head of A&R), Jackie Joseph (Head of Legal) and Martin Nelson (TV & Radio plugger extraordinaire). It turned out they were planning to release a TC compilation album anyway, which would later be titled The Definitive Collection. *Brian told me that if TC would be up for coming back to the UK to promote it, they would TV advertise the album as a campaign for the following Mother's Day at the end of March 2005. I asked Brian if we could add to the album new songs that TC had written. He replied, "Your dad is still unrecouped from his old terrible MCA deal, so yes. That way he will see some positive accounting from those tracks." I left the office with a big grin and butterflies in my stomach.*

I had never felt so intimidated as when I had walked in to meet Brian and the team in his big glass corner office at UMG's headquarters, which back then was next to the Hammersmith Odeon. I was still, in my head, a drummer in a band with long hair and a green parka and jeans. I'd just had what was my first ever meeting with top echelons in the British music Industry. Brian is an old drummer himself, so we ended up good pals.

We were still in need of TV promotion for the upcoming tour, which was to start in Autumn, so I began approaching newspapers to try and get stories or magazine features. The Daily Mail *came back with an offer to do an interview with journalist Peter Robertson for their* Mail on Sunday *magazine. This helped a great deal and we began picking* up more and more press and even got a radio interview with Steve Wright on BBC Radio 2.

It was around this time Chanel 4 TV were advertising Peter Kay's live recorded show at G-Mex Arena in Manchester. The advert showed Peter with his two tour managers walking through the backstage corridors miming to 'Amarillo'. That was what gave me an idea. I immediately emailed Phil McIntyre, who was Peter Kay's then manager. I wrote and asked if Peter would be up for doing a video with TC for 'Is This the Way to (Amarillo)'. I told him that Universal were going to put out a greatest hits album and that it would be great to copy the TV advert airing at the time, but instead of Peter and his two managers walking to the song, how about TC with Peter and Paddy McGuinness, in character as Max & Paddy, acting as bodyguards. Taking inspiration from Paul Whitehouse's 'Brilliant' character in The Fast Show sketches, where Paul is walking saying random things are "brilliant", I thought we could use green screen to change the background in the same way.

I got a reply within a few hours saying that Peter would be up for this, but that he also had another idea for TC to sing the theme tune to his next TV show, Max & Paddy. We obviously agreed, as I saw this as a sort of 'you do me a favour and I'll return a favour by doing the video for Amarillo'. I quickly called David Rose and told him I had got the green light for Peter to be involved with the video. David was absolutely thrilled and this then changed Universal's plan completely. They were going to bring forward the release of the album to November 2004 and TV advertise it through to Xmas, the biggest-selling peak period for album sales. They had previously decided to avoid this period in our first meeting as they thought that the market would be saturated with huge-selling artists. They were concerned the album would get 'buried' and wouldn't stand a chance of getting any of the limited, most prized radio, TV and press slots. All was looking and feeling good.

Off we went, Mum, Dad and I, to a recording studio in Warrington to record the theme tune to Max & Paddy. This is where we first met

Peter and Paddy. It was a very friendly atmosphere. Peter was sitting on the couch next to Mum, talking about his love of his mum's old record collection and how he first heard The Best of Tony Christie. *He said he always found the album cover funny; TC in a white suit very badly superimposed on a beach with a sunset behind him. Peter said that he always thought TC had two throats to sing with such power. He came over as very a genuine fan and a really nice guy. Paddy is, as he comes over on the telly, a genuinely warm and friendly guy. Phil McIntyre later popped by the studio and Dad and he had a catch-up as they hadn't seen each other in years. When Dad started singing the first verse of the theme tune in the vocal booth, Phil said, "God I've missed that voice." That's always stuck with me. He's a great guy. I felt so proud to be in the studio with Peter and Paddy of* Phoenix Nights. *I was a huge fan. The recording done, we went our separate ways and everyone was happy with the results. In the end, the version TC sang of the theme tune was used only as the outro music of the last episode to* Max & Paddy *as a sort of surprise.*

A few weeks passed and I emailed Peter Kay's office, asking about when Peter would be available to begin discussions for the 'Amarillo' promo video. I was told that Peter was now too busy to do it that year and would think about it the following year. This was a huge blow and I felt physically sick. I had told the guys at Universal he was on board and they had moved the whole campaign forward. I was going to look like a fool, but they were actually cool and we went back to plan A.

Moving forward to around the second week in January 2005, I received a call from Jackie Joseph. She told me that Richard Curtis had been in touch to ask if they could use 'Is This the Way to (Amarillo)' for Comic Relief. This would mean signing away all TC's royalties for the song to the charity. Incidentally, Neil Sedaka also kindly gave up his writing royalties too. At that time, we did not know what Comic Relief's plans were for using the song. All we were told was that it was something to do with Peter Kay. Once Dad had agreed to give his royalties to the charity, a meeting was scheduled for January 27th between Universal, Richard Curtis, Phil McIntyre, Kevin

Cahill (ITV) and some Comic Relief people. After the meeting (which I did not attend) we were told that Peter would be making a video that would be shown during the evening of the Comic Relief TV show and that the filming would take place over two days, the first day held at the old ITV Granada Studios in Manchester, and the second day at Dave Stewart's 'The Hospital Studios' in Soho London.

The day before the filming, I called Jackie and said that I had not received a call sheet so had no idea what time, day or venue TC was supposed to be there for the filming. She said she would make a call and get back to me. However, when she did call back, she relayed to me that Comic Relief had told her TC wasn't needed for the video. I was dumbfounded and really hurt. I said something along the lines of, "Oh right, well they can forget it then. We will revoke our permission." Though I think my language may have been a little more colourful, to be honest. I was so angry and deeply upset. I was thinking how the hell was I going to tell Dad, especially when I had asked Peter to be involved in the video that Universal were going to release as a Christmas single a month before. It only took about 30 minutes for Jackie to call me back with a time and address. We were told to be at The Hospital Club, Dave Stewart's place in Covent Garden, two day later.

When we got there, I remember Danny Baker and Heather Mills were sitting in the dressing room next to a big mirror with all the bulbs around. I held up a beautiful Ozwald Boateng suit and Peter Kay said, "No, it will only work if you wear this," holding out his infamous purple jacket and Hawaiian shirt. The way the plot went meant it had to switch to Dad being in Peter Kay's clothes with Peter being at one side and a Peter Kay lookalike on the other side. Dad took one look at the suit and said, "I can't wear that, I'll look silly!" It was so funny because he locked eyes through the mirror with Danny and Heather who were dressed as the scarecrow and Dorothy out of The Wizard of Oz . Danny just shrugged his shoulders and smiled. Dad had to wear bulldog clips to hold in Peter's jacket at the back and it was done in one-take. In, out, done.

The rest is history, I suppose. 'Is This the Way to (Amarillo)' went on to be the biggest single of the Millennium, selling in excess of 1.3 million and with all master and copyright royalties going to charity, raising over two million pounds for Comic Relief.

CHAPTER 23

I'm coming home, I'm coming home —
Christie's coming home

Even 1971, when all the media hit first time around, couldn't have prepared me for 2005. Thirty-four years on, it was crazy, but seriously good crazy. I loved being back on *Top of the Pops* and if you watch my performance again on YouTube, you'll see just how much it meant to me. I don't think I stopped grinning for all the 7 weeks 'Amarillo' was No 1. It was how people describe having all your birthdays come at once, but the album, *The Definitive Collection*, reaching No 1 as well was seriously fantastic news. I now had everyone young and not-so-young coming to my shows. It was, as they say today, seriously off the scale.

One minute, I was appearing singing Schlager songs on TV in Northern Germany as their 'gentleman of pop'. The next minute, I was selling out venues I'd never played when I was a million-seller the first time around. In those days, I never played tours that included the Royal Albert Hall, Manchester's fabulous Bridgewater Hall, Leicester De Montfort Hall, Ronnie Scott's with the fabulous Martin Taylor Quintet, and I was never booked for festivals.

It was a different age back in the '70s. In those days, Glastonbury had only just begun in 1970 and Woodstock and the Isle of Wight Festival had only been around a few years. Today, an appearance at V Festival and Glastonbury is a measure of your talent and appeal.

To be offered V Festival and sing in front of 50,000 that same year as everything was still going wild was more than amazing. What a day we had. There were some amazing experiences throughout 2005, with everything from V Festival to playing for Thunder Sunday at The Rock race circuit in Northamptonshire in June.

I'd always wanted to feel accepted back in the UK and I had felt very rejected after the MCA deal finished. Fortunately, as one door has closed another one has invariably opened fairly soon elsewhere.

I love dearly the German, Austrian and central European fans, TV companies, record companies who brought about great records, like *Sweet September* and *Kiss in the Night* and my *Welcome to My Music* albums. But for all the millions of copies of records I've sold everywhere, I still wanted to be accepted back home.

It's not like I've ever craved stardom. I've never seen it that way and I'm not bothered about that kind of thing. I've always just wanted to be known as a good singer who interprets songs to the best of his ability.

After the spring tour in 2005, Sean took me back with Kennedy Street. Harvey was by then ensconced in Palm Springs with his lovely wife Carole. Danny Betesh was the agent, as he still is today.

We were touring while 'Amarillo' and the *Definitive Collection* were No 1, and again in winter when we played 14 dates across November and December. The Bridgewater Hall date in Manchester apparently had a night that was booked 114 per cent. I didn't even know anyone could go over 100 per cent, but they did so by opening the choir seating area. That was the tour that included the Royal Albert Hall, Cardiff International Arena, Belfast Waterfront Hall, Dublin Olympia, Edinburgh Usher Hall, Harrogate International Centre and home ground with Sheffield City Hall. All fantastic venues.

My great mate, Mike Ryal, my bass player from the '70s and '80s, drove me around from gig to gig that year and we had some lovely times back together.

Sean and Lisa were living in Lichfield, not far from our old stamping ground of Sutton Coldfield, so the logical thing was for us to stay with them, or at least be close to them while we made decisions on returning to the UK permanently.

We stayed in The George Hotel in Lichfield for two months and rented for six months in The Friary House while we found our new home in this lovely city.

The success of 'Amarillo', the album, the tours and future possibilities for new recordings back in the UK, had brought me back.

I'd loved Mojacar, we both had, but the opportunity that had presented itself was just what I needed. We'd had great years out in Spain and made friends for life, but it was also nice to be back nearer the kids again and their kids. Sue suffers from fibromyalgia and used to suffer quite a bit from the humidity during summertime over on the Med, so the move back was a help and after so many years in the sun it made a change to be back where the seasons change by the day!

Sue went back to Spain, once we'd made the decision, and organised the move while I was on tour. We also knew I could still fly over to do my European work from here and so we put down a deposit on a place in Lichfield and we've lived in the city ever since.

Lichfield is a big village really, but because it has an amazing cathedral it is officially a city. It has fantastic facilities, great real ale pubs (always a prerequisite of mine), restaurants and the obligatory wonderful golf courses. It has that same artisan feeling as we used to get in Mojacar and the festivals in the city are so cosmopolitan.

'Amarillo' had already been a million-selling single around the world one-third of a century ago, but it went on to eclipse that from sales purely in the UK and Ireland where it was also No 1 with 1,280,000 sales, making it twice-over platinum the second time around. It was the biggest selling record of 2005 and the third biggest selling record of the decade from 2000–2009. The video has had over 6 million hits. Not bad for a song Neil Sedaka hadn't finished writing!

'Amarillo' also reached No 25 in Germany as a duet by Tony Christie and the Hermes House Band from Holland. It has a really good cartoon video to it also, although I'm not so sure about a couple of the wackier things in it. Take a look. The whole thing was such a crazy time and crazy times lead to even crazier things.

I'd mentioned in passing, while being interviewed by *The Sun* journalist, Sally Brook, in March 2005, that in all the time I'd been singing 'Amarillo' I'd never been to the Texan city, although I'd had people come up to me over the years saying they came from there. The cheeky people at *The Sun* had put together a little guide alongside the interview when it was published showing the flight options available and before I knew what was happening the newspaper had arranged for myself and Sean to fly over and meet the mayor.

We exchanged Sunny Skeggy for where 'the day is dawning on a Texas Sunday morning', although I can't remember which day of the week it was. I'd performed for 18 of the past 25 days in March and we'd just finished playing to another full house at the Embassy Theatre in Skegness on 26 March. We had five days until our next date, the Albert Halls in Bolton, but we were headed for Gatwick courtesy of the Super Soaraway Sun.

They'd not just published the details, they were now sending me there! Four hours on the road later and we were at Gatwick ready to fly to Amarillo at 7am the next morning via Fort Worth Dallas and then Route 66.

Mayor Trent Sisemore III greeted us with a 'Howdy', or something like that. He was very welcoming, and I was given the keys to the city in an official ceremony. Apparently, '(Is This the Way to) Amarillo' has provided their city with its biggest boost to tourism. It has a population the size of Middlesbrough or Milton Keynes. If only Neil Sedaka had known about our cities instead of Amarillo, it could have been a whole different song!

Trent bought me a Stetson and a pair of ostrich leather boots, as well as a pair for Sue. They are absolutely magnificent and are so heavy. It was a real cowboy town and I had to get on this horse at the River Breaks Ranch — my first time since getting on one for the filming in the '70s and I was just as useless. They wanted a picture of me with 'Marie who waits for me' and they had a Marie all set and ready.

Trent said at the ceremony, attended by local businessmen and women: 'Tony, I know you have had trouble finding your way to Amarillo, but it's great to have you finally here with us.' And I was showered with even more gifts, from local wines to shirts.

We were taken to the Big Texan Steak Ranch where, if you can eat the whole 54 dollar, 72oz steak and all the trimmings in an hour, you get it for free. I didn't even manage a quarter of it, but I did try the local delicacy of fried calves' testicles. Funny thing though, the photographs of those who have managed to eat it all in that time are all slim people. We were only in Amarillo a day and a half, but what an experience it was. We exchanged Amarillo for Bolton, Doncaster and Darlington as the next three nights on tour.

And then there was *Emmerdale*. One or two of the show's writers came to see me during the spring tour at the sadly now bulldozed Futurist Theatre in Scarborough. I was offered the part of Tony Christie! The idea was that I was supposed to have had a fling with the character Diane, played by Elizabeth Estensen, back in the '60s. In the show, I performed 'Avenues and Alleyways' at the Pub Chef Awards Ball, which was filmed in a hotel in Ilkley, but in the storyline was set in Newcastle.

I spot Diane, catch up with her and dedicate a song. There's some thought from her son that I may be his long-lost father, but that's it really. My first few lines as an actor on a TV soap. I was starting to tick a few boxes of an unwritten bucket list. The funniest thing about filming *Emmerdale* was that my mum was more proud of me appearing on the show than anything else I've ever done. She was thrilled to bits.

While in Leeds making the show, I also made an appearance in another video of 'Amarillo' and had a great time. It features the cast of *Emmerdale*, with Danny Miller, who plays Aaron Dingle in the show, playing the lead role. I already knew Danny through his dad, Vince Miller, who compered the functions for the celebrity golf days in Manchester. Danny raises funds for the Once Upon a Star charity and came up with the idea to do his own version with the *Emmerdale* team. I think it's pretty good and it's had over a million hits. I appear in it several times with my mate Vince, Danny's dad.

August 2005 was a pretty good month all round. I appeared at V Festival with my fabulous band of superb musicians and later a DVD and CD of my set was released. We played 'Las Vegas', 'Walk Like a Panther', 'Avenues and Alleyways', and of course 'Amarillo', as well as a cracking version of 'If It Feels Good Do It', and a mix of Beatles classics, including 'Lady Madonna', 'Hey Jude' and 'Sgt Pepper's Lonely Hearts Club Band', and the reaction was amazing. My *Emmerdale* appearance was broadcast, we were still playing festival dates and Universal re-released 'Avenues and Alleyways', which reached No 26, higher than it had reached first time around. Unbelievable. I was on Cloud Nine. We made a fantastic video for it with Nick Moran from *Lock, Stock and Two Smoking Barrels*.

The video was very retro-Bond style in its opening, with me wearing a tux and singing, while all the girls are either dancing or doing something or other in silhouette, and then there's the obligatory gun. It moves into a pastiche on the '70s cop and detective TV series, such as *The Sweeney* and *Starsky and Hutch*. I even got to put a flashing light on the top of the car as I was driving, like they used to do. It was an absolute giggle to do and I loved the Jensen car.

You know, it's a funny thing, 'Amarillo'. I always said it wasn't really me, it wasn't what I do, but one day it dawned on me that thousands of singers would give their right arm or back teeth, or whatever description you like, to have been given a song like it. Sue and I used to describe it as our naughty child. It makes you smile, it can sometimes irritate, but you will always love it and it just keeps coming back for more. Our friend Yvonne's clairvoyant proclamation had come true.

There isn't another song like it and that's what makes it unique. Since its success the second time around, I started looking properly at the audiences and now fully see the joy and unbridled pleasure it brings to people. I don't think I'd ever fully appreciated it the first time in the '70s. Sure, I knew it was a hit song from the moment I heard it, but it's a phenomenon.

It's a piece of pop history. And it brought me back to the UK and gave me back my career over here, and for that I will always be truly grateful to all those concerned — to Neil Fitzmaurice, Dave Spikey and Peter Kay for including it in *Phoenix Nights* originally; to Sean for having the fortitude and tenacity to bring about the idea that surfaced as the song for Comic Relief and that raised over £4m for charity; to Peter for including me in the video and the loan of his jacket; but most of all, to Howard Greenfield, who generally gets forgotten about, and my good friend Neil Sedaka for writing the song that has proved far more than a naughty child.

CHAPTER 24

Time for something new, some things slightly altered and something simply in love

Everything that had taken place in 2005 involved songs I'd recorded years ago, and it was fantastic to have them all appreciated. I'd been amazed that the new younger audience I was now attracting, in addition to those who had followed me for many years, actually knew the other songs and were singing along too, but when you're a singer you want to record new material and you're always looking for what might be either the next big hit or purely something you feel good about when you sing.

Universal had been terrific with their TV campaign for *The Definitive Collection*, but there was no recording deal for anything further and Sean knew I needed to be back in the studio to start pulling something together. In the months that followed, we flew to Nashville, recorded several songs for a new album, recorded an album of classic love songs back in the UK and managed to release a couple of turkeys along the way as singles — one of them even providing me with another UK Top 10! Mad, I tell you. Totally mad.

I'd never released a Christmas single before. I'd had the Christmas album recorded with the Stuttgart Radio Orchestra in Germany, but no single. Then the idea came to re-record Slade's 'Merry Christmas Everybody' as a big band swing number. It was a nice idea, but in all fairness it didn't really work for me. It reached No 49 in the UK, but that's not what I mean about it not working. I didn't feel it added anything to the original by Noddy (Holder) and the boys. It's such a fantastic feel-good song and, like 'Amarillo', one of those that brings so much joy and never needs to be released in a different style. The video was fun, but seriously now, I know the song was not my best moment. I enjoy eating turkey, but not making one. Fortunately, there were enough that did like it.

Next stop Nashville. You'll remember I'd recorded an album of country classics with Graham Sacher in the mid-80s at Strawberry Studios, but this time we actually went to the home of country music with the intention of singing and recording completely new songs. Grammy Award-nominated and Ivor Novello winner, Graeme Pleeth, was producer and wrote songs with the equally legendary Graham Gouldman. When we'd started working with Graeme and discussed where to make it, he'd said we should go there. His songs are lovely and the musicianship from the Nashville guys we used was just brilliant. Graeme had worked with Shania Twain's guitarist, who also got involved in our recordings at the Sound Emporium in Nashville. Such a beautiful studio.

We were there a week and songs like 'Dancing Days', 'Early Morning Memphis', 'When All Is Said and Done' and 'Damned', that all appear on my *50 Golden Greats* collection, are all great country music. We now had something fresh to put out, or at least songs that might get me that next record deal, but blow me if 'Amarillo' didn't resurface again for summer 2006, but in a different guise.

The World Cup was to be held in Germany and these two guys who were radio presenters, Big George, as he was known, although really George Webley, and Ian Stringer, had come up with a version of 'Amarillo' called '(Is This the Way to) the World Cup'.

We didn't have a record deal, but Sean felt if we said yes to this it might lead to getting an album deal for the country music album we had planned. Big George, who was known for writing and producing theme tunes for TV series, like *Have I Got News for You* and *Room 101*, and had been musical director at EMI, as well as having his own band, had played a demo to BBC Radio 1's Chris Moyles, who got behind the idea and I was approached to record it.

I really wanted to get the album under way and it was Tug Records who came good through a contact Sean had from his band. Tug had fantastic worldwide success under their other name, Gut Records, with Right Said Fred's 'I'm Too Sexy' and several more big hits for them and other acts. They were keen on the World Cup version of 'Amarillo' with me singing. Chris (Moyles) had plugged the idea too, being a friend of Big George.

We went in to Angel Studios in Islington, where Big George recorded the guide vocal. He said later that when he'd been asked to do it in front of me in the studio he felt like he was 'naked in the high street on a cold day.' Two days later, we relocated to a place I'd been familiar with many years before, Olympic Studios in Barnes, where I put down the new version. I remember George being taken with my broadsheet crossword competence, as I had my head stuck in various newspapers while not singing.

The video was another fun shoot, filmed at Barnet FC's Underhill Stadium, with a mock football match where every player wore a mask of my face. It was very surreal. I appear in the video as a rather intense England football manager. Again, it wasn't my finest hour, or three minutes come to that, on record, but with the video shown on all manner of TV programmes, including another appearance on *Top of the Pops*, and airplay on every radio station in England, it did far better than I had ever imagined.

'(Is This the Way to) the World Cup' sold over 50,000 CDs and downloads and also became another UK Top 10 hit, peaking at No 8. In the words of Chris Kamara on a Saturday afternoon on Sky Sports, 'Unbelievable, Geoff.' I have been quoted in the press as saying the song was not something I really liked. Those weren't quite the words, but you probably get the drift. The other great thing though was that once again all the profits went to charity, so it had a positive effect — maybe not on the England team though, as we went out to Portugal on penalties in the quarter-finals.

But singing the song did bring about a new record deal. You could say the ends justified the means by which we got there, but it wasn't to be the country music album that was taken up. Guy Holmes, the owner of Gut Records and the chap Sean knew from his band days, decided that if he was going to back an album by me, he wanted an album that his mum and dad would buy. I knew that fitted for me, singing classic songs I'd always loved, even though the new songs we were recording were great.

That's how *Simply in Love* came to be my first new album to be released in the UK since the '70s. We recorded it at Lansdowne Studios in Holland Park, London, with Paul Flush on piano, Dave Adams on drums, who had been musical director for *The Lion King* in the West End, the brilliant Martin Taylor on guitar, Guy Barker came in on trumpet, Duncan MacKay on trumpet and flugelhorn, and we had a fabulous upright bass player, Christophe Devisscher from Belgium.

We are talking seriously world-class musicians and the album became the basis of our next tour. The whole thing was class from beginning to end. It wasn't big band, but very expertly played by everyone and a tour that was a joy. The songs include 'Moon River', 'My Funny Valentine', 'I Left My Heart in San Francisco' and 'Stranger in Paradise'. We even included 'Danny Boy', my dad's favourite.

It was a lovely album to make with wonderful, talented musicians and I dedicated it to all the great musicians I'd had the pleasure of working with over the years, and to Sue as we approached our 40th anniversary of being a couple. It was officially released in November 2006 in conjunction with the tour with the Martin Taylor Quintet. It's an album I still love today.

On the CD notes I wrote:

'When I started singing back in the '60s, I cut my teeth on the 'standards'. In fact, I used to open my set with 'Stranger in Paradise'. Most of the songs on this album I sang back in the days when I used to record late night sessions for BBC Radio 2's easy listening programme, *Night Ride*. I feel so happy this style of music is back in vogue, giving me an opportunity to make the type of album I have wanted to make for a long time. I am just sorry that my dad Paddy could not be here to hear my version of his favourite song, 'Danny Boy'.

'We sang it together at my daughter Antonia's wedding to Raphael, which meant a lot to me, to my mum Iris and my brother Neal. I want to thank my wife Sue for her love and support throughout the ups and downs of my career. I'd also like to thank my kids. Sean, his wife Lisa, Antonia, her husband Raphael, Sarah and her husband Martin, who collectively gave me my beautiful grandchildren, Joby, Caius, Paddy, Thais, Isaac and Deià. I love you all. TC 23 August 2006.'

Isaac and Deià had added to our joy the previous year, when they had been born to Sarah and Martin, and Sean and Lisa, respectively. They were both beautiful, healthy grandchildren.

Sue and I were, and are, so proud of them both, as we are of all our children and grandchildren.

Family is the most important thing in my life. And just so that you don't think I've miscounted or left anyone out, Louis hadn't been born to Antonia and Raphael at that time. He's the youngest of our grandchildren.

The *Simply in Love* tour was very different to the tours of 2004 and 2005, with 10 dates starting in Felixstowe and ending at the Liverpool Philharmonic Hall, but also included another highlight — performing at Ronnie Scott's Club in London.

We still played all the hits, but the emphasis was very much on the songs from the album and all the other standards I'd sung over the years with this stripped down sound we'd used. We played Michael Parkinson and his son Nick's Royal Oak pub in Maidenhead, where Amy Winehouse and Katie Melua had also played.

The TV show *Countdown* was a favourite of mine too and I'd just got back from finally tying things up over in Mojacar, when I went over to record five programmes with Des Lynam in the chair and Carol Vorderman. I wasn't bad at the anagrams, something you need to be good at when doing cryptic crosswords in *The Times* and *Daily Telegraph*.

It was television that was to feature again for me at the start of 2007, but more importantly, it turned out to be the year that brought me my greatest ever acclaim by the UK music industry.

CHAPTER 25

The road that led back to Sheffield

I've 'Dined', 'Antiqued' and 'Barged' in the past decade, as well as appearing on countless game shows, but my first TV reality show was *Just the Two of Us*, hosted by Vernon Kay and Tess Daly in January 2007. It was a kind of pro-celebrity golf for singing, with eight celebrities teamed up to sing duets with well-known singers. I appeared in series 2 and my celebrity partner was Julia Bradbury, presenter of TV's *Watchdog* and *Countryfile* programmes.

Just the Two of Us was a live show and we managed to get through the first three days. Carol Decker of T'Pau, Alexander O'Neal, and Natasha Hamilton of Atomic Kitten, were the three professional singers knocked out before we left the show. Julia was lovely and it turned out she had connections with Sheffield and had been to school there. She came to our house to rehearse. Julia did really well on the show and we got on together right from the start. I've read that she was chuffed to bits to be partnered with me as I was Daddy Cool with a fantastic voice. She was very kind and we both had fun doing the show. We weren't the ideal match voice-wise, but we gave it our best shot. Marti Pellow ended up winning with Dennis Waterman's daughter Hannah.

I was back in New Zealand and Australia in February 2007 with The Drifters as my support act and there was more TV once again in Germany and across central Europe, as well as some great appearances with the full 10-piece band at two great events in Middlesbrough and Gateshead. The latter of those was the Bandstand evening at The Sage in Gateshead. It was a fantastic evening of music and comedy with Roger Daltrey, Vic Reeves, Jimmy Nail, Ruby Turner and Roland Gift all on the bill and all in aid of Teenage Cancer Trust.

Anne Robinson's *The Weakest Link* show was another TV appearance, albeit a brief one for me! I was knocked out in the first round by what I said afterwards was a little bit disappointing, as I felt, in the best tongue-in-cheek way I could, that it was all down to professional jealousy because I was so fabulous! Ha Ha!

I was on a special music edition with Matt Willis from Busted, Bonnie Langford and Darren Day. It was all going so well when I answered my one and only question correctly, but the time I took answering, a matter of a split second, deemed me to be the weakest link and three of my fellow contestants voted me off.

Leo, one of the three hatchet men who sealed my fate, was very funny when he gave his reason for getting rid of me. He said if I hadn't found my way to Amarillo by now, 'what with there being a lot of GPS systems about,' then I was better off going to buy one straight away. Matt was straight to the point, he just said 'Amarillo' had done his head in a bit. Charming! It was all in great spirit and my time on the show ended with me leading a rendition of the song once again. Anne felt I'd been unjustly picked on by the younger gentlemen. For the record, I never got a question wrong!

The Greatest Hits Tour was my next official tour in October 2007, taking in seven great venues from the South East to Scotland, this time reverting back from the jazz style of the previous year with the *Simply in Love* tour to the full sound. We started at the lovely Birmingham Symphony Hall and finished at the grand Royal Concert Hall in Glasgow.

I was delighted to be able to fly out to Tenerife in the Canary Islands in December to play a concert with the full band on behalf of the K9 Animal Sanctuary. We played the Magma Art and Congress Centre in Playa de las Americas, alongside iconic Latin American singer, Rosanna.

During the year, we had also been making progress on recording new songs. Sean had felt that after *Simply in Love*, we needed something that was simply different, something he could go to record

Christmas at Badgers Bar,
Mojacar Playa 1991. Antonia
was my surprise present all the
way from Brazil!

Pulling my own pint at Badgers Bar in Mojacar with Keith and Gill Bradley, 1991.

Great day out with the family.

Receiving a Gold Record from Lothar Matthäus for the *Welcome to My Music* album. Seehaus, Munich, 1992. (Alamy)

With Jerry Toger (manager) Seehaus, Munich, 1992. (Alamy)

Above: My darling Max sulking! He
hated me going away.

Top right: Our lovely nieces and
god-daughters Jackie and Samantha.
Sammy was taken from us too soon.

Middle right: Me and Sue.

Below: Happy times with Irene,
Keith and Angela.

Above: A Gala Dinner in Munich where I chaperoned the beautiful Gina Lollobrigida.
Below:–
Top Left: With Midge Murray, Phil Coulter and Gerry Marsden.
Bottom left: Graeme Pleeth, me and Andrew Gold at Townhouse Studios, London, June
3rd 2006. Andrew Gold and Graham Gouldman (not pictured) were adding backing
vocals to 'Dancing Days'.
Right: One of our wonderful trips to Beijing.

Another happy day at El Cantina, Mojacar Playa with my mum and brother Neal.

A wonderful evening with my mum and dad in Mojacar.

Great day out with my brother Neal at Kontiki Beach Bar, Mojacar.

Sue and I with our old friend Max Schautzer, well-loved German TV presenter, en route to Australia, circa 1995.

Good times with my old mates Norman Collier and Vince Miller.

Howard Keel Charity Golf hosted by Don Felder of the Eagles, with myself and Sue.

Lisa and Sean's wedding. The happy couple and (left) with their little drummer boys at Le Grand Roche, Paarl, Cape Town, SA, 14th Feb 2002.

Above: With our dearest mums Iris and Irene, March 2002.

Right: So Proud! Celebrating our daughter Sarah's wedding blessing with her husband Martin, Mojacar Playa, 26 March 2002.

Our daughter Antonia and her husband Raphaël on their wedding day.

Above left: My four lovely girls – Sarah, Sue, Lisa our daughter-in-law and Antonia at our godson Carl Bown and Catherine's wedding.

Above right: Me and my girls.

Above:
The Prono Family – my daughter Antonia with her husband Raphaël and my grandchildren, Paddy, Thais and little Louis.

Right:
The Keefe family – my daughter Sarah, husband Martin and grandson Isaac.

With Neil Sedaka at The Royal Albert Hall, 7th April, 2006. (Alamy)

Right: With the Feeling at Goodwood, 2010. (Alamy)

Below: This wonderful picture of my family on stage at Sheffield City Hall was taken by Shaun Bloodworth. Gone but not forgotten. Shaun had taken many photos for me over the years and was taken from this earth far too soon. A dearly missed friend.

With Bob Harris at Radio 2.

With Jarvis Cocker at the 2010 MOJO
Honours List award ceremony. (Alamy)

With Richard Hawley during the recording
of *Made in Sheffield*. (Chris Saunders)

Elvis in the Park. Hyde Park, 12th September, 2012. (Alamy)

With Franz Beckenbauer. Party at The Eagles Golf Cup, at the Nobilis Robinson Club, Belek, Turkey, 16th November, 2012. (Alamy)

With Arthur Abraham, former World Super Middleweight and Middleweight Boxing champion, on *Willkommen bei Carmen Nebel*, September 2015. (Alamy)

With the legendary Terry Wogan, together with Irish Folk group and close friends, Ranagri. Terry was, as always, the most welcoming gentleman and a delight to work with.

With Carmen Nebel on her show *Willkommen bei Carmen Nebel*, 2016. (Alamy)

Me with the lovely Beate Okunowski from Munster in Germany. I call her 'Beate, my old friend.'

Above: Golf professional Simon Smith on my right, with Tony Hadley and great friend and organiser of my golf charity, Roger Partridge on my left.

At the *Willkommen bei Carmen Nebel* show in Berlin, 2019.
Above: with Jan Stephan 'superfan', friend and the man who has translated this book into German and singer Ireen Sheer, who I surprised on the show for her recent 70th birthday.
Left: with the singer Paul Potts.

Above: CarFest, 2019:– (L – R) Just before walking out front to 40,000 people; Onstage; Backstage with the Jacksons; and with Rick Astley and Chris Evans.

Right: Camper Calling Festival, 25th August 2019.

companies with for the next deal. That's how eventually a fellow Sheffield man emerged who would prove the inspiration for my next album.

Richard Hawley had released his album *Coles Corner* in 2005 and had sent it to me via Sean. The title track is all about a popular meeting place on the corner of Fargate and Church Street in Sheffield and is so-called because it was once home to the Cole Brothers department store.

Sean was keen for me to sing the title track, but at the time, back in 2005, we were riding the crest of a wave created by 'Amarillo' and I didn't give it my full attention.

I mention Richard now because you'll see how everything developed into what many regard as the best album I've ever made just a year later.

Sean had been working on a few new ideas that included synchronisation, getting my back catalogue, including *Simply in Love*, out into the film and TV world. He'd seen that other bands and artists like The All Seeing I had made more out of their music being used in TV commercials and thought there may be opportunities worth exploring.

At the same time, he had also made contact with a couple of producers who had just worked on Shirley Bassey's great *Get the Party Started* album, with the view to finding something different. They had reworked and remixed all her hits as well as giving a new sound to songs like the title track.

The producers, Chuck Norman and Bob Kraushaar, suggested I record three songs initially: 'Wild Is the Wind', which Johnny Mathis had recorded for the film of the same name and had been written by Dimitri Tiomkin and Ned Washington (Nina Simone and David Bowie had also recorded the song); 'Wild Ones', written by Brett Anderson and Bernard Butler of Suede; and 'Stupid Thing' by Grammy Award winner Aimee Mann. I'm up for most things, so we agreed and joined them at Real World Studios in the delightful village of Box in Wiltshire.

Peter Gabriel founded the studios and they are fabulous. Recording with new producers is always challenging, as everyone has their own ideas about what they want from the singer. The tracks came out fantastically well, brilliant production all round and all three appear on my *50 Golden Greats* album. Once again, I was also working alongside fabulous musicians, this time of a completely different music genre to the Martin Taylor Quintet and one of them it turned out was from my home town of Conisbrough, or at least close by, bass player Stan White.

After hearing the first three tracks and everyone at the studio being excited about them, there was talk of recording more in a similar vein before taking them to a record company as the basis of an album.

That's when Richard Hawley came back into the frame. I heard 'Coles Corner' again on the radio on the way back home from the studio with Sean and happened to say that the production on it was the sort of production I should be getting with its lush arrangement.

Sean politely reminded me that Richard had sent us the song a few years ago when 'Amarillo' had taken over our lives. He looked at me in the way he sometimes does, and that's when I knew why he had been so enthusiastic about it from the start.

We mentioned 'Coles Corner' as another song to try with Bob and Chuck. They asked whether we could get Richard to play the guitar solo, as they felt it would work having him involved. Sean made the contact through his manager and so began the next part of my journey that led me back to Sheffield.

CHAPTER 26

The Making of
Made in Sheffield

Richard met with Sean and he had talked enthusiastically about working with me from that moment. Sean and I then both went to see him in concert in Oxford. Afterwards, we talked and hit it off immediately.

He told us he didn't want to just play guitar on 'Coles Corner' and that he wanted to produce a whole album with me singing songs written by singer-songwriters from Sheffield. Sue and I were married in the city and our children were born there. The whole concept appealed to me straight away. It struck me right to my heart. It was like coming home.

When I popped into the studio with a mug of tea in one hand and a bag of chips in the other, Richard told me he knew we'd work well together. He's a bit like me in that he shares the passion for creating good music while also not too bothered about the glitzy side. We both work hard at what we do and he worked exceptionally hard on the album.

The album was produced almost wholly in Yellow Arch Studios in Sheffield by Richard and Colin Elliot, who put their hearts, souls and amazing talents into every second of every song, just as the 'little mesters' had done in the same buildings years previously as craftsmen of produce such as scissors. It was a great feeling to return to the city in which I had spent some of the best years of my life, had met my wife and grown a family. Yet it was also strange to drive around a place that I knew like the back of my hand only to find, like most other cities, that streets had been pedestrianised, or made into one-way systems, or had even completely disappeared and been replaced by huge office complexes.

That's why one of the great parts about recording at Yellow Arch was that it is situated in the old manufacturing district of Neepsend. The studio used to be a series of small fine engineering workshops.

It took me a while to get into the songs, but I just kept reading, absorbing and feeling the lyrics, until I was totally immersed in every line, syllable and intonation. That's my style. You should always feel like there is nothing left in you to come out when you're recording and the songs on this album made me want to keep giving more every time I sang. These songs were to be my greatest interpretations since I began recording.

One of the major differences with the production of the recordings came right at the start when Richard said, 'Your speaking voice has a nice warm timbre and a deep tone, why don't you sing like that, lower down?' Nobody had ever said that to me before and one of my little grouches with record producers over the years is that they always had me singing in as high a register as possible. Richard's comments were quite literally music to my ears. I knew I had someone I could trust with my voice.

We had a problem with the song that became the opening track. We had wanted the opener to be something from Sheffield's hottest property at the time, The Arctic Monkeys, but I hadn't heard anything that suited me until Richard mentioned 'Only Ones Who Know', written by Alex Turner. It was a track on their second album and he reckoned we could work with it, but I found it hard to put a rhythm to. I found it a bit all over the place, kind of al fresco.

I'd tried working on it on the way home to Lichfield for several nights and hadn't been able to work out what to do with it until I suddenly had this idea about giving it the feel of 'Love Letters (Straight from Your Heart)' by Ketty Lester, that Alison Moyet had also recorded.

I'd seen Ketty at Sheffield City Hall way back in my teens and knew it would work. When the penny dropped, I rang Colin who owns the studio and asked him to listen to Ketty Lester's version. He came back saying 'brilliant,' as it gave the rhythm we were lacking, and we were on our way.

I met Alex at the Q Awards the following year and he said he loved what we had done to his song. He wished the Monkeys had done it that way and that he'd played it over and over to his mum on the train on the way back from London.

Every song on the album is a gem. 'Louise', recorded by the Human League and written by Phil Oakey, Jo Callis and Philip Adrian Wright, is far different to the band's original and was the last song we recorded. I'd taken a bit of convincing because it was a great song already.

If we were going to do it, I wanted to get it across as the serious, sad song that it truly is. It's an emotional song that touches anyone who has ever lost the one true love they had, sees them once again and then parts once more without ever feeling whole. We stripped it right down.

We took away the techno side of it and Colin said it would work with piano and strings. After I'd sung it, I went back to the others to listen. There were four grown men in there, all misty-eyed. I was thinking, 'Bloody 'ell, what just happened?' People since then have told me they've had to stop the car and weep when they've heard it on the radio. When I sing 'Louise' in concert, I get emotional too, let alone the audience.

There are songs that still do that to me, that bring me to tears even now. 'Daddy Don't You Walk So Fast', 'Someone to Watch Over Me' by Ella Fitzgerald, and 'My Little Girl' from 'Soliloquy' in *Carousel*. Just thinking of those or singing 'Louise' all send me. I think I need a whisky right now, as well as a tissue. Richard loves that kind of heartstrings rendition in the same way.

Sue and I used to see Phil and his girlfriend near to where we lived. The Heaven 17, ABC and Human League boys and girls were all students in Sheffield and would often be seen in the cafes and bars.

Every day in the studio at Yellow Arch was special. This wasn't an album or a time when you're thinking of anything other than the music you're creating and your craft of putting together something beautiful. That is what is in your core. As soon as I had started listening to the amazing talented songwriters Sheffield has, I was blown away.

Everyone knows the city has produced and continues to produce legends in the music business, from Joe Cocker to Jarvis Cocker and Alex Turner to Phil Oakey, Paul Carrack to Martin Fry and the bands Def Leppard, ABC, Pulp, Human League and Heaven 17, but there are many who will never, not through any failings on their part, achieve a hit, because it's a funny old world and some of us are more fortunate than others.

One songwriter who I was extremely fortunate to come across in listening to all the songs that led to the album is Martin Bragger. We included two of his compositions: 'Danger Is a Woman in Love' — a dark song which carried such fabulous lyrics about going through tough times in a relationship — and 'Paradise Square', where all the lawyers have offices in Sheffield. It's probably not the most apt address, is it?

Richard had told me that Martin was good. What he didn't tell me was just how good. 'Danger Is a Woman in Love' sounds like a Bond movie theme with a big '60s string arrangement that Colin went down to London to have recorded. We still use it regularly in the act today, along with 'Louise'. That's how good a song it is and how good a song Martin Bragger writes.

I make no excuses for mentioning every one of the songwriters here. Richard's concept was fabulous, it captured the hearts of everyone who was involved, and all the songwriters deserve full credit. 'Perfect Moon' is a lovely ballad and one of two songs written by Sara Jay and Mark Sheridan on the album, the other being 'How Can I Entertain'.

Mark Sheridan also wrote 'I'll Never Let You Down' with John Stuart. Mark plays guitar with Richard on other projects. Mike Ward, who wrote 'Weak in the Presence of Beauty' with Rob Clarke, that became a big hit for Alison Moyet, wrote two songs, 'Streets of Steel' and the big sound of 'Every Word She Said', both written with Richard Barratt and also Kay and McCall for the latter.

'Coles Corner' is there too, Richard's classic that set the ball rolling, and 'Born to Cry', written by Jarvis, Richard and the team of Banks, Doyle, Mackey and Webber. The original was used in the soundtrack to the film *Notting Hill*.

There was never any way that this album could have been called anything but Sean's title, *Made in Sheffield*. I like to think that we have mirrored the power, industry, talent, guile and love that exists in the city.

I said I wouldn't leave anybody out on the songwriting credits and the last to mention is me. Richard is such a nice bloke and so inclusive of everyone. A lot of producers will claim everything as their idea or will just want everything their way. He allows everyone to have their input and he asked whether I had any songs. Two of mine appear on the album, 'All I Ever Care About Is You' and 'Going Home Tomorrow'. No prizes for guessing who the first one is all about, as when this was recorded it was our 40th wedding anniversary year. Sean had bought me this banjolele and I wrote the song in half an hour while getting used to the instrument in my office at home.

'All I Ever Care About Is You' I wrote originally thinking of it as a trad jazz arrangement, but the way it went evokes the sentiments I had right from the start of a wartime forces sweetheart song with a slightly out of tune upright piano, of the type that may have been in a NAFFI or RAF canteen or bar. Jon Trier plays a fantastic piano solo on the recording. 'Going Home Tomorrow' saw me going back towards country and rockabilly with Johnny Wood on rockabilly bass.

Dean Beresford on drums, Richard and Shez Sheridan on guitars, Colin on double bass, Jon on piano, Guy Barker on trumpet, Danny McCormack on Hammond, Camilla Pay on harp and the strings under the conductorship of Thomas Watson, arranged through Eliza Marshall of Ranagri, who haven't come into my story yet — you all played your significant parts in the making of *Made in Sheffield*.

It was truly a labour of love from beginning to end, with a

generous, talented producer and gifted people. In my CD notes, I wrote: 'I am not and never have been an excitable type, but this album has me jumping up and down'. I dedicated it to my niece, Samantha, who was tragically taken away from us at just 37, as I mentioned earlier. It seemed fitting, since she was also from Sheffield.

The reaction we received from the music industry aficionados, musicians and fans was to be the most amazing I'd ever received. More importantly, though, there were so many magic moments in the making of *Made in Sheffield* it was a joy. The production was great and still sounds fantastic now over a decade on. It's the real Tony Christie hopefully interpreting what the writers intended the songs to be when they were inspired to write the lyric and the melody.

We played a three-date tour, including an album launch gig at the Memorial Hall, which is within the Sheffield City Hall complex, Cadogan Hall in London and in Dublin, playing purely the album tracks. Richard wanted it to focus on the quality of what we had all just produced — but we nearly had a riot in Dublin when I wouldn't sing 'Amarillo'!

Richard wasn't at the launch gig in Sheffield, but his band were amazing. Colin was on bass, Shez Sheridan on guitars, Dean Beresford on drums, Jon Trier on keys and Bryan Day on guitar. I introduced 'Louise' as the song that made four grown men cry in the studio.

There was a documentary made of the making of *Made in Sheffield* that was shown after the gig, at which point Richard was there, and after the screening, as we were both involved with a Q&A session, I'd said quite sentimentally, 'All my kids were made in Sheffield,' at which point Richard added, 'I bet you stamped them as well.'

The album was released in November 2008 on the Decca music label through Autonomy Recordings, part of Universal, and if I had thought what we were producing was fabulous to me, I was soon to find out that I'd made something, together with all of these fantastic Sheffield people, that was to fill me with an even greater sense of achievement. When I was in Spain, I'd wanted acceptance from my home country. *Made in Sheffield* and Richard Hawley gave me just that.

I finally appeared on *Richard & Judy* on Channel 4 when the album was released and, picking up on my popularity in both Germany and the UK, they asked questions of the Superfans from both countries, Phil Fletcher from the UK and Jan Stephan from Germany.

It's at this point I should make a special thank you to Jan, as he has undertaken the massive job of translating this book into German. Thank you so much, Jan. You are a true friend.

Jan's name was shouted loudly by the audience when Richard and Judy asked who was the No 1 fan, but they are two really lovely people, both he and Phil, regardless of who took the honours on the day, and it was all in good humour. I remember Larry Lamb was on the show too and the video of 'Born to Cry' was featured.

CHAPTER 27

Made in Sheffield — *The Reaction*

Iwas playing at the inaugural Vintage Festival at Goodwood in Chichester in the summer of 2010. The Feeling were acting as backing band to stars such as Sophie Ellis-Bextor and Glenn Tilbrook of Squeeze. It was a lovely day made even lovelier when Glenn came in the dressing room after he'd been on and told me he'd been in bother with his record company because he'd been on the radio to plug his new album, but he'd spent more time plugging mine! That's when I began realising how far-reaching *Made in Sheffield* had become and what we had done was way beyond simply something by people from South Yorkshire.

It wasn't until putting this book together with Chris (Berry) that I'd ever been aware of the review *Made in Sheffield* received by Barry Nicolson in the *NME*, probably the most revered of all music publications.

I was flabbergasted when Chris read it to me and I'm still waiting for the punchline now. Here's how Barry put his review in its entirety, and I thank you Mr Nicolson:

'People forget that before Rick Rubin captured the sound of Johnny Cash embracing his own mortality, the Man in Black was a fading figure of fun who fought ostriches and made cameo appearances on Columbo, *rather than the monolith of cool he's become today. Icons of an older generation turning to icons of the new when the credibility crunch hits is hardly an innovative idea, but it's one that more often than not works; recent memory alone throws up records such as Loretta Lynn's collaboration with Jack White on* Van Lear Rose *or Neil Diamond's Rubin-produced* 12 Songs. *The problem with Tony Christie*

pulling the same trick, of course, is that the man has never had any credibility to speak of, let alone reclaim.

'Which is what makes Made in Sheffield *such an unexpected delight. It is — and we never thought we'd say this about a Tony Christie album — a genuinely great record. Brilliantly co-produced by longtime fan Richard Hawley, it's as far from the beery karaoke of '(Is This the Way to) Amarillo' as you can get; a wistful paean to his hometown's musical heritage featuring songs by artists as diverse as Pulp, Arctic Monkeys and The Human League lavished with sumptuous strings and Christie's own world-weary pipes. Not only that, but in the wake of The Last Shadow Puppets' recent orchestral manoeuvres, it even sounds weirdly contemporary. Opening Arctics cover 'Only Ones We Know' is a case in point, with the combination of Hawley's lush production and Christie's ghostly voice turning the song into something otherworldly.*

'Whereas Christie could have gone for novelty kitsch and covered, say, 'Fluorescent Adolescent', the songs are remarkably well-chosen; Pulp's 'Born to Cry' gets the grandiose treatment. The Human League's 'Louise' is spectral and heartbreaking and Richard Hawley's 'Coles Corner' sounds like it was written especially for him, which it practically was.*

'But it's the songs by some of Sheffield's lesser-known songwriters that really surprise; Martin Bragger's clutch of offerings — the spiky, Walker Brothers-esque 'Danger Is a Woman in Love' and the simple but beautiful waltz of 'Paradise Square' — are both standouts, and Christie's own 'Going Home Tomorrow' — a bouncy, electrified slice of melancholy country — suggests he gets a bad rep as the quintessential karaoke crooner and nothing else. Believe us, we're as surprised as you are by all this, but Made in Sheffield is a surprising record, lovingly conceived and beautifully executed. Thank God Peter Kay didn't get anywhere near it.'*

Wow! Ally Carnwath of the *Guardian* also gave this far briefer but nonetheless wonderful review:

'This is no cheesy croonfest from the '(Is This the Way to) Amarillo'*

singer, but a beautifully crafted album produced by Richard Hawley.
All songs are written exclusively by Sheffield's finest, including Alex
Turner and Jarvis Cocker, and Christie's voice soars throughout, Roy
Orbison-style. 'Danger Is a Woman in Love' could be a Bond classic,
while Phil Oakey's 'Louise' has a trumpet solo to die for.'

Sir Lucian Grainge, CEO of Universal, called the reviews for *Made in Sheffield* the best collectively he had seen in a decade.

I've made music that I'm proud of and some music I'm not so proud, that's the way it goes, and with *Made in Sheffield* we all made an album that was definitely in the former category. I thank everyone who said really good things about it from *The Times*, who called me 'the senior Sheffield Sinatra' and hailed the album as 'an unlikely triumph'; Stephen Trousse of Uncut magazine, who said I'd swung with the times: '60s power balladeer turned '70s Eurovision crooner; revived as Britpop survivor by Jarvis and The All Seeing I; as quintessential entertainer by Peter Kay and with impeccable timing returns as a kind of South Yorkshire Roy Orbison. It's a perfect match with producer Richard Hawley; the *Sunday Express* also touched on the big O influence too, saying: Christie's Orbison-esque voice of experience bleeds passion and intensity on a captivating record; and the *Daily Telegraph*, who said I transformed 'Louise' from merely a good song to a masterpiece.

What I said at the time still remains true today, eleven years on from the release of *Made in Sheffield*. The songs aren't intended to be fashionable, we just went for pure quality. I've always wanted to get across that I'm not just about one fabulous party song. I'm so, so proud of *Made in Sheffield* and I promise I've plenty of years and albums left in me, but if I never do anything else again, this will do as my legacy.

CHAPTER 28

From Glastonbury to the West End ...
and a little culinary chaos

Chris Evans was so taken with 'Every Word She Said', that was released in March 2009, he played it twice consecutively on his BBC Radio 2 show. That's unheard of in the broadcast world. It's such a big powerful song and was on the A list for radio plays for seven weeks. We also played it at Glastonbury in 2009, my first time on what is now the iconic legends Pyramid stage.

If I'd wanted acceptance in the music world, then this was it. There's no finer moment than playing in front of tens of thousands of people at the world's favourite festival and I enjoyed myself immensely. In the 12-song set we played the '70s hits 'Las Vegas', 'I Did What I Did for Maria', 'Avenues and Alleyways' and 'Don't Go Down to Reno'; a few classic covers — 'You've Lost That Loving Feeling', 'Can't Take My Eyes Off You'; two of my all-time favourites, 'So Deep Is the Night' and 'Daddy Don't You Walk So Fast'; 'Walk Like a Panther' and two songs from *Made in Sheffield* — 'Every Word She Said' and 'Danger Is a Woman in Love'.

And then I announced, 'It's time for that song,' which was met with the kind of joy it has always done. But to have, I don't know, maybe 70,000 people singing it all the way through, dancing and having a great time, was a fabulous feeling. I mentioned cheekily that it was very annoying that everyone always joined in, but of course that's the beauty of it and why it just keeps giving after all these years. One YouTube follower put, 'I think it's the most popular song in the history of the world.'

I don't think the chap was talking about 'Every Word She Said', but it received this fabulous little review when it had been released in March 2009 from *OK! Magazine*: 'In a market flooded with artists recreating a Ronson-esque faux 1960s vibe, Tony Christie blows us away with a huge voice that swells over dramatically rolling drums, rattling guitars and a massive chorus. This spine-tingling track shows they just don't make 'em like him anymore.'

From Glastonbury to *Musikantenstadl,* I now had the two careers that have continued to run side-by-side since coming back to the UK in 2005.

Although it may seem a little bizarre, and I'm still the same person, there have been two Tony Christies for many years — one, the singer that keeps coming back for more in the UK; and the other, the Schlager singer in Central Europe. Actually, there are of course three — the family man.

The same year I appeared on the Legends stage at Glastonbury, I was also having fun on the ever popular *Musikantenstadl* TV show, that was transmitted into all the Central European countries, singing a medley of 'Sweet September', 'I Did What I Did for Maria' and 'Amarillo'; and also 'Every Word She Said'. I also sang a German/English duet of 'Moonlight and Roses' with the host Andy Borg, one of the loveliest and funniest men you could ever wish to meet. We worked together on the lovely Carmen Nebel tour, along with the amazing Paul Potts and two great singers, Beatrice Egli and Ella Endlich. We recently all met up on the *Carmen Nebel* TV show, when I was a surprise guest to sing 'Happy Birthday Baby' to my dearest friend, Ireen Sheer, on her special birthday.

It's a funny old world. Tours of Germany, Austria and Switzerland, singing lovely Schlager songs and tours of New Zealand, Australia, South Africa and the UK and Ireland, singing new songs. But now here I was singing one of my new songs in Germany too. My fans have really taken to them.

Closer to home, the Lichfield Garrick Theatre is a personal favourite. I've played there many times and became president of the Friends of the Lichfield Garrick in 2016, but it was a visit to watch

Ladies' Day, performed by the Lichfield Garrick Repertory Company in 2009, that may have set wheels in motion somewhere along the way for what was to happen nearly a decade later that saw me 'tread the boards' once more in my acting career, that had started on TV with *Emmerdale* and would soon now see me hit the West End.

Sue and I had seen the rock 'n' roll musical *Dreamboats and Petticoats* at the Savoy Theatre in The Strand on its opening night in July 2009. I loved the storyline of young musicians competing to win the hearts of adoring female fans and, quite appropriately for me, the girl they were after was the gorgeous Sue! I also loved the music. They were all songs from the artists I'd grown up listening to — Roy Orbison, The Plattters, Marty Wilde, Eddie Cochran and The Everly Brothers.

Songs trigger memories and I saw how, when certain songs were played, couples looked at each other, the way they do when they are looking back fondly and put their arms around each other and were swaying. It was beautiful!

Brian Berg of Universal was involved with putting on the show, along with theatre impresario Bill Kenwright, and it was Brian who had invited us. As soon as I saw the show, I really fancied being in it. I think Brian uttered some words along the lines that it was full of kids, but there were some parts for a not-so-young singer.

I was offered not one but two parts for three months at The Playhouse Theatre in Northumberland Avenue, where it had moved to after its run at The Savoy Theatre. I seem to recall we played golf while Brian checked out if I was serious and I think he's still got my clubs!

I had existing commitments before joining the cast and we were already getting under way with songs and ideas for the follow-up to *Made in Sheffield*, but I was ready for my first acting role on stage since I'd appeared as the third witch in the cauldron scene from *Macbeth* back in school at Conisbrough when I was about 14 years old. I was to go from a school part to the West End in one move! Okay, it may have taken 53 years, but who's counting?

Dreamboats and Petticoats is about two male characters, Norman and Bobby, who are competing for the affections of Sue. My role was two-fold: to play Older Bobby and Phil, Bobby's father who runs the St Mungo's Youth Club where the action is based. Unfortunately, I think I was too ripe to get the girl in the production. I was to start my run on July 5, 2010.

I found the whole production and what goes on behind the scenes amazing and the young cast were all so talented, truly fabulous and I learned so much from them all. It was in every way a fantastic experience and also required terrific energy levels because it was so fast-paced. I found it quite daunting initially, not just learning the lines, but the interactions and timings. It's all about interpretation, whether singing or acting.

There were two and sometimes three shows per day and many costume changes for everyone, and as I was playing two roles that increased my number of changes, but it really is a great show. It still tours the UK from time to time. If you like the music of the late-'50s and early '60s, you will love it, as I do.

I sang 'Dream Lover' by Bobby Darin and 'Shop Around' by Smokey Robinson and The Miracles in the show, which I added to my shows afterwards. There was another Neil Sedaka song in the show too — 'Happy Birthday Sweet Sixteen', which once again he had written with Howard Greenfield. They get everywhere those guys — and in fact Neil was over in the UK again just as I finished my three-month run, as came to my final night. He was honoured with the Silver Heart Award by The Variety Club in The Palace Hotel in Manchester that same week.

Ironically, the man who had given me my first TV break in the '60s was to take my roles in *Dreamboats* the following year — Des O'Connor. Des was 79 years old when he joined the cast, so maybe I wasn't so ripe after all at a mere 66!

Sue and I stayed at The Groucho Club in Soho for my three-month stint in the show, where I ticked the thespian box on my curriculum vitae or bucket list. By the time my run in *Dreamboats* was over, we were ready for getting back home, but that's not how it turned out.

Now you may recall my adeptness at jobs around the house, amazing DIY skills, making meals for everyone. No? Well, that's never really been me. I have tried — and failed miserably on occasions. Just ask Sue about a shelf I managed to put up, upside down! Certainly not my vocation. Give me a microphone or a golf club and I'm in my comfort zone. Anything else, not really.

So why, might you ask, and quite justifiably I might add if you do, did I accept the invitation to take part in *Celebrity Come Dine with Me* on Channel 4, that was broadcast on 22 December 2010, but like all good Christmas programmes was filmed much earlier.

I thought it might be fun to do and it was hilarious in some respects, especially if you weren't me! I'd been offered a few celebrity programmes. Sue and I had been approached to do *Celebrity Wife Swap*. We'd seen the episode with Paul and Debbie Daniels and Vanessa Feltz and her partner. Even if we had ever considered it, which we didn't, that was as good a reason as any not to take part — and anyway, I'd never swap Sue for anyone or anything.

Celebrity Come Dine with Me was bad enough!

When I tell you that at one stage I had my head in my hands, muttering the words, 'I've lost the will to live,' you'll get the general idea that things weren't exactly going so well. Apparently, the producer whispered to Sue that I was 'doing really well' as she saw me in that state through the glass door.

The day did not start well. We had been staying at Groucho's while the *Dreamboats* job was on and this followed it, so we weren't filming in our own house. We were using a house in London that was meant to appear as though it was ours. As it was a Christmas programme, the place needed festive decorations.

They'd told us not to bother bringing anything with us, they would set it all up. It was horrendous. It looked like something you would find at your granny's house in the 1950s. In Sue's words, it looked like 'a lot of old tat', but it was too late to do anything else, we just had to go with it.

It was a lovely house, but the cutlery and crockery that we were allowed to use left a lot to be desired, and Sue was understandably not happy with how things might look, as though odd cutlery, odd glasses and chipped crockery was our normal way of entertaining. She didn't want people thinking that's what we used.

We'd stayed at a hotel near to the shoot for the night beforehand, so that we were there on time.

We had arrived at 9 o'clock in the morning, ready to start filming at 9.15.

The film crew turned up at midday! In all fairness, when they arrived they were all very helpful. I was asked whether I needed any help with the meals. I think they'd worked me out fairly easily. I was able to tell them I was perfectly confident as I had my sous chef with me! A very real Sue chef!

Sue had already been put under pressure, as the producer had asked me to change the starter, which was going to be a prawn linguini, because one of the guests, Goldie, was allergic to shellfish.

I'd left my suit back at Groucho's and Sue, while going back to collect it for me, had unbelievably managed to bump into celebrity chef, Aldo Zilli, who she pumped for information about what she should do instead. Aldo suggested stuffed portobello mushrooms, using sundried tomatoes, olive oil, spices. Exactly my thoughts, being the culinary wizard I'm not.

I remember whimpering something along the lines of, 'Don't leave me,' before she had left.

My Portobello mushrooms were not the pleasing-to-the-eye dish my 'Sue' chef wanted, as there was nothing appropriate in the kitchen utility range to give them the necessary extra boost to zhoosh it up, as we chefs say.

Sue had taken our own crystal bowls for the passion fruit parfait dessert and they looked great, but my main course masterpiece of duck breast never stood a chance!

We would have been better leaving the little things waddling around somewhere, rather than the train wreck my dishes they became. Sue ... sorry, *I*, had just got the duck breast sizzling in the pan when the producer shouted, 'Stop!' calling a halt to proceedings. Sue was mortified.

The choir had arrived. They had booked a local choir to sing a Christmas carol with me, mercifully at last something I could do successfully. The only problem was they were supposed to have come after the main course had been served and before dessert, but they had another gig to get to. They'd said they could only do it at that time or they couldn't do it at all. So much for the legendary power of television over everything else! Times had clearly changed. We were all in the hands of these lovely choir people who were calling the shots and had effectively 'cooked my goose' — well, duck actually, but either way we were going quackers!

The carol went well and the carollers were hot — unlike the duck, which was by now colder than it had ever been in a chiller! It was like leather. Even that wasn't the end of it. We, sorry, *I* set it all out as best I could and then I was asked to do it all again, pretending that I was cooking it — something had been wrong with the camera. I don't recall James Martin having these kinds of problems on *Saturday Kitchen*. The meal was annihilated. The producer promised not to make it look so bad. Thanks for saving our disaster!

I came second, but my sous chef reckoned I didn't deserve to even come fourth — and there were only four of us! I can see how funny it was now, but at the time I really was wondering why the hell I'd taken it on, and although I wasn't helped by all the events of the day, I'd never want to go through it all again. Janet Ellis, Sophie Ellis-Bextor's mum and ex-*Blue Peter* presenter, won. I came second with Susie Amy from *Footballers' Wives*, with DJ Goldie fourth. The programme was shown on 22 December 2010 and the producer was so kind to me. I didn't come out anywhere near as badly as I thought I would, but maybe *Wife Swap* would have been easier — they kept putting the money up to try and entice me! But that was always a half-baked idea, a bit like my cooking! Let's move on, because now is the time.

CHAPTER 29

Now's the Time for a return to Northern Soul

How do you follow up what many in the music business regard as the greatest album in your career? During 2010, we set about a different project and one that gave me just as much satisfaction as *Made in Sheffield*, and in some respects even more so because I felt it had captured my sound and with all the appropriate nods back to what had put me where I was.

Sean had contacted Eddie Piller at Acid Jazz Records in East London, who was also a popular Northern Soul DJ and had produced many albums inspired by the Motown and Mod sounds of the '60s. Sean had worked in Eddie's studio in Denmark Street with his band and we had these great songs written by Richard Barratt and Michael Ward.

When Eddie heard I was Sean's dad, he told him he regularly still played 'Give Me Your Love Again', the B side to 'I Did What I Did for Maria' and album track on my first album in 1971 at Northern Soul nights and weekenders. It had been so well received over the years that, even without a video to go with it and just a picture of the 45rpm single, it has picked up over 20,000 'views' as people have sought it out on YouTube.

Eddie was taken with the songs we had in mind. They definitely fitted with his record label.

I signed to Acid Jazz Records with Richard Barratt — DJ Parrot — also producing it as he'd wanted to a few years previously and had written these great tunes with Michael. These were the sounds I grew up with and gave me some fantastic new energetic songs that really do get the party started.

The title track, 'Now's the Time!' sets any concert under way in great style and is a life-affirming happy song. It has a nod in the direction of Sammy Davis Jr and is all about how your life is changed when you find the love of your life. Audiences love the song, as it is such a big opener to a show with the brass section blasting away, but it can equally be the perfect song after a ballad.

We released my first 7-inch 45rpm single in years, 'Nobody in the World', in November 2010, before the album was released in February 2011. This has Northern Soul stamped right through it with that big Motown sound and fabulous backing vocals. The beat, the rhythm, everything about it is a dancefloor song.

Michael Ward wrote it, played on it and sang backing too. What a feller. He did such a fantastic job. The CD single features a '60s song that I'd never previously released, 'Concrete and Clay'. Acid Jazz talked of 'Nobody in the World' being the first Mod single I'd released since Shel Talmy produced my first ever single 'Life's Too Good to Waste' in 1966. It had only been 45 years, after all!

'Seven Hills' was the other track on the CD single and was also on the album. It's so good we include it along with 'Now's the Time!' in concerts even today, and is a duet I sang with Irish singer-songwriter Roisin Murphy, who wrote the song and was in the duo Moloko, who had a massive dance hit with 'Sing It Back'. 'Seven Hills' sounds to me like a song that's from one of those gritty Northern kitchen sink dramas of the '60s.

Two of the album's other songs we still play regularly in concert are 'Key of U' and 'Workin' Overtime', both written by Richard Barratt and Michael Ward. 'Key of U' is in the Ramsey Lewis soul vein, that brought the American great fame, and 'Workin' Overtime' has that real Detroit sound that sends me back to my roots. Jarvis got involved in the album too, contributing another pastiche song, 'Get Christie', playing on the classic Michael Caine gangster movie, *Get Carter*.

'Money Spider', 'Steal the Sun', 'Longing for You Baby', 'Too Much of the Sun', 'I Thank You' and 'Something Better' are all fabulous songs too. I honestly don't think there's a single song on *Now's the Time!* that I didn't enjoy recording. Some are just great Northern Soul/Mod dance songs, others could be film themes in the style of the spaghetti westerns made in the '60s and '70s. Special thanks must go to Richard Barratt, Michael Ward, Roisin Murphy and Steven 'Boycey' Boyce, for a lot of the arrangements that make this album so big, bold and brassy — and Sean even got to play percussion on it too!

We knew it wasn't the kind of album that would make the charts. *Made in Sheffield* had only just made it into the Top 100, but *Now's the Time!* became a good crossover album in Germany, where it was picked up by Sony who put it out on the Columbia label because they perhaps saw the potential in the Northern Soul '60s style. I finally appeared on some of the big TV shows over there playing something other than my old hits.

Over in the UK, the reviews were great. *All Music*'s journalist reviewer, Jon O'Brien, said I could have just made one of the best albums of my career, and Martin Townsend of the *Daily Express* said it 'oozed wit and style'. I was receiving 4-star and 8 out of 10 reviews. Before *Made in Sheffield*, I was lucky if they had been reviewed at all. I had become a singer who made not just interesting, but also well-respected albums with terrific songs.

The *Guardian*'s reviewer, Caroline Sullivan, hit the nail on the head when she wrote that I'd returned to brassy pop. She actually put lounge pop, but I don't know what that is, but where she hit the mark was when she wrote, 'and he sounds pleased to be there.'

It just shows that what you put into songs when your heart and soul is into something others can read that way. Caroline called the album's songs a 'uniformly good bunch' and singled out a trio for special praise — 'Seven Hills' with Roisin, 'Too Much of the Sun' and 'Get Christie'. I know Eddie was the owner of the record company, so you'd expect him to say something nice about one of the albums on his label, but he was extraordinarily pleased with it. He was quoted as saying, 'The spread on the album is amazing, quite filmic, but with some nods to spaghetti westerns and a classic soul sound.'

I enjoyed everything about *Now's the Time!* because of the type of music we were all creating. It was exciting and provided me with great new songs. Michael Ward pretty much wrote everything. Later in the year, we released a special arrangement of 'Steal the Sun' as a charity single for Afghan Heroes, supporting British forces on the frontline in Afghanistan. Michael wrote it in memory of his friend.

CHAPTER 30

50 years and 50 dates

When I first started in this business, on the stage with Dave at the Ivanhoe WMC in my home town of Conisbrough in 1961, even before we gave ourselves the name of the Grant Brothers, I could never have imagined that fifty years later I would have sung and had hits all around the globe. I've never had vocal training. I've never been a manufactured pop star. I'd never been on *Opportunity Knocks*, *Search for a Star* or *New Faces* — the *X Factor* and *Britain's Got Talent* of the past. I changed my name to a stage name, the way a lot of people used to, but that's been about it — and somehow, half a century after I'd started, I was about to embark on probably the longest tour I'd ever done.

We began the fifty-date tour — that I think ended up at fifty-two or more, by the way — back at the Ivanhoe! Fifty years later, on 16 March 2011, I was back in the club where we supported Lynne Perrie and Norman Collier. Lynne had passed away some years earlier. We have since lost our dear Norman.

It was nostalgic and a good way of getting the tour under way, with one or two people who still remembered being there for the career debut. I don't get over to my home town that much and so it was nice to see people I hadn't seen for years, decades, aeons! All of the proceeds from the evening went to Teenage Cancer Trust and St Peter's Church, Conisbrough.

The tour went all around England, Scotland and Wales, from the Leicester Square Theatre in London's West End to Blackpool Opera House and Winter Gardens, where I'd first been approached by Harvey Lisberg. We were visiting all those places that had made a massive difference to my career and also great places like Falkirk Town Hall. Falkirk FC had adopted 'Amarillo' as their anthem years before and the sound inside the hall when we finished with the song that night truly raised the roof. I doubt that 'Flower of Scotland' would have been sung with more gusto, certainly in Falkirk, at any rate.

Apart from the support of your family, the most important people I've ever had in my life have been the musicians I've worked with, and during that 50th anniversary tour I had one of the most experienced bands it has been my pleasure to work with, led by musical director, Daniel McCormack, who played keys on tour and has also performed with music legends Van Morrison, Roy Wood and the brilliant Imelda May. Daniel transcribed and arranged every song on the tour and is just such an amazing man.

Elliott Henshaw was on drums, Richard Hammond on bass, Oliver Darling and Dave Day on guitars, and the amazing horn section was made up of Bryan Corbett on trumpet and flugelhorn, who is a regular at Ronnie Scott's, John 'Boysey' Battrum on tenor and baritone sax, and Chris 'Beebe' Aldridge on tenor and baritone sax as well as flute. Shell Naylor was on backing vocals. Every single one of them has an impeccable background in live and recorded music and every single night it was a pleasure to be with them all.

The really great thing about the 50th anniversary tour was to be playing new songs from albums that were fresh, as well as the hit songs from the previous decades that I'd played thousands of times. *Made in Sheffield* and *Now's the Time!* had given me a whole new set of material that had begun with 'Walk Like a Panther'. Maybe I'd never left Sheffield after all — or it had never left me.

I was asked time and time again by journalists and TV presenters about how I geared up for a 50-date tour. Did I have a fitness plan? How much did it take out of me? I answered that I'd laid off beers down at my local.

My standard reply was that I'd been used to playing over 320 dates a year in the '60s and '70s when I was doing the clubs and I was seriously loving every minute. Who wouldn't? I was playing the songs people knew, as well as playing the new songs I loved and wanted to play for them — and the really great thing was the fans all knew them.

It wasn't just the 50 dates in the UK I played that year, either. We also played dates in Germany where my audience was now moving with me from the Schlager music to my new uptempo songs from *Now's the Time!*

One of my favourite lines of the time came from a journalist who wrote: 'Christie celebrates his 50th year in music with an album of original tracks marinated in the sounds and style of the '60s.' I'd go with that. While ever I am able to sing I will always go into the studio and record. It's exhilarating and what comes out of it can sometimes be as fulfilling as both *Made in Sheffield* and *Now's the Time!* In many ways, I'm just getting started!

I'd been offered pantomime since the '70s and had always resisted, but now it was different. I'd appeared on stage in the West End and, following my run in *Dreamboats*, Bill Kenwright approached me to play the King in *Sleeping Beauty* at his Theatre Royal in Windsor, where he is executive producer. Well, how could I turn Bill down? Christmas performing close to the Royal Family, being a royal myself in the panto, and with the lovely and beautiful Anita Harris as my queen. Something great for my family too. All the grandchildren could come along.

I just thought everything was right for me to do it. The timing, the theatre itself which is fantastic, the fact that it was in Windsor really appealed and I'd tick another box. So I signed up for the run which opened on Wednesday 7 December through to Sunday 8 January 2012.

It was a wonderful cast. Anita was terrific and is one of the icons of the pantomime world, whose appearances as Peter Pan were legendary. Britt Ekland played the Wicked Fairy. To appear alongside two such stunning and talented ladies on stage was a real treat for me. And it wasn't just two either, as Chloe Madeley, daughter of Richard and Judy, and television presenter in her own right, played my daughter Princess Beauty — appropriately beautifully. We also had Noddy, the children's book character and now TV star.

I really had a ball. We had Christmas Day off, but made up for it on Boxing Day with three shows, as well as two shows most days. I don't think any of us had any idea where we were after the first show on Boxing Day, or maybe that was just me! So many costume changes and three times over. My head was spinning.

The local press seemed to enjoy it, as Sophie Flowers from the *Maidenhead Advertiser* wrote: 'If you love good old pantomime fun then you'll love *Sleeping Beauty*. Movie legend Britt Ekland is fabulous as the wicked fairy who places a curse on the pretty princess on her 16th birthday. Duo Tony Christie and Anita Harris are perfect as the doting King and Queen determined to protect their darling daughter by removing all spinning wheels from the kingdom. The long-running 'Amarillo' joke, prompting Christie to threaten to burst into song more than once, is great fun and makes it all the more satisfying when he finally sings his popular hit. Kids' favourite Noddy helps save the day. For panto fun and action, and Tony Christie singing 'Is This is the Way to Amarillo?', you won't have a better night out.'

Fleet of foot from Windsor on New Year's Eve, I made it to The Savoy in London as one of the special guests at the Stompin' at the Savoy evening broadcast on BBC Radio 2, hosted by stand-up comedian and presenter Patrick Kielty, where I appeared and sang with The Guy Barker Orchestra. It was a glittering occasion that also saw performances by the UK's Queen of Soul, Beverley Knight and Paloma Faith, and with the amazing Buddy Greco playing piano. What a star-studded way of bringing in the New Year. I was back on stage in Windsor the next day. No rest for the King, you know. My subjects needed dealing with.

CHAPTER 31

The Hippodrome, Nashville and Germany ... and a little golf classic

I'd loved playing at The Talk of the Town in London's Hippodrome in the '70s and, just as my career had come full circle in 2005, so too did this world-famous venue make its own comeback in July 2012. I was honoured to be the opening act of its new life. It had been the Las Vegas of the Thames back in its heyday, with Sinatra, Sammy Davis and Judy Garland all appearing, as well as Shirley Bassey and Louis Armstrong, when it was a sell-out every night.

It had been around 40 years since I'd played there for the second of my two runs and it was now much more intimate as its main purpose is now as a casino. The Matcham Room has a much smaller capacity than The Talk of the Town had all those years ago, but boy does it still have bags of atmosphere. TV chef, Barry Vera, was in the audience. His dad and I were golfing pals in the old days in Sheffield. Young Barry, as he was known, was the chef at The Hippodrome and we were served some of the best food in the world.

For me, The Talk of the Town was always hallowed ground, a place where if you played it was like another notch on the bedpost. In the '70s, there was a huge stage and a balcony and it was like working a theatre. It's now up close and personal and the Matcham Room has been built on what was the stage.

We had a brilliant week playing songs old and new. It was wonderful to once again be performing where my idols had all graced the stage.

I've been extremely fortunate to have been in a position where I have met and talked with famous people, everyone from Franz

Beckenbauer, one of my all-time favourite footballers; to Tony Bennett in London; chaperone for Gina Lollobrigida at a charity ball in Munich; to having lunch with Larry Hagman; but nothing beats a great venue and it was an absolute pleasure to set the ball rolling for the Hippodrome's rebirth.

Around that same time in summer 2012, I was also offered the opportunity to play a gig with Ronnie Scott's Orchestra at Preston's Charter Theatre in Lancashire. I hadn't realised the concert was going to be as big as it was. I'd taken the gig on because it was Ronnie Scott's band and somebody had asked whether I fancied singing a few songs and it was a good excuse to get out and sing with a big band.

Having performed all over the UK in 2011 for the 50th anniversary tour, we couldn't leave out Germany, Austria and Switzerland and released an album, *Best of Tony Christie — Die Größten Hits Aus 50 Jahren* in 2012. I appeared several times on TV programmes, singing medleys of the big hits, including everything from the '70s singles to 'Sweet September' and 'Kiss in the Night', as well as a number of the songs from the Jack White era.

It was now that Sean and I were planning for the next albums. An Irish album of classic tunes was something I'd always wanted to record, having grown up with the music at weddings and Christmas occasions — and I particularly wanted to put it together for my dad. The other album was to go back to Nashville and record more country songs. We'd gone so far with what we had done the first time around, but we wanted to get back under way with what will eventually be a country album.

I had become host of the Howard Keel Golf Classic by this time. Don Felder, lead guitarist with The Eagles, had taken over from Howard originally. I hosted it on 9 September 2012 at Carden Park Golf Resort in Cheshire, with Willie Morgan once again organising and promoting the event, raising charity funds for the NSPCC and the Christie Hospital in Manchester.

Celebrity players included Jasper Carrott, Alan McInally, Robert Powell and Gordon Banks. These were always great days followed by fabulous nights and have raised millions of pounds for charity over the many years. Willie was a great player for Manchester United and Scotland, but he is also a fabulous and dedicated charity fundraiser.

CHAPTER 32

Grugahalle, Essen — 15 December 2012

I had always been very fortunate with injuries. Broken noses, as you know by now, and I broke my thumb falling off my bike when I was about 15, but otherwise nothing. Sue and I have been skiing many times. Nothing, not even a pulled muscle. I'd had near misses.

I'd never had anything more, no catastrophes, until Grugahalle, Essen, 15 December 2012.

I was nearing the end of a tour with a number of '60s and '70s acts all performing our hits and giving everyone a great time in the concert hall that holds nearly 10,000. I was standing next to the on-stage sound mixing desk to one side of the stage. I was announced and made my entrance.

What an entrance it was! Sue said she heard the roar that went up when I'd come on and had a feeling that it had been much more enthusiastic than normal, either for me or the rest of the acts that had been on so far. She'd not seen the entrance I'd made and probably just as well that she hadn't, otherwise she may have rushed on stage to check I was okay, which it turns out I wasn't for the next two years.

I had run on to the stage, which was in darkness, or at very least semi-darkness, with the lights about to go up centre stage. Bounding on with all the enthusiasm and adrenaline pumping, I hit a monitor speaker that should not have been there and, due to the pace I was moving, flew into a somersault, landing on my hip and elbow. But the audience seemed to think it was all part of the show, which is why the roar went up, although there were also probably just as many who were giving out a shocked sound that mingled with the rest and made the whole thing sound much louder.

When you're performing, the adrenaline sees you through, and so it proved that night. I leaped up and carried on. Like many before me and since, you sometimes don't feel the pain on stage that you do immediately after spotlight goes off, but I could see the blood.

I played my whole set, but my musical director had alerted Sue while I was on that I'd had a bad tumble and would need a medic quickly when I came off.

After I'd completed my 50 minutes, and with blood running down my left arm from my elbow and dripping off my fingers from underneath my shirt and jacket, it was time to see the damage.

When I came off stage, the medics took over. First off was the jacket, that revealed my shirt covered in blood. Next was the shirt. The skin was ripped off from the elbow and the medics cleaned it up, put the skin back in place, bandaged me up and sent me on my way.

And that was that, you might think. Just a fall, others have had them before, we all have accidents, everything should heal.

I woke up the next morning and was black and blue from my hips to my legs. I know it's normal for bruising to come out later, but two weeks, four weeks and six weeks later, I was experiencing excruciating pain in my back and hip and finding it hard to either stand up or bend down.

Once we were back in the UK and at home, I went to see my GP, who sent me for X-rays and an MRI scan. The results came back that the three bottom discs of my spine had herniated with one pointing inwards and two away from me. Spasms and nerve pressure is what causes the pain.

My doctor told me that in most cases herniated discs do repair on their own and in their own time. I was prescribed painkillers, physiotherapy and regular exercise.

I couldn't undertake either of the last two of the three because I was in so much pain. I took the medication, which included morphine and gabapentin, but I was getting worse. We are talking months now. I wasn't able to do anything, sing, perform, it was even a struggle for me to feed the birds. Sean was telling everybody how busy I was, because you never say you're ill, otherwise the phone stops ringing, but I was feeling worse. I was now officially a zombie.

When I did venture out of the house to buy a newspaper at our local shop, Waitrose, the staff told Sue they were really concerned because of the way I looked. It was like I hadn't recognised them or made conversation the way I would normally.

Sue sometimes reckons my social skills could be improved when I'm not on stage, but this was way beyond all that.

It got so bad that one day I told Sue very sincerely and honestly that 'I don't want to be here anymore.' I really truly felt I wanted to die. I was just rocking in my chair, shaking with the pain. Sue came and put a shawl around me. I was so depressed and close to being suicidal. I knew everyone was worried about me, but I was also past caring what people thought. The pain was too much.

Sue looked at the paperwork and leaflets for my medication and found that the side effects of taking gabapentin could include anxiety, depression and suicidal thoughts. She stopped me from taking it straight away and my doctor upped the morphine patches. My mental health improved, but my hip began hurting again and I returned to hospital where I had cortisone injections after it was revealed I had painful swelling in the joint.

I couldn't work properly for two years. A 90-minute show was impossible, but I could usually get by with doing a short stint for a TV show or a shortened set and none of this had affected my voice in any way. Prior to the accident, I'd always been fit, either through running, cycling, skiing or playing golf, but this was not as easy to shake off as the odd dead leg or twisted ankle that are more normal injuries.

Spiritual healing and reiki wasn't something I'd initially thought about, but Sue's grandmother was into spiritualism. Both Sue and I love to go to church, but we're not regular churchgoers. We have lots of friends who are spiritual healers and reiki experts. It's as though we've been thrown together over the years and, although I can't explain it fully, it is all about channelling positive energy into your body. Whether it is someone practising reiki, either placing hands on or near a body, or whether it is some kind of force sent through good thoughts, wherever your combined number of healers happen to be, for us it works.

In Mojacar, we met Sylvia and John Stannier from Stourbridge when they were visiting our friends Betsy and Arthur Lees. I'd had a headache for days and couldn't shake it off. Sylvia, with her wonderful healing hands, made my headache disappear and I hadn't had another until I started writing this book!

John and Iris Taylor were also living in Spain. They are reiki masters and have also been there for Sue and I many times.

When I was really bad with my back and hip, Sue rang John, Sylvia, Iris, Yvonne and Martin Young in Nuneaton, who all sent positive energy through thinking about me. Martin, being local, came over regularly. Martin is one of our best friends and is a wonderful healer, life coach and a most amazing person. He is like family.

I was willing to try anything and hoped that at very least reiki and the physiotherapy might speed up the healing.

One day, knowing that everyone was thinking about me, I sat back, closed my eyes and relaxed. The medicine wasn't helping. I sat, eyes closed, floated off into a kind of trance with Sue sitting on the opposite sofa. Suddenly, my eyes opened wide and I sat bolt upright. Sue asked what was happening. I said that I'd felt something push at my back and something had moved. After that, the pain didn't go away, but became less severe and was even better over the next few days.

We went to the hospital three or four days later. An X-ray was taken and the consultant told me it looked like everything had gone back into place. It was as though that push I'd felt had made everything right again and I was gradually weaned off the medication, thanks to my wonderful healing friends.

This certainly doesn't mean in any way that I don't go down the normal routes when illness and injuries arise, and after nearly 70 years of needing hardly any help at all, in the past half dozen years, I seem to have become close to a regular.

The news that I hadn't been paid for any of the tour where I'd had the fall was like rubbing salt into my wounds. It was also pretty much the end of my golfing days. I've hardly swung a club since.

Lovely German TV presenter, Carmen Nebel, was particularly supportive in interviews around the time after my fall in Essen, and has invited me on her shows many times. I'm looking forward to seeing her again in the coming months, along with Ireen Sheer and their husbands, Norbert and Klaus.

CHAPTER 33

The Great Irish Songbook *via Nashville, Sheffield, Denaby and Germany*

It's surprising what the body can take. I wasn't one hundred per cent immediately after the herniated discs went back in place and couldn't cope with too much, but I was able to perform again and played in some memorable concerts.

There's also a fabulous YouTube clip of me playing an outdoor concert along the side of a river in Austria. The whole night, filmed for TV, called *Starnacht aus der Wachau* and hosted by Alfons Haider, on September 21, 2013 at Rossatz-Arnsdorf alongside the River Danube in Austria, was just great fun and with such a receptive audience. The Austrian singer, Conchita Wurst, who won Eurovision in 2014 with 'Rise Like a Phoenix', performed too. Close by is Castle Durnstein, where King Richard the Lionheart was held captive by Duke Leopold V. It is only a small village, but what a great night we all had.

Sheffield called me home again too, this time playing to honour the city's Women of Steel, the women who kept the steel mills working during the two World Wars, by raising funds to pay for a bronze statue in their memory.

Some of those amazing ladies were at the concert held at Sheffield City Hall in November 2013, and amongst them was 91-year-old Kathleen Roberts, who built parts for the Spitfire; and three 92-year-olds, Kit Solitt, a tanks and battleships parts maker, Ruby Gascoigne, who worked in the steel rolling mill, and Dorothy Slingsby, an overhead crane driver.

My old mate, Graham Walker, from Sheffield's main newspaper,

The Star, was one of the organisers of the show that included Heaven 17's Glenn Gregory and Martyn Ware; ABC's Martin Fry, who I sang with, and who also brought along his mother-in-law, Nora Awoko, who worked in Firth Brown steelworks; and John Parr of St Elmo's Fire fame, along with many more once again showing off the great talent that exists in this wonderful city. It was a fantastic night and over £50,000 was raised. Once again making me feel proud to call Sheffield my adopted home city.

There were other one-off gigs and TV appearances, but I really wasn't in a fit state for anything that would take too long — but you know, sometimes not being able to do something can help you concentrate on other things and, since the extreme agony had subsided and I was able to deal with getting healthier, I focused on the recordings — and that's how more country recordings in Nashville took place and *The Great Irish Songbook* emerged with the amazing contemporary folk band, Ranagri.

So far, even today in 2019, as we're about to embark on a book tour, tour of Germany and a UK tour from autumn onwards, and with Chris Evans' Car Fest dates in summer, the new country album with songs from Graeme Pleath and Graham Gouldman is still a work in progress, but we did make more headway in 2013 by returning to Nashville to put together another set.

This time, we went to the Blackbird Studio in Azalea Place in Nashville, where anyone who is anyone in the modern era and in the past has recorded — Adele, Taylor Swift, Bryan Adams, Kelly Clarkson, Buddy Guy, Alicia Keys and country legends like Keith Urban and Tim McGraw. It is owned by country singer Martina McBride's husband, sound engineer John McBride. They have quite literally the biggest collection of microphones I had ever seen and with the clearest sounds you will ever hear. It was a vocalist's dream. Don Henley of The Eagles was there when we recorded. Great company to be around and in the heart of possibly the best known country music city of them all.

The Great Irish Songbook was a different matter. A seed planted so many years previously had taken a long while to grow and mature, but was about to blossom into another fabulous album.

Three decades previously, that initial seed had come from starting life in a 'very late night and into the early hours' session back at our house, including a melodeon. There may have also been an occasional whisky and beer infusion, and a good old-fashioned singalong of Irish songs we all had in common. That night had been like being back with all the Fitzgerald grandparents, aunts, uncles and cousins and brought happy memories.

I'd thoroughly enjoyed the company of Donal and Tony Rogers all those years ago, who'd come to one of my concerts, but not, would you believe it, to see me! Uncanny. Instead, they'd been checking out a fantastic drummer they heard about, wanted to work with and who just happened to be my son.

Donal and Tony were on the lookout for a new drummer — not for Ranagri, as that was a long way off Donal's radar at the time, but for their rock band, and they'd had, as Donal described, a tip-off from their manager about Sean's prowess with the sticks.

Donal told me afterwards, when they came back stage to meet Sean, that he'd been in awe of my voice, something he'd not expected, saying, 'Wow, you can sing!' and that while he'd heard of me and knew my hit songs, what he hadn't been expecting, he'd said, was the 'depth of power and emotion.'

When they came back to the house that night, at our invitation, Donal was immediately taken with the melodeon, the button accordion my grandfather Martin Fitzgerald had brought over from Co Mayo in the west of Ireland, that still takes pride of place at home as my favourite family heirloom.

That's when he heard my real name was Fitzgerald, and that's when the night suddenly turned to the green hue of Ireland and the amber hue of Bushmills single malt whiskey from Co Antrim, Ireland's oldest distillery. It's very rude to ignore your heritage, you know.

I told him my grandfather had come over to England, like many Irishmen before him, to seek work and had found it in the coal mines of South Yorkshire in 1915 during WWI, when there was little work to be had in Ireland. My cousin Eileen, who now lives in the small town of Tuam in Co Galway, but who was born in Maltby near Rotherham, tells me our granddad Martin came from a hamlet called Carrasteelaun near the town of Claremorris. It is close to the border with Co Galway. She recalls he was lame because of being trampled by a horse and cart and that he had been a gardener in a convent in Claremorris. Ballindine is just south of Claremorris and is the county border town between Mayo and Galway.

My dad, Paddy, would play the piano when we had the Fitzgerald family gatherings with granddad Martin on the melodeon and grandma Mary Anne on fiddle. She was from Maltby and played in a ceilidh band. My cousin Eileen's mum was Molly, one of my dad's sisters. Dad was the eldest of six siblings, including my uncles Michael and aunties Theresa, Kath and Eileen. When we were all together, things regularly turned musical. Eileen recalls 'A Mother's Love Is a Blessing' and 'Star of the County Down' being sung. At family weddings, 'Star of the County Down' and 'The Parting Glass' would be sung.

That night back home in our house in Streetly, Sutton Coldfield, in the mid-80s, was to be a moment that would turn into *The Great Irish Songbook* many years later, that I would dedicate to my mum and dad, Iris and Paddy, and my brother Cornelius — Neal's full name.

The next morning, Donal and Tony left our house having signed up their new drummer and having suggested that one day we should record the songs we had sung that night. Apparently, I'd smiled, as I do occasionally, and had said, 'Maybe, someday.' And that was that. The melodeon was put away.

Ranagri — made up of Donal, flautist Eliza Marshall, who is also currently playing 27 instruments in *The Lion King* in the West End, world-renowned harpist Jean Kelly, who has played everywhere, including at Buckingham Palace, and world-famous bodhran player Tad Sargent — are now one of the UK's leading folk bands, who play traditional tunes in a contemporary style, as well as writing their own material.

They had signed to Gunther Pauler's Stockfisch Records label in Northeim, Germany, in 2014, where they had recorded their debut album. A chance conversation with Sean, since he and Donal were in Germany at the same time, probably me too actually, but not with the two of them that night, brought a familiar conversation for Sean.

Donal knew the answer already, of course, but when the question came from Gunther it rekindled Donal's flame for the album he'd mentioned making while at Streetly. Gunther, knowing how popular I was in Germany and having a love of Irish music, saw an opportunity.

Gunther had asked Sean why his surname was Fitzgerald and not the same as mine, Christie. Sean relayed the familiar tale of how I'd changed my name, something incidentally my father understood, but would have still preferred me to be under my real name, plus Sean added the story of our family roots.

An album deal of Irish songs featuring myself with Ranagri was agreed. You cannot beat working alongside great musicians and these guys and girls are the best in their field, of that there is no doubt.

In many ways, it was also the ideal time. I wasn't running around — as I couldn't since Essen — and this led to another highly enjoyable experience making the music of my family's heritage. I'd never thought of myself as a folk singer, as they can sometimes be a bit 'tiddly-eye-ay', if you know what I mean, but folk songs are also a bit like country songs.

They tell stories, and story songs have so much more appeal about them than many others. You're not just interpreting, you're relating the song and it progresses. It was just as my dad had wanted me to record all those years ago and I was thrilled. He passed away in 2000. I think he would have been proud of what we produced. Rod (Stewart) has done many albums of *The Great American Songbook*; I look forward to more of *The Great Irish Songbook*.

Donal, Jean, Eliza and Tad came over to Lichfield before we went over to Germany to begin recording in what was once an abbey. That night back in Lichfield, we returned to the time when Donal and Tony had come round nearly thirty years ago, sitting together singing, each of us in turn, some of our favourite Irish songs and this time embrocated with a little Tullamore Dew, another favourite Irish whiskey from the town of Tullamore in Co Offaly between Dublin and Limerick, where Daniel E Williams (hence the Dew of Tullamore Dew) created the legendary triple distilled single malt.

That night, we began whittling down our initial shortlisted 40 songs that, if you travel to Dublin, Cork, Tipperary or Galway, you will still hear in nearly every bar. Ireland has always been a live music paradise and it has been my good fortune to play over there many times.

The songs we steered away from were the slightly more over-used songs of recent time, such as 'Fields of Athenry'. We wanted the album to be about our heritage. Some of the classics are there, along with others we all just really liked.

We also wanted a good mix of rousing songs and that made 'The Black Velvet Band' a shoe-in and the poignant 'The Parting Glass' an excellent farewell song as the last track on the album. 'Star of the County Down' was a family favourite and was released as a single on download in September 2015. There's a promotional video of it on YouTube.

'When You Were Sweet Sixteen' was in. Who couldn't want that on their album, such a beautiful song. One of my proudest moments on the album is 'She Moved Through the Fair', that I remembered from childhood days. It's one of those moments when you can look back and think I would never have imagined recording that, but I'm glad I've had the opportunity.

A lot of people in England and Germany or Austria won't know too many of the songs, but in Ireland they will probably know them all. When we played them at Dublin's Bord Gais Energy Theatre in 2015, it was just a lovely night performing Irish songs in Ireland — I bet there weren't many who even knew about my Irish background beforehand, but back in Tuam, up in the west of Ireland, Eileen tells me there are two dancehalls that carry the names Amarillo's and Las Vegas.

I spoke with Ed Power, a journalist on an Irish newspaper, backstage at the Bord Gais, and it suddenly brought back a memory of being in Australia with another great Irish singer and performer, Joe Dolan, who had a No 3 hit single in the UK with a song called 'Make Me an Island' in 1969, and a couple of Top 20 hits with 'Teresa' and 'You're Such a Good Looking Woman'.

It makes me smile just thinking of him, as Joe really was a bit of a lad. I was playing a club in Sydney on a four-week run and he was due to play four weeks there also and we overlapped. We were staying at the same hotel. He'd arrived 'well-watered' from the flight and immediately went out on the town. He arrived back in a taxi some time later and he was black and blue, and bleeding. I think he must have upset someone. He was a character in the true Irish sense of the word. He was known as 'Boots', but I think that night it was him who had been given a bit of a kicking! He had a few well-documented run-ins along the way, but was such a popular singer and his live show always carried the slogan, 'There's no show like a Joe show!'

Ranagri bring so much to a recording — including their love of whiskey. They have such a unique sound that allows a singer to express themselves, as well as creating an atmospheric beauty to each song, and it was a pleasure to spend time with them, not only in the studio, but socially and in concert in Ireland, England and Germany, when we took the album on tour. These songs have been recorded many times before and it is down to Ranagri's skills and Gunter's that the production, along with the arrangements they created, sounds so fresh and tender. Maybe another night round at ours in Lichfield sometime? I can feel it coming on. I'll supply the bottle — or two!

What a fabulous project, going back to my family's roots and putting something together for the Fitzgerald family, wherever we all are throughout the world.

And our good friend Yvonne, who had foreseen me having the hit once again with 'Amarillo', had also amazingly told Donal years before when Sean was in their then rock band, that one day Donal's band would change to something that would involve two girls and they would be playing what she termed weird instruments. Amazing!

I really feel so blessed that my career has offered up so many opportunities and when you read some of these later chapters you'll see that these new ventures, even more fortunately, just seem to keep on coming.

Whilst putting *The Great Irish Songbook* together, I was also able to take another step back in time, returning to Conisbrough, or more accurately Denaby, thanks to BBC's *Songs of Praise*, which offered another chance for reflection when I revisited my youth at St Alban's Church, where I sang in the choir at the back of the church, having joined from the Glee Club.

I was baptised at St Alban's and drifted into religion because of my voice. I do believe in there being one God, as I've said before. Sue and I, while we don't go to church regularly, enjoy going to Lichfield Cathedral for evensong occasionally.

I once sang 'So Deep Is the Night', otherwise known as 'Tristesse' by Chopin, at a mass there. Such a fabulous place to sing it. When we are away, we will often find a church and go and pay our respects and simply sit a while. It's our connection, very peaceful and we will light a candle.

The *Songs of Praise* programme was broadcast in July 2014 and was a special programme, with me leading the congregation in a selection of favourite hymns, plus a song written by Graham Gouldman. It was a lovely show, very affectionately produced by Jonathan Mayo, with Aled Jones as presenter.

Aled is a lovely, gentle man and started his interview of me, knowing I'm a very private person and not one for letting too many people inside my life — until now in these pages — by asking how someone so shy and private could alternately then stand up in front of thousands of people performing every night.

I'm certainly not a flamboyant person, not that I have anything against those who are. We are all different, no matter who we are, and I've always been happy being who I am. I certainly wouldn't have wanted my personal life splashed all over the place all the time, as happens to some entertainers. My family mean more to me than to have their lives splashed about, as sometimes happens in the music world.

There were some really nice tributes paid to me on the programme, by Sir Tim Rice and BBC Radio 2 DJ, Tony Blackburn. Tim was very kind, saying I had a timeless voice and there was no-one better at telling a story through song; while Tony weighed in with feeling that the older I was getting, the better my voice.

The live music recording and interviews with Aled all took place at Christ Church, Spitalfields in East London, where I led the congregation in 'Praise My Soul the King of Heaven' and 'How Great Thou Art', an acapella version of 'Amazing Grace' and Graham's 'You Are My Lifeline', where I was accompanied by Michelle John and Janet Ramus.

In the part of the programme that saw me clambering the steps up to where I sang at St Alban's, I met former work colleague, Jim Beachill, who, in typically South Yorkshire wit, said that I used to sing at work in the office and it was sometimes a bit annoying. That's what you get from Yorkshire people. We generally tell people what we think, quite honestly and with varying degrees of dry humour. Jim went on to say that he could tell I had a good voice though.

Being back in the church where I'd sung at 16–17 years old, brought back all those memories of standing on the back row wearing my Italian suit, that was all the rage, and hearing the church organ. When the choir used to join forces with the organ, I was literally in heaven.

I can see why many American singers who grew up singing in chapels and churches were similarly inspired. Churches are magical musical places where the acoustics are often so good, where people believe in what they are singing and wherever that happens it is a perfect marriage.

The sound of a church organ holds a special place in my heart. Singing at St Alban's showed me, before I began working the clubs with Dave, what my voice could do, but it meant much more. It was a great time of my life and brought me some fantastic mates, as well as providing me with a platform to set me on my way towards what has been a really great life.

I'd become one of the Grand Order of Water Rats in 2009 and, on 13 November 2014, Sue and I were particularly proud to have been invited to the 125th anniversary of the organisation that raises charity funds at Buckingham Palace. HRH The Queen and HRH The Duke of Edinburgh Prince Philip were both there and I was introduced to the Queen.

The Queen said they played 'Amarillo' at all their parties and said it was one of those songs you can't get out of your head. Sue says that she, Sue not the Queen, was so excited about being at the Palace. It was great to be there and Prince Philip, who is a Companion Rat, quipped he and the Queen had another gig after the Water Rat reception. Rick Wakeman was King Rat that year. It's an amazing organisation to be a part of and current Water Rats include Alfie Boe, Brian May, Roy Wood and Barry Cryer.

CHAPTER 34

50 Golden Greats, The Golden Anniversary Tour and TV Shows

I've lost count of the number of greatest hits compilations that have been released over the years all around the world since the mid-70s. If some fans have been collecting them all, they've probably ended up with 'Amarillo', 'I Did What I Did for Maria', 'Avenues and Alleyways', 'Don't Go Down to Reno' and 'Las Vegas' about two dozen or more times.

The *50 Golden Greats* album we put together through the Wrasse record label in 2015 was what I would call a proper compilation.

My long-time friend and sadly departed writer, Richard Havers, who wrote the notes for the *50 Golden Greats* CD booklet, called it my musical autobiography, as it includes that very first recording for CBS Records, Barbara Ruskin's 'Life's Too Good to Waste', through to all the songs that made me famous, and some of the many fantastic songs I've recorded since coming back from Spain, including tracks from *Made in Sheffield, Now's the Time!, The Great Irish Songbook* and the yet-to-be-released new country album.

The album was released in the same year as *The Great Irish Songbook* and together with *50 Golden Greats* led to an amazing tour that saw Ranagri join me for the first half of the show each night as we travelled the length and breadth of the UK, Ireland, Germany and Austria.

I've always enjoyed giving audiences something different to what they expect and as well as the Irish songs I also included as many different songs as I could, including 'Like Sister and Brother', 'Jezebel' and 'Mr Bojangles', complete with a little whistling soft shoe routine celebrating Sammy Davis Jr. We also played many of the more recent numbers, like 'Key of U', 'Damned' and 'Now's the Time!' The really great thing I've found is the new songs go down just as well as the hits from the '70s.

It was especially good to play a series of dates throughout Ireland — Northern Ireland and the Republic — going back to my family's roots and including Tullamore, complete with the Dew, as you might expect. I only wish I could have stayed longer, seen more of my heritage, performed even more. We'll do it again when *The Great Irish Songbook 2* is released. It will be a privilege to record for the first time with Ranagri's other performers, Joe Danks on bodhran and bouzouki, and Ellie Turner on harp, who I've performed with on tour.

What wasn't such a privilege was what happened in France at the end of the tour. We'd played to packed houses in Central Europe with audiences loving the Irish flavour Ranagri brought to the show.

We were returning to the UK, having had a great time, and my band and Donal were all together in the tour bus. It had been Sue's birthday, so we'd had a party on the bus in December 2016.

Sue and I were asleep, until we were woken by this racket and our driver saying, 'Don't be stupid, you're being filmed.'

It was a bunch of illegal immigrants from the nearby Grande-Synthe migrant camp, who were trying to get into the bus while we were parked to fill up with fuel near Dunkirk.

In the melee that followed, one of the biggest of the illegal immigrants went for our sound guy, Paul, and Donal fell, breaking his wrist.

It would have been even more frightening for me, but I'd taken a sleeping tablet and was a bit out of it, thank God.

Sue said she held my hand as we were going through Customs and that I was a bit like Andy Pandy. Well, I certainly wasn't handy. At least no one picked up anything more serious than Donal's injury, which was bad enough for him.

But I did pick up something else the following year.

In 2017, I received *The Irish World* newspaper's People of

Distinction Award. The year previously I'd picked up a Legends of Industry Award from The Variety Club of Great Britain. I've not done too badly for awards over the years, thinking back to Blackpool Winter Gardens where Harvey first introduced himself to me as The Penmen picked up our award; and the *Club Mirror* awards that I received in the '70s and '80s.

The heaviest award I've ever received was from a radio station in the port city of Kiel on Germany's Baltic Sea coast. When we brought it over with us to the UK, we had problems getting it through Customs. It looks like gold and, although I've never held a gold bar, I can imagine it being a similar weight. It's bloody heavy. We eventually got it through, but with some very strange looks.

Mentioning strange items brings me to another of my TV appearances. I really have enjoyed being invited and then taking part in a number of celebrity TV programmes since coming back from our ex-pat lifestyle in Spain, and while there are some that I'd never go on, like *Celebrity Wife Swap* or *Celebrity Big Brother*, I do enjoy the game shows and will have a go at any others that sound interesting and where I can have fun. I haven't won many of them, but I did beat Jimmy Osmond in *Celebrity Antiques Road Trip*.

The programme was a giggle. We both travelled around the Midlands visiting places where we bought old stuff and then had to see whether we made a profit at auction.

Our journey started at Loughborough, visiting Nottinghamshire, Leicestershire and Shropshire, before finishing at the auction room in Stoke-on-Trent. I had Margie Cooper on my team and Jimmy had Catherine Southon. The ladies are both antiques experts. The cars we'd been given to drive were a Bentley and a DeLorean.

I ended up purchasing a satin and lace Victorian lady's evening coat, as you do, a silver sugar shaker and a few other things. Jimmy bought an old record player, a pile of old records, including a *Top of the Pops* LP that had 'Long Haired Lover from Liverpool' on it, but not recorded by him.

It was one of those records that used to come out with the hit songs of the time, but sung by session musicians. We had a nice journey around, in good company, visiting interesting places, and having spent £400 on basically a load of old tat, mine sold for a bit more than that and after taking off the auctioneer's percentage I made £8.54 profit.

My first comment was, 'You mean we've done all that just to make less than a tenner!' It was meant tongue-in-cheek, but at least we made a profit. Jimmy made a loss. I don't think either of us will be pursuing a career in antiques any time soon.

After facing a first round exit in *The Weakest Link*, my next game show was the BBC show *Pointless*, and the best that can be said is that I couldn't fare any worse. I didn't, but I didn't fare any better either. It was a *Celebrity Pointless* featuring people from the music business and I was teamed up with Ben Adams, a nice lad, from the boy band A1, who had a couple of No 1 hits in 2000. I was very much the older statesman of the participants, that included Sinitta and Claire Richards and H (Ian Watkins) from Steps. Ben and I went out in the first round.

My favourite celebrity show came more recently. I had such a great time and it involved an experience I'd missed out on years before when I'd had to play The Talk of the Town and couldn't go on holiday with the family to the Norfolk Broads. You remember the one? That one where my golfing mate took the holiday and told me he'd had the best time ever!

Five Go Barging was the programme and for me it was the holiday I never had. We were in France. The first week we were on the beautiful River Lot and the second week on Canal du Midi. One of the stopping-off points was Cahors, known for its production of many excellent deep red wines. My fellow shipmates were actor Tom 'The Admiral' Conti, TV gardening guru Diarmuid Gavin, Olympic gold medal javelin star Tessa Sanderson, and zany TV presenter Penny Smith.

The idea of the show, so they said, was to learn how to live life together on a narrowboat in cramped conditions, with relative strangers — and to be responsible for navigating and not sinking the boat. Well, the good news is we didn't, but to be fair, it probably looked at times as if we were having a bloody good try!

You're probably wondering what your hero, that's me by the way, would do considering my prowess at nothing much other than singing. I'll tell you.

I crashed it. Yep. Penny, bless her, said they should have called it *Celebrities Go Crashing*. I took it all in my stride. I was there for a holiday, not all this running about nonsense, and anyway, Tom was having a ball. He loved every minute of being captain, which is why we started calling him Admiral. He said he'd been on boats before, so I kind of left it to him and drank tea. He knew all the terms, like port and starboard, forward and aft. Sue found it hilarious when she watched it on television, with everybody running about while I clutched my cuppa and completed crosswords.

Tessa, bless her too, is a bit hard of hearing and couldn't hear instructions half the time; Penny, as always, by her own admission, was a bit bossy; Diarmuid was good value and also became my fall guy. I'd been the cause of this accident that had seen an anchor go straight through my bedroom window.

I knew full well I'd pressed this button I shouldn't have when opening these lock gates, but with the straightest face I could manage, my family would say my normal face, I said to him, 'What did you do there, Diarmuid?' He took it in good part.

The producers loved it, and even more so when Tom said at the end, 'Now, Tony, can you tell me what happened?' I was a combination of the naughty schoolboy and a granddad just happy to be there while everyone else enjoyed being sailors.

What actually happened was I was standing at the front of the boat when they opened the lock gates. I saw the water coming down like a tsunami. So I turned around and dived inside the boat and closed the doors. Everyone thought I'd gone over the side! It was a lovely two weeks with a really fun group. I enjoyed it immensely, plus I got my barging holiday at last.

Even more recently, I recorded another celebrity game show, *Impossible* with Shaun Ryder of The Happy Mondays, Lesley Joseph from *Birds of a Feather*, sporting legends Martin Offiah and John Hartson, and Sally Lindsay, who played Shelley Unwin in *Coronation Street* and appeared in the 'Amarillo' video. Let's just say my game show record wasn't troubled by the appearance in six programmes and my mates in my 'local' loved it. I think, 'Don't give up the day job,' may have been one of the nicer suggestions.

Sally has invited Sue and I to her place for dinner, as her family likes my music.

Summertime, since those heady days of V Festival and Glastonbury, has more often than not seen me performing at festivals in the UK, Holland, Belgium, Germany and Austria and I've thoroughly enjoyed being a part of this scene that was only properly getting underway when I first hit the charts. They are now an essential part of summer for all artists and something we all enjoy.

By the time you read this, I will have performed at Chris Evans' highly popular Car Fest weekends in the north and south of England, but just as pleasurable have been those I've performed closer to home.

In 2017, I headlined the new Wentworth Music Festival, set in the incredible grounds of Wentworth Woodhouse stately home, with Heaven 17, Lemar, T'Pau and Dodgy, all on in the same day. It was a fantastic line up for a debut festival and I hope they go on to have many more.

And as if that wasn't close enough to home, I also played Conisbrough Music Festival and, further afield, the Priory Park Festival in Chichester with Georgie Fame, The Christians, Chris Farlowe, Dodgy and S Club. I played the Godiva Festival's 20th anniversary in Coventry in 2018, with Ronan Keating and Hazel O'Connor.

CHAPTER 35

Panto beckons once again — oh yes it does —
Ladies' Day — and a blood bath!

Having ticked the thespian box twice with Dreamboats and Sleeping Beauty in the West End and Windsor, I was to take my treading the boards career total to four productions with my second pantomime from 30 November 2017 to 7 January 2018 with a show that revolved around me, called *Ladies' Day* at The Grand Theatre in Wolverhampton, but the bigger drama of them all came in between the two productions.

Once again I was the King, this time in *Jack and the Beanstalk* at Cambridge Arts Theatre. I was officially King of Amarillo. Well, I'd been treated like royalty when I'd visited with Sean in 2005, so why not? There were various treats for me in playing the role. Firstly, who wouldn't want to do panto? Christmas, having fun, with the opportunity for the family to be there — both children and grandchildren. Also, Cambridge is only half an hour from where our daughter Sarah lives, so that was great — and you get to meet lovely people like *Bergerac* star Liza Goddard, who was in the Australian TV show *Skippy the Bush Kangaroo*. Liza was the Good Fairy Beansprout and Stephen Beckett from *Coronation Street* played Fleshcreep. Matt Crosby stole the show as Dame Trott.

Recording for a new album was well under way in 2017 and 2018. We were working with amazing Grammy Award-winning songwriters and people who'd written hit songs for the biggest stars of today's music business, like Amy Wadge, who has written stuff for Ed Sheeran and Kylie Minogue; Jimmy Hogarth, who has written for Amy Winehouse and Tina Turner; and Paddy Byrne for Paloma Faith and

Olly Murs.

The album, called *Pop Nonsense*, is due to be released around the same time as this book. It's me doing something a bit different once again and it's very exciting. We've recorded in the UK, the US and Portugal, getting it all together and when I came back from my panto kingdom, I was right back in the thick of it all.

It was time for another great UK tour, this time playing places as far flung and different as possible. It was a lot more up close and personal and I found that audiences were enjoying me talking about my career. It's not something I've done a lot of during the years, preferring to get on with my job of singing and entertaining, but it was a very pleasant surprise receiving such a nice reaction to giving out some of the stories that have coloured my life.

We played Findhorn on the Moray Firth in Scotland and for the first time ever I played in Orkney at the Orkney Theatre in Kirkwall. We just wanted to get to all the places we've never been, myself and Sue, and this was such a great way to do it.

Now, as you probably already know, if you know your history, some of our kings have met a very bloody end. Well, I'd only been a panto king, but mine wasn't too far away in 2018.

Like quite a few of my age group, I now seem to take quite a few pills for various things and go for tests regularly to make sure all is as it should be or as close to as it can be. Vitamins, remedies, glucose, fish oils, homeopathic stuff, you name it, I seem to take it. Sue and I are also on the ginkgo tablets for our memory — at least, we are when we remember to take them!

The tablets are all fine — and a lot better than those I was taking when I had the herniated discs — but I'd had a gastroscopy for Barrett's esophagus, a reflux condition, that I've suffered from for some time.

I have a gastroscopy every two years where an endoscope is used to look into the gullet, stomach and small intestine. In June 2018, I came back not feeling well. I'll let Sue tell you the tale because I was unconscious part way through.

'Tony had the procedure at 2.30 in the afternoon where they took a small biopsy. He'd had this procedure previously a few times and had always been okay. This time he wasn't well when he got home. He started passing a lot of blood, which was black, so I rang 111 and they told me the doctor would call me back. The doctor told Tony to go straight back to the hospital, but by then it was 10.30 at night. So Tony went and they said his stomach was distended and sore and he would pass blood, but I don't think they realised how much.

'His blood pressure was fine so they sent him home. He was restless through the night and at 5 o'clock in the morning he sat bolt upright and tried to get to the bathroom. He told me that he needed to get to hospital. And as he stood up, he passed a lot of blood and his legs buckled beneath him and he passed out. I laid him on the floor and rang 999, but before I could speak to them I heard a gurgling noise and I told them I could hear gurgling and blood was coming out of his mouth like Vesuvius. I'm sorry this is maybe a little too graphic, but it was very upsetting.

'And she said to just put the phone on the bed, not hang up, and to keep telling them what was happening. The paramedics were here in a couple of minutes, they must have been in the area and they took photographs of the state of the bedroom that looked like a crime scene.'

Thank you, darling. Back to me now. I came round in the hospital and don't remember much about the rest of the next few days. The next morning, although I was very anaemic, I asked if I could go home and they knew I would be well looked after, as Sue had never left my side all night.

Fortunately, I recovered and was told that when they take the biopsy it is very close to an artery. This had probably blistered an artery that had popped a few hours later and that was all. The necessary checks were completed, including another gastroscopy. I was in hospital on the Saturday and on the following Wednesday I had my golf charity tournament. I've held the event for the past few years, raising funds for the Sutton Coldfield Cancer Care Centre and Birmingham Children's Hospital. I couldn't play golf, but I performed the evening show at Aston Wood Golf Club. Andy Bennett from Ocean Colour Scene has played every year and my mate Tony Hadley, formerly of Spandau Ballet, regularly attends. I would also like to record my thanks here to my good mate, Roger Partridge, who organises the charity golf day each year. Panic over. Just a few days later, I started a 17-night run back treading the boards.

I was to appear in a new adaptation of the brilliant *Ladies' Day* at The Grand Theatre, Wolverhampton.

I won't spoil the plot, but it involves a bunch of ladies from a fish filleting factory going to the races. The production was written by Amanda Whittington for Hull Truck Theatre, where it was performed originally in 2005 before going on a nationwide tour.

One of the themes of the 2018 show involved a girl who is a fan of Tony Christie, gambling a six-horse accumulator at Wolverhampton racecourse based on song titles of my hits. In the show, I came on to sing songs that were previously played from recordings. It was a great idea, a really poignant play and I loved it. I was like Frankie Valli's Teen Angel character in *Grease*, appearing from time to time amongst great actors like Cheryl Fergison, who played Heather in *EastEnders*, and Deena Payne who played Viv in *Emmerdale*.

CHAPTER 36

How the world can turn full circle —
and dreams can turn to reality

You will know well enough by now where my singing heart lies: with Sinatra, Ella, Nat — proper singers. That's where I've always seen myself, in their world, singing in their era. Why do I mention this now? Well, I don't know when you will be reading this book, hopefully not too long after it is published, in which case this next bit won't necessarily come as a surprise, but for quite a few months now since a chance meeting last year (2018) Sean has been working hard behind the scenes to bring about yet another exciting time that could see quite possibly the next big chapter in my musical journey. No letting the cat out of the bag just yet. Read on.

It's funny how these things come about, but I have to say Sean has a good instinct for following an idea once it appears.

We had been invited to a charity event at the Belfry golf club by Geoff Littlefield, who is a film producer. Sean had told them I would sing for my supper and it turned out to be a great move. When I sang 'Solitaire' it went down a storm.

Later, Geoff said I was the last of the real singers and asked why I didn't just go out and sing the big songs with a big band. Having explained that it didn't pay the bills, he came back to Sean and asked whether I would like to sing with the Nelson Riddle Orchestra. I was gobsmacked. This is the great Frank Sinatra's band and, okay, there will have been many changes in personnel, but it is still a massive name and now led by his son Christopher, who has all the rights to his dad's arrangements for Sinatra. Would I like to? You must be joking.

Since that initial approach, I've met Christopher and the strangest thing that really knocked me out was he'd travelled over especially from the States to meet me in this pub.

He's a real ale fan too, into hand-pulled ale like me, and we are currently working on a show, something that will be taken on the road initially around the UK and will be something we could take to the West End.

It's the 50th anniversary of 'My Way' hitting the UK charts this year, so what better time to honour the governor, the man who I've always revered. We're thinking something along the lines of Sinatra's Life and Music, celebrated by Tony Christie with the Nelson Riddle Orchestra, possibly also including some Nat King Cole songs too. Crazy. Things might have come around full circle for me.

So we've *Pop Nonsense* due for release at the time of this book, with songs for today's generations, and if all goes according to plan there will then be not just a tour and the West End, maybe even Broadway or Vegas, and an album with the Nelson Riddle Orchestra. Then there's the country album to complete, another *Great Irish Songbook* and in four years, when I turn 80 — that will be the new 70, by the way — a whole package of albums, boxed set of hits, favourite songs and maybe even a farewell tour.

If you're going to bow out at any time, then you may as well do what you love doing and I'm looking forward to the next four years, so long as I can remember what I'm supposed to be doing. We're back to the ginkgo again.

And there's my German and Central European career too, with a whole back catalogue of songs I released in the '80s and '90s, with hits like 'Sweet September', 'Train to Yesterday' and 'Kiss in the Night'. These and others are still popular today, and only recently we have been approached by one of the biggest DJs in the world, who has remixed 'Sweet September', bringing it back in line with today's music.

Last Christmas, I also had the sheer joy of being part of a magnificent evening — Christmas Carols with Bloodwise at the Royal Albert Hall. I'd appeared there in my own show in 2005, just after the whole 'Amarillo' thing; with Neil Sedaka in 2006; and I'd also appeared there with Richard Hawley around the time of *Made in Sheffield*, when I sang 'Danger Is a Woman in Love', but this was all for the blood cancer charity, and what a night.

I sang 'The Christmas Song', that Nat made famous — 'Chestnuts roasting on an open fire' — but it was a pure delight to be there and, backed by the Royal Philharmonic Orchestra, it couldn't have been better. Maybe we should add another Christmas album to the release list? I certainly have no intention of ever stopping singing until I simply cannot. I might forget, but that's another story.

CHAPTER 37

*I knew I was going to call this chapter something —
where's the autocue?*

I do get concerned over my memory. And I'm not joking. Writing this book has made me think more about it. I've been trying to remember things from decades ago, and that's tricky for most people, but I've lost count of the number of times when I've said I just can't think. It's not just remembering things from a long time ago, though. In more recent times I've forgotten lyrics, the tools of my trade, and the last thing I want is for people to feel I'm losing it, even if I am. I'm also aware of how Alzheimer's affected Glen Campbell's memory for lyrics. If you think about it too long though, you can frighten yourself.

I have autocue available now for everything when I'm on stage, every song. I'd been using it a few years for songs I didn't sing regularly, but now it's there all the time and is there as a safety net. I don't want to disappoint audiences by forgetting things. I remember how I felt when Sue and I were watching Frank Sinatra in concert near the end of his life. I'm sure most people in the audience are very generous when they see someone struggling, especially when that person is a legend like Sinatra, but you don't want people to have to be generous.

Autocue is a fantastic addition for those of us who are in our not-so-young years, and it is really great when I'm in Germany and fans ask for a song that you haven't sung in years. That's nothing to do with any memory problems, it's just a useful way of fulfilling someone's request. I've seen some concerts where the artist has the autocue on several screens all around the stage and in front of the singer in the auditorium. It can be a little disconcerting when you see half the audience staring more at the autocue than the singer.

All I want to do is put on what I've always tried, the best show I can, and I don't want anything messing it up. If that means I need autocue, then I'm all for it. Now where did we put that ginkgo, Sue? I'm making light of it here, but I am concerned about my own memory and if you have loved ones going through something similar, or have been diagnosed with Alzheimer's or dementia, I really do feel for you.

CHAPTER 38

The Superfans, lovely people and my guilty secret

It is wonderful to have fans, people who enjoy your music so much they follow you in the nicest way and just want to see you and hear you. I've had many lovely people follow me for years, both here in the UK, in central Europe and in other parts of the world, like New Zealand and Australia. Some have become close friends of Sue and I, and might like a photograph taken with them, others just want to say hi, maybe exchange a few words. I try to make time for everyone.

If you consider yourself a big fan, but you're not mentioned here, I apologise. Put it down to what I wrote in the previous chapter, but I want to at least mention a handful of the many who have followed my career.

Ray and Margaret Smyth from Wigan didn't just run my fan club in the '70s, they instigated it. I'd stay over with them from time to time when I was playing a series of nights in Lancashire. It was they who asked whether I had a fan club and when I replied I hadn't they organised one for me. Ray had his own transport business until recent times. He and Margaret ran the fan club for many years. Time for a public acknowledgement of that right now. Great couple. Great friends.

Ray was with me in a concert in Germany in the '80s at the city hall in Braunschweig on the old eastern border of West Germany and where they make the famous Schimmel pianos we've used on tour. One night we'd finished the tour and we were invited to go to this lovely little pub around the corner. So, the musicians and I and Ray were all there. I sat in the bar with the musicians and Ray and the technical crew sat at a table with some German guys.

We were sitting quietly, but Ray, the crew and the German locals started drinking and became quite merry. Then football came into the conversation and they started mentioning footballers. The Germans would say, 'Franz Beckenbauer,' and they'd all say, 'Jah!' and they'd all stand and give a toast. Then Ray said, 'Bobby Charlton,' and they all said, 'Jah!' again and drank to Bobby. More footballer names were mentioned with a similar reaction. Then suddenly Ray Smyth said, 'Billy Wright!' and there was silence.

Ray said, 'Billy Wright! Wolverhampton Wanderers!' Then still no reaction. Then, he said, 'You know Billy Wright. He married one of the Beverley Sisters.' Still no reaction. He turned around to me at the bar and shouted, 'Tony! What's the German for Beverley Sisters?' And then myself and my musicians almost fell off our stools laughing.

Dot Harrison from Warrington has followed me from right back in the '70s through to today, and a really special thank you must go to Dot for the use of her scrapbooks crammed full of places I'd forgotten ever playing and TV shows I would never have remembered for this book. Heaven knows how much it must cost any fan to get to as many concerts as Dot has over the years.

Barbara and Elizabeth Wheat and their mum Elsie from Cheshire, but now live in Wales. They started following me in the early '70s. They will come to several shows each tour and every year they make a calendar from photographs of my past shows.

They all become family friends, like Phil and Pamela Fletcher who live in Crawley, but Phil is originally from Sheffield, and has quite probably more knowledge of me than I do! They met at one of my shows and are now happily married.

Charlotte Fischner and her husband, who has also now sadly passed away, came to a remarkable 17 dates of a 31-date Germany and Austria tour in the 2000s and is still a regular today. Her husband made a rocking horse for our grandson, Joby.

Beate Okumowski from Munster in Germany knows just how much I think of Sinatra and once bought me one of his ties as a gift. She writes us the most beautiful letters; and Angela Schneider has a massive collection of my recordings. Helen Schwink is one of many

German fans who come over to see me when I'm on tour in the UK. Helen was a friend of Brigitte Duncklau, one of my backing singers. Ricarda Wolfe ran my fan club in Germany for many years. I apologise Ricarda if I have the wrong spelling.

And, of course, there's Jan Stephan who I've already mentioned previously.

I have sometimes spoken a little German in concerts, just a few words, and it always gets a good reaction when I do, but the German people don't seem to mind and my work over there has always been appreciated. That's why I give them all the time I can. I'm often surprised when people come up and say they have been fans for years. I really feel quite humbled that they have kept coming to my shows. I understand more German than I can speak.

Werner Schoder and his wife Marlene were another fabulous couple and rather than being fans as such, they were a couple that Sue and I held a lasting friendship for many years.

If you're not mentioned here, but you've followed me for whatever length of time, please don't be offended. Just come up and see me at my next concert and say hi!

My guilty secret is that I have two more ladies in my life! Without their perfect grooming of my hair and eyebrows I would look more like Worzel Gummidge and politician Denis Healey. Thank you so much Zoe Haynes and Lynn Parker.

CHAPTER 39

Sean

I've never been one for going over the top about things. I've had some great help in my career, people who have advised me or given me opportunities. First up must be Sue's dad and my dad when I was all set for giving up in the late '60s. Their help and advice kept me going.

Tommy Sanderson gave me my first airplay on BBC Radio 2; Harvey Lisberg propelled me to the charts; Mitch Murray and Peter Callender gave me the songs; Neil Sedaka gave me *that* song; Graham Sacher gave me that first big Central Europe hit in the '80s; Jack White made sure the '90s went brilliantly in Europe; Jerry Toger and Derek and Debra Franks looked after me on tour all around the world; Jarvis Cocker came up with the song that brought me back to the UK charts after over 20 years; Peter Kay's *Phoenix Nights* made 'that song' a monster hit; Richard Hawley and Richard Barratt gave me new albums of original material that I would never have thought would have come about while playing golf and enjoying life in Spain — but there has been one man who has been with me since 1968, and who Sue and I would never want to be without, and that's our son, Sean.

We never formalised that he was my manager, even though that's what he has now been for the past 14 years, but everything that has happened with my career since 'Amarillo' second time around is more directly attributable to Sean's tenacity and ability to spot an opportunity than anything I've done. Without Sean it is quite possible 'Amarillo' wouldn't have even become an idea in Peter Kay's mind for Comic Relief. Sean had contacted him, we'd agreed to do the song for *Max and Paddy's Road to Nowhere* in exchange for a video. I was nearly not involved in the video until Sean intervened. Sean had approached Brian Berg about the album that went simultaneous No 1 as the single.

Sean has guided my career ever since and into areas it would never have dawned on me. He's certainly got Sue's organisational skills and he's a far better trader and negotiator than I could ever be. I just provide the voice. We've also had a fabulous time together travelling the world.

There was an interview where Sean is quoted as saying, 'Dad is a man of few words. You know he loves you, but he doesn't say it very much. It's the same with praise. I don't have to be told. I just know.' I'm so pleased he said it that way. He's right. I am a man of few words, which sounds daft when putting together a book like this, but for the record, Sean, you've done and continue to do such a great job and your mum and I can't thank you enough for all the effort you and Lisa put in.

CHAPTER 40

Sue

There is one name you will have read more than any other in this book and that is the lady who I first cast eyes upon in the 1960s while singing with The Trackers. The girl I knew I was going to marry from that moment and the girl who has been by my side every step of the way ever since. The girl who grew into the woman who is mother to our three beautiful children who, together with their partners, have given us seven fantastic grandchildren.

Sue is everything to me and always has been since I first saw her. When I started thinking about my autobiography, I knew it would be quite a task for whoever was going to write it with me, because we are a family without any of that kind of sensation. There are no skeletons in my cupboard. Sue and I have been happy together, no matter what life has thrown in our way. We've had the good times, and certainly more of them have been good than bad, but where the poorer times have come we've never split, parted, fallen out. We've got on with life.

I was interviewed by John Barrett, a journalist on the *Weekly News*, in 2006 at the time we released *Simply in Love*, and this is what I said then, so that you know I'm not making this up for the sake of the book: 'I always wanted to dedicate an album to Sue and, with our 40th anniversary coming up, this was the perfect time. I asked Sue to draw up a list of her favourite songs and I wrote down my own. There were about 40 in all, so we put them together and came up with the 14 recorded for the album.

'The one track I particularly wanted to include was 'Stranger in Paradise', because that was the first song Sue ever heard me sing. She came to a show in Sheffield. She was just 18 at the time and was into

The Beatles and The Stones and had never heard of me. Few people had. I was just a band singer in those days. I hadn't gone solo. Sue sat on the front row as we came onstage and I clocked her straight away. She was a stunning girl with gorgeous legs. We always opened with 'Stranger in Paradise' and I sang it straight to her. In fact, I sang every song to her that night, it was like a private concert. I was smitten. I was 24 at the time.

'Later we were introduced backstage and I asked her for a date. She gave me her phone number and that was it. A few months later we were married. We've had ups and downs like anyone else, but I really wanted to say thank you to her for all the love and support she's given me over the years. My favourite track on *Simply in Love* is my own version of the Beach Boys' song 'God Only Knows'. And it contains the line, 'God only knows what I'd be without you,' and that's just for Sue.'

That's exactly how I still feel today. We've had an amazing journey and it's still going on, but even if I hadn't had the success I would still have considered myself a lucky man to have found Sue. Things would have been very different for sure, but I know she would have been there regardless. I didn't have much when I was with The Trackers, but we were, as they used to call it, an item, and we are very much two halves, where when we are put together we are whole.

This is the chapter where we close the book, like a happy ending kind of book. There are many songs still to record, albums to release and I will enjoy all of them, as long as Sue is by my side.

THE FAMILY TREE

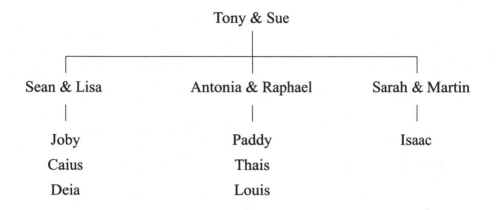

Tony & Sue

Sean & Lisa   Antonia & Raphael   Sarah & Martin

Joby   Paddy   Isaac
Caius   Thais
Deia   Louis

DISCOGRAPHY

SINGLES (UK)

The first ever record release:
Tony Christie and The Trackers
7" 45rpm vinyl
A: Life's Too Good to Waste
B: Just the Two of Us
CBS 202097
1966

Tony Christie
7" 45rpm vinyl
A: Turn Around
B: When Will I Ever See You Again
MGM 1365
November 1967

7" 45 rpm vinyl
**A: I Don't Want to Hurt You
Anymore**
B: Say No More
MGM 1386
March 1968

7" 45rpm vinyl
A: My Prayer
B: I Need You
MGM 1440
October 1968

7" 45rpm vinyl
A: God Is On My Side
B: A Thing Called Love
MCA MK5049
June 1970

7" 45rpm vinyl
A: Las Vegas
B: So Deep Is the Night
MCA MK5058
October 1970

7" 45rpm vinyl
A: I Did What I Did for Maria
B: Give Me Your Love Again
MCA MK5064
April 1971

7" 45rpm vinyl
A: (Is This the Way to) Amarillo?
B: Love Is a Friend of Mine
MCA MKS5073
October 1971

7" 45rpm vinyl
A: Don't Go Down to Reno
B: Sunday Morning
MCA MKS5089
April 1972

7" 45rpm vinyl
A: My Love Song
B: Celia
MCA MKS5095
August 1972

7" 45rpm vinyl
A: Avenues and Alleyways
B: I Never Was a Child
MCA MKS5101
October 1972

7" 45rpm vinyl
A: Love and Rainy Weather
B: Life Without You
MCA MUS1199
May 1973

7" 45rpm vinyl
**A: You Don't Have the Magic
Anymore**
B: By Tomorrow
MCA MUS1217
September 1973

7" 45rpm vinyl
A: A Lover's Question
B: Underneath the Covers
MCA MCA123
March 1974

7" 45rpm vinyl
A: (Is This the Way to) Amarillo?
B: Las Vegas
MCA MCA122
April 1974

7" 45rpm vinyl
A: Happy Birthday Baby
B: Who Am I Fooling?
MCA MCA157
September 1974

7" 45rpm vinyl
A: If I Miss You Again Tonight
B: A Man Will Cry for His Woman
MCA MCA187
April 1975

7" 45rpm vinyl
A: Easy to Love
B: My World Is Yours
MCA MCA212
October 1975

7" 45rpm vinyl
A: Drive Safely Darlin'
B: Sweet Summer Souvenirs
MCA MCA219
December 1975

7" 45rpm vinyl
A: Queen of the Mardi Gras
B: Wall of Silence
MCA MCA231
March 1976

7" 45rpm vinyl
A: On This Night of a Thousand Stars
B: Bewitched, Bothered and Bewildered
MCA MCA269
January 1977

7" 45rpm vinyl
A: Smile a Little Smile for Me
B: It's Good to Be Me
MCA MCA296
April 1977

7" 45rpm vinyl
A: Stolen Love
B: First Love Best Love
MCA MCA312
August 1977

Tony Christie (featuring Dana Gillespie on A side)
7" 45rpm vinyl
A: Magdalena
B: Half a Moment
MCA MCA331
November 1977

Tony Christie
7" 45rpm vinyl
A: I Did What I Did for Maria
B: (Is This the Way to) Amarillo?
MCA MCA709
August 1980

7" 45rpm vinyl
A: I Did What I Did for Maria
B: (Is This the Way to) Amarillo?
OLD GOLD OG9212
July 1982

7" 45rpm vinyl
A: The Wind Beneath My Wings
B: Dancing in Shadows
A1 A1291
July 1985

The All Seeing I — featuring Tony Christie
CD single
1: Walk Like a Panther (featuring Tony Christie)
2: Snake I
3: Sweaty Walls
London FFRR FCD 351
1999

Tony Christie — featuring Peter Kay
CD single
1: (Is This the Way to) Amarillo?
2: Amarillo (Club Mix)
3: The Laughing Record
4: (Is This the Way to) Amarillo? (Red Nose Day Video)
Universal 9828606
March 2005

Tony Christie
CD single
1: Avenues and Alleyways
2: Santa Maria
3: Avenues and Alleyways (Love to Infinity Radio Mix)
Universal 9831670
2005

CD single
1: Merry Xmas Everybody
2: (Is This the Way to) Amarillo? (Big Band Swing Version)
3: If It Feels Good Do It (Live at V Festival)
Video: Merry Xmas Everybody
Video: (Is This the Way to) Amarillo? (Big Band Swing Version)
Amarillo CD1
2005

CD single
1: (Is This the Way to) The World Cup? (Final Whistle)
2: (Is This the Way to) The World Cup? (Extra Time Edit)
3: (Is This the Way to) The World Cup? (Penalty Shoot Out Version — Karaoke)
Tug CD SNOG 16
2006

CD single
1: Born to Cry (Radio version)
2: Born to Cry (Album version)
Autonomy AUT003
2008

7" 45rpm vinyl
A: Nobody in the World
B: Seven Hills
Acid Jazz AUX246S
November 2010

CD single
1: Nobody in the World
2: Nobody in the World (Instrumental)
3: Concrete and Clay
Acid Jazz AJX246CD
November 2010

CD single
1: Now's the Time
2: Season of the Witch
3: Beautiful Woman
Acid Jazz AJX254CD
February 2011

SINGLES (GERMANY)

7" 45rpm vinyl
A: Las Vegas
B: So Deep Is the Night
MCA MCS3146
January 1971

7" 45rpm vinyl
A: I Did What I Did for Maria
B: Give Me Your Love Again
MCA MCS4739
May 1971

7" 45rpm vinyl
A: (Is This the Way to) Amarillo?
B: Love Is a Friend of Mine
MCA MCS5391
November 1971

7" 45rpm vinyl
A: Don't Go Down to Reno
B: Sunday Morning
MCA MCS5981
1972

7" 45rpm vinyl
A: My Love Song
B: Celia
MCA MCS6187
1972

7" 45rpm vinyl
A: Avenues and Alleyways
B: I Never Was a Child
MCA MCS6333
1972

7" 45rpm vinyl
A: Love and Rainy Weather
B: Life Without You
MCA MCS6828
1973

7" 45rpm vinyl
A: You Just Don't Have the Magic Anymore
B: By Tomorrow
MCA MCS7063
1973

7" 45rpm vinyl
A: Happy Birthday Baby
B: Who Am I Fooling
MCA 6.11 535 (AC)
1974

7" 45rpm vinyl
A: If You Stay Too Long in Oklahoma
B: It's Good to Be Me
MCA MCS7261
1974

7" 45rpm vinyl
A: A Lover's Question
B: Underneath the Covers
MCA MCS7304
1974

7" 45rpm vinyl
A: A Man Will Cry for His Woman
B: If I Miss You Again Tonight
MCA 6.11 656 (AC)
1975

7" 45rpm vinyl
A: Drive Safely Darlin'
B: Sweet Summer Souvenirs
MCA 6.11 619
1976

7" 45rpm vinyl
A: Queen of the Mardi Gras
B: Wall of Silence
MCA 6.11 857
April 1976

7" 45rpm vinyl
A: (Is This the Way to) Amarillo?
B: Avenues and Alleyways
MCA 32 014 (The Original Oldies)
1977

7" 45rpm vinyl
A: Happy Birthday Baby
B: Don't Go Down to Reno
MCA 0032 054 (The Original Oldies)
1978

7" 45rpm vinyl
A: Sweet September
B: I'm Not Chained by You
RCA Victor PB5668
1979

7" 45rpm vinyl
A: Train to Yesterday
B: Summer in the Sun
RCA Victor PB5695
1980

7" 45rpm vinyl
A: Mexico City
B: What a Little Love Can Do
RCA Victor PB5741
1980

7" 45rpm vinyl
A: (Is This the Way to) Amarillo?
B: I Did What I Did for Maria
MCA 101 833 (Original Double Hit series)
May 1980

7" 45rpm vinyl
A: Don't Go Down to Reno
B: Happy Birthday Baby
MCA 101 834 (Original Double Hit series)
May 1980

7" 45rpm vinyl
A: Summer Wine
B: I'm Coming Home
RCA Victor PB5825
1981

7" 45rpm vinyl
A: Put a Light in Your Window
B: Paradise
RCA Victor PB5895
1981

7" 45rpm vinyl
A: Me and Marie
B: Caribbean Nights
RCA Victor PB69001
1982

7" 45rpm vinyl
A: Long Gone
B: Time
RCA Victor PB9960
1982

7" 45rpm vinyl
A: Te Voglio Mi Amor (I Want You My Love)
B: Higher on Your Love
RCA Victor PB69072
1983

7" 45rpm vinyl EP
A1: Sweet September
A2: What a Little Love Can Do
B1: Put a Light in Your Window
B2: Long Gone
Amiga 556062
1984

7" 45rpm vinyl
A: (Is This the Way to) Amarillo
B: I Did What I Did for Maria
MCA 259 552-7
September 1984

7" 45rpm vinyl
A: Keep On Dancin'
B: Strangers
Polydor 885 265-7
1986

7" 45rpm vinyl
A: Battle of Wounded Pride
B: Memories
Polydor 885 722-7
1987

7" 45rpm vinyl
A: Kiss in the Night
B: Kiss in the Night (instrumental)
White 113 365
1990

12" 45rpm vinyl
1: Kiss in the Night (long version)
2: Kiss in the Night (radio version)
3: Kiss in the Night (instrumental)
White 613 365
1990

CD single
1: Kiss in the Night (long version)
2: Kiss in the Night (radio version)
3: Kiss in the Night (instrumental)
White 663 365
1990

7" 45rpm vinyl
A: September Love
B: September Love (instrumental)
White 113 694
1990

12" 45rpm vinyl
1: September Love (long version)
2: September Love (radio version)
3: September Love (instrumental)
White 613 694
1990

CD single
1: September Love (long version)
2: September Love (radio version)
3: September Love (instrumental)
White 663 694
1990

7" 45rpm vinyl
A: Moonlight and Roses
B: Moonlight and Roses
(instrumental)
White 114 218
1991

12" 45rpm vinyl
**1: Moonlight and Roses (long
version)**
2: Moonlight and Roses (radio
version)
3: Moonlight and Roses (instrumental)
White 614 218
1991

CD single
**1: Moonlight and Roses (long
version)**
2: Moonlight and Roses (radio
version)
3: Moonlight and Roses (instrumental)
White 664 218
1991

7" 45rpm vinyl
A: Come with Me to Paradise
B: Island in the Sun
White 114 389
1991

CD single
**1: Come with Me to Paradise (single
version)**
2: Come with Me to Paradise (long
version)
3: Island in the Sun
White 664 389
1991

7" 45rpm vinyl
A: Sweet September
B: Coming Home
White 114 783
1991

12" 45rpm vinyl
1: Sweet September (radio version)
2: Sweet September (long version)
3: Coming Home
White 664 783
1991

CD single
1: Sweet September (radio version)
2: Sweet September (long version)
3: Coming Home
White 664 783
1991

7" 45rpm vinyl
A: Going to Havana
B: Tomorrow Manana Manana
White 115 015
1991

12" 45rpm vinyl
1: Going to Havana (radio version)
2: Going to Havana (long version)
3: Going to Havana (instrumental)
4: Tomorrow Manana Manana
White 615 051
1991

CD single
1: Going to Havana (radio version)
2: Going to Havana (long version)
3: Going to Havana (instrumental)
4: Tomorrow Manana Manana
White 665 051
1991

7" 45rpm vinyl
A: You Are My Darling
B: You Are My Darling (instrumental)
White 74321 10694 7
1992

CD single
1: You Are My Darling
2: You Are My Darling (instrumental)
3: In San Jose
White 74321 10694-2
1992

7" 45rpm vinyl
A: Arrivederci
B: She Took Me to the Mardi Gras
White 74321 12178-7
1992

CD single
1: Arrivederci
2: She Took Me to the Mardi Gras
3: The Summer Rain
White 74321 12178-2
1992

7" 45rpm vinyl
A: Down in Mexico
B: Passion
White 74321 13247 7
1993

CD single
1: Down in Mexico
2: Passion
White 74321 13247-2
1993

7" 45rpm vinyl
A: Dancing in the Sunshine
B: Got to Be Mine
White 74321 14567 7
1993

CD single
1: Dancing in the Sunshine
2: Got to Be Mine
3: Dancing in the Sunshine
(instrumental)
White 74321 14567-2
1993

7" 45rpm vinyl
A: Come Back Diana
B: Too Young
White 74321 16472 7
1993

CD single
1: Come Back Diana
2: Too Young
White 74321 16472-2
1993

7" 45rpm vinyl
A: Got to Be Mine (remix)
B: Got to Be Mine (instrumental)
White 74321 17067-7
1993

CD single
1: Got to Be Mine (remix)
2: Got to Be Mine (instrumental)
3: Jenny My Love
White 74321 17067-2
1993

CD single
1: Solitaire (radio version)
2: Solitaire
White 74321 17069-2
1993

7" 45rpm vinyl
A: Calypso and Rum
B: A Morning in December
White 74321 22800 7
1994

CD single
1: Calypso and Rum
2: A Morning in December
3: Calypso and Rum (instrumental)
White 74321 22800-2
1994

Vicky Leandros and Tony Christie
7" 45rpm vinyl
A: We're Gonna Stay Together
B: We're Gonna Stay Together
(instrumental)
White 74321 24287-7
1995

Vicky Leandros and Tony Christie
CD single
1: We're Gonna Stay Together
2: We're Gonna Stay Together
(instrumental)
3: We're Gonna Stay Together (special
TV mix)
White 74321 24287-2
1995

Tony Christie
7" 45rpm vinyl
A: Dreaming of Natalie
B: Kiss Me Maria Elena
White 74321 29483-7
1995

CD single
1: Moon Over Napoli
2: Torero
3: Moon Over Napoli (instrumental)
White 74321 33316-2
1995

CD single
1: Never
2: How Much You Mean to Me
Intercord 810.455
1996

CD single
1: Oh Mi Amor
2: This Is Your Day
3: Oh Mi Amor (instrumental)
Intercord 825.063
1996

CD single
1: Mona Lisa's Smile
2: Too Many Times
3: Mona Lisa's Smile (instrumental)
Intercord 825.084
1996

CD single
1: Knocking On Your Door
2: Hasta Manana
White 74321 37944-2
1996

CD maxi single
1: Hit Mix (radio edit)
2: Hit Mix (long version)
Includes mash-up of *Down in Mexico,
Come Back Diana, We're Gonna Stay
Together, Kiss in the Night, September
Love* and *Come with Me to Paradise*
on both tracks
White 74321 49775-2
1997

CD single
1: Never Say Auf Wiedersehn
2: Sweet September (version 1998)
3: Never Say Auf Wiedersehn
(instrumental)
JTC EMI 620529
1998

CD single
1: Baby Come Back
2: Only Heartache
3: Baby Come Back (karaoke)
Da Music 873607-2
2002

CD single
1: The Eyes of a Woman in Love
2: Our Love Is Forever
3: The Eyes of a Woman in Love
(karaoke)
Voice B0000691SA
2002

**Hermes House Band and Tony
Christie**
CD single
**1: (Is This the Way to) Amarillo?
(summer party mix)**
2: (Is This the Way to) Amarillo?
(summer karaoke mix)
Polydor 987 3567
2005

SINGLES
(Selected releases never
released in UK or Germany)

7" 45rpm vinyl
A: What Becomes of My World?
B: What Do You Do?
MCA D1189
Released in Japan 1972

7" 45rpm vinyl
A: No Vayas A Reno
B: Domingo Por La Manana
MCA SN20722
Released in Spain 1973
Tony singing *Don't Go Down to Reno*
in Spanish

7" 45rpm vinyl
A: Gifts
B: Words (Are Impossible)
MCA 40408
Released in USA and Canada
1974

7" 45rpm vinyl
A: Here Comes My Baby Back Again
B: Mary Lee
MCA 40253
Released in USA and Canada
1974

7" 33rpm flexi disc
A: This Is Our Lager (one side only)
Tennents Lager
No code available
1983

ALBUMS (UK)
The major releases — there have been many compilations
Authorised and unauthorised

12" 33rpm vinyl
TONY CHRISTIE
Side 1:
I Did What I Did for Maria
Have You Ever Been to Georgia?
Las Vegas
Frankie
Smile a Little Smile for Me
Give Me Your Love Again
Side 2:
My Sweet Lord
Home Lovin' Man
What Do You Do?
God Is On My Side
Walk Like a Panther
Didn't We?
MCA MKPS2016
1971

12" 33rpm vinyl
WITH LOVING FEELING
Side 1:
You've Lost That Loving Feeling
Daddy Don't You Walk So Fast
Is This the Way to Amarillo?
Life Without You
Solitaire
On Broadway
Side 2:
A House Is Not a Home
Avenues and Alleyways
God Bless Joanna
My Love Song
Don't Go Down to Reno
So Deep Is the Night
MCA MUPS468
1972

12" 33rpm vinyl
IT'S GOOD TO BE ME
Side 1:
If It Feels Good — Do It
Sittin' On the Dock of the Bay
Love and Rainy Weather
Tie a Yellow Ribbon
The Janes, the Jeans and the Might-
Have-Beens
It's Good to Be Me
Side 2:
I'm Gonna Make You Love Me
You and I
If You Stay Too Long in Oklahoma
Baby I'm A Want You
A Year and a Wife and a Kid Ago
Here's That Rainy Day
MCA MCF2534
1974

12" 33rpm vinyl
FROM AMERICA WITH LOVE
Side 1:
Vado Via
Here Comes My Baby Back Again
Can't You Hear the Song
Gifts
The Most Beautiful Girl
Drift Away
Side 2:
Happy Birthday Baby
Tequila Sunrise
Stained Glass Blue
A Lover's Question
Mary Lee
Underneath the Covers — In Between
the Sheets
MCA MCF2577
1974

12" 33rpm vinyl
**TONY CHRISTIE 'LIVE' (at The
Fiesta, Sheffield)**
Side 1:
Avenues and Alleyways / You've Lost
That Lovin' Feelin'
Ol' Man River
If It Feels Good — Do It
Las Vegas / Don't Go Down to Reno /
I Did What I Did for Maria
MacArthur Park / Didn't We?
Side 2:
(Is This the Way to) Amarillo?
'West Side Story' Medley:
Something's Coming / Maria /
Somewhere / Tonight
(Your Love Keeps Lifting Me) Higher
and Higher / Help Me Make It
Through the Night
So Deep Is the Night
Hey Jude / Land of a Thousand
Dances
Solitaire (play-off)
MCA MCF2703
1975

12" 33rpm vinyl
I'M NOT IN LOVE
Side 1:
Queen of the Mardi Gras
Like Sister and Brother
Love Hurts
I'm Not in Love
Nobody Cried
Feelings
Side 2:
No Other Love
Wall of Silence
The Way We Were
Drive Safely Darlin'
Somewhere in the Night
Part Time Love
MCA MCF2755
1976

12" 33rpm vinyl
BEST OF TONY CHRISTIE
Side 1:
(Is This the Way to) Amarillo
Avenues and Alleyways
Solitaire
I Did What I Did for Maria
Don't Go Down to Reno
So Deep Is the Night
Side 2:
Las Vegas
Happy Birthday Baby
The Most Beautiful Girl
Words (Are Impossible) (Vado Via)
Drive Safely Darlin'
I'm Not in Love
MCA MCF2769
1976

CD
THE BEST OF TONY CHRISTIE
I Did What I Did for Maria
Drive Safely Darlin'
Didn't We?
On This Night of a Thousand Stars
Happy Birthday Baby
Baby I'm A Want You
Daddy Don't You Walk So Fast
Las Vegas
Avenues and Alleyways
Drift Away
Feelings
A House Is Not a Home
I'm Not in Love
Love Hurts
Solitaire
(Is This the Way to) Amarillo?
MCA MCBD19529
1995

CD
DEFINITIVE COLLECTION
Is This the Way to Amarillo?
Avenues and Alleyways
Las Vegas
Solitaire
Happy Birthday Baby
I Did What I Did for Maria
Drive Safely Darlin'
On This Night of a Thousand Stars
Daddy Don't You Walk So Fast
Most Beautiful Girl
Don't Go Down to Reno
The Way We Were
So Deep Is the Night
Didn't We?
You've Lost That Loving Feelin'
Home Loving Man
Walk Like a Panther '98
Vienna Sunday
Loving You
Almost in Love
Street of Broken Dreams
Universal 9827867
2005

CD with DVD
TONY CHRISTIE LIVE
at the V Festival
Avenues and Alleyways
If It Feels Good — Do It
Walk Like a Panther
Part Time Love
Las Vegas
Drift Away
The Long and Winding Road
Let 'Em In
Lady Madonna
Hey Jude
Sgt Pepper's Lonely Hearts Club Band
(Is This the Way to) Amarillo?
(Is This the Way to) Amarillo? (Big Band Swing Version)
Time for Love
Prism PLATCD2739
2005

CD
CHRISTMAS WITH CHRISTIE
Let It Snow! Let It Snow! Let It
Snow!
White Christmas
Winter Wonderland
A Winter's Tale
Have Yourself a Merry Little
Christmas
The Christmas Song
I'll Be Home for Christmas
Silent Night Blue Christmas
(Is This the Way to) Amarillo?
Plus additional tracks by other artists
The Sun newspaper freebie
2005

CD
SIMPLY IN LOVE
People Will Say We're in Love
Moon River
My Funny Valentine
The More I See You
You've Got a Friend
I Left My Heart in San Francisco
Light My Fire
This Guy's in Love with You
Danny Boy
Stranger in Paradise
Every Breath You Take
Life On Mars
We've Only Just Begun
God Only Knows
Tug SNOGCD03
2006

CD
MADE IN SHEFFIELD
Only Ones Who Know
Perfect Moon
Born to Cry
All I Ever Care About Is You
Going Home Tomorrow
Louise
Danger Is a Woman in Love
I'll Never Let You Down
How Can I Entertain?
Paradise Square
Coles Corner
Every Word She Said
Streets of Steel
Decca 478 1410DH
2008

12" 33rpm vinyl
NOW'S THE TIME
Side 1:
Now's the Time
Money Spider
7 Hills (featuring Roisin Murphy)
Nobody in the World
Steal the Sun
Longing for You Baby
Side 2:
Get Christie
Too Much of the Sun
Key of U
Workin' Overtime
I Thank You
Something Better
Acid Jazz AJXLP249
2011

CD
NOW'S THE TIME
Now's the Time
Money Spider
7 Hills (featuring Roisin Murphy)
Nobody in the World
Steal the Sun
Longing for You Baby
Get Christie
Too Much of the Sun
Key of U
Workin' Overtime
I Thank You
Something Better
Acid Jazz AJXCD249
2011

CD
Tony Christie and Ranagri
THE GREAT IRISH SONGBOOK
Cliffs of Doneen
On Raglan Road
The Banks of the Lee
Spancil Hill
Star of the County Down
When You Were Sweet Sixteen
Lord Franklin
She Moved Through the Fair
Carrickfergus
The Black Velvet Band
Wild Mountain Thyme
The Parting Glass
Stockfisch 357.4087.2
2015

CD
50 GOLDEN GREATS
CD1
(Is This the Way to) Amarillo?
Every Word She Said
My Prayer
Las Vegas
Life's Too Good to Waste
Love and Rainy Weather
Born to Cry
I Did What I Did for Maria
Happy Birthday Baby
Home Loving Man

Drive Safely Darlin'
My Sweet Lord
God Bless Joanna
Solitaire
Just the Two of Us
Walk Like a Panther (with The All
Seeing I)
So Deep Is the Night

CD2
Avenues and Alleyways
Now's the Time
All I Ever Care About Is You
Don't Go Down to Reno
Say No More
On Broadway
Star of the County Down
Daddy Don't You Walk So Fast
When Will I Ever Love Again
Turn Around
Smile a Little Smile for Me
Key of U
Didn't We?
Working Overtime
Carrickfergus
Most Beautiful Girl
I Need You
CD3
Early Morning Memphis
Just Like Yesterday
Hangin' Around
Have You Ever Been to Georgia?
Dancing Days
Drift Away
Wild Is the Wind
Stupid Thing
Tequila Sunrise
Only Ones Who Know
Wild Ones
Louise
I Surrender
You Are My Lifeline
Damned
When All Is Said and Done
Wrasse WRASS344
2015

ALBUMS (GERMANY)
The major releases — there have been many compilations
Authorised and unauthorised

12" 33rpm vinyl
LAS VEGAS
Side 1:
I Did What I Did for Maria
Have You Ever Been to Georgia?
Las Vegas
Frankie
Smile a Little Smile for Me
Give Me Your Love Again
Side 2:
My Sweet Lord
Home Loving Man
What Do You Do?
God Is On My Side
Walk Like a Panther
Didn't We?
MCA MAPS4738
1971

12" 33rpm vinyl
WITH LOVING FEELING
Side 1:
You've Lost That Loving Feeling
Daddy Don't You Walk So Fast
Is This the Way to Amarillo?
Life Without You
Solitaire
On Broadway
Side 2:
A House Is Not a Home
Avenues and Alleyways
God Bless Joanna
My Love Song
Don't Go Down to Reno
So Deep Is the Night
MCA MAPS6268
1972

12" 33rpm vinyl
IT'S GOOD TO BE ME
Side 1:
If It Feels Good — Do It
Sittin' on the Dock of the Bay
Love and Rainy Weather
Tie a Yellow Ribbon
The Janes, the Jeans and the Might-
Have-Beens
It's Good to Be Me
Side 2:
I'm Gonna Make You Love Me
You and I
If You Stay Too Long in Oklahoma
Baby I'm A Want You
A Year and a Wife and a Kid Ago
Here's That Rainy Day
MCA MAPS7256
1974

12" 33rpm vinyl
FROM AMERICA WITH LOVE
Side 1:
Vado Via
Here Comes My Baby Back Again
Can't You Hear the Song
Gifts
The Most Beautiful Girl
Drift Away
Side 2:
Happy Birthday Baby
Tequila Sunrise
Stained Glass Blue
A Lover's Question
Mary Lee
Underneath The Covers — In
Between the Sheets
MCA MAPS7572
1974

12" 33rpm vinyl
TONY CHRISTIE 'LIVE' — 20 Great Songs
Side 1:
Avenues and Alleyways / You've Lost That Lovin' Feelin'
Ol' Man River
If It Feels Good — Do It
Las Vegas / Don't Go Down to Reno / I Did What I Did for Maria
MacArthur Park / Didn't We?
Side 2:
(Is This the Way to) Amarillo?
'West Side Story' Medley:
Something's Coming / Maria / Somewhere / Tonight
(Your Love Keeps Lifting Me) Higher and Higher / Help Me Make It Through the Night
So Deep Is the Night
Hey Jude / Land of a Thousand Dances
Solitaire (play-off)
MCA 6.22.240
1975

12" 33rpm vinyl
I'M NOT IN LOVE
Side 1:
Queen of the Mardi Gras
Like Sister and Brother
Love Hurts
I'm Not in Love
Nobody Cried
Feelings
Side 2:
No Other Love
Wall of Silence
The Way We Were
Drive Safely Darlin'
Somewhere in the Night
Part Time Love
MCA MCF2198
1976

12" 33rpm vinyl
LADIES' MAN
Side 1:
Sweet September
Devil in Me
Mexico City
What a Little Love Can Do
Train to Yesterday
Ladies' Man
Side 2:
With Just a Piano and a Song
Summer in the Sun
Tobago
I'm Not Chained to You
I Will Remember
Once More from the Top
RCA Victor PL28382
1980

12" 33rpm vinyl
DAS BESTE VON TONY CHRISTIE
Side 1:
(Is This the Way to) Amarillo?
I Did What I Did for Maria
Don't Go Down to Reno
Walk Like a Panther
Smile a Little Smile for Me
You've Lost That Loving Feeling
My Sweet Lord
Frankie
Avenues and Alleyways
Side 2:
Happy Birthday Baby
Las Vegas
Tie a Yellow Ribbon
Have You Ever Been to Georgia?
Daddy Don't You Walk So Fast
A House Is Not a Home
On Broadway
Solitaire
My Love Song
MCA 204 794-502
1980

12" 33rpm vinyl
TIME AND TEARS
Side 1:
Long Gone
Caribbean Nights
Can't Get That Feeling
Me and Marie
Paradise
Time
Side 2:
Tears on My Pillow
Put a Light in Your Window
No One in the World But You Tonight
Summer Wine
I'm Coming Home
Another Lonely Day
RCA Victor PL28511
1982

12" 33rpm vinyl
COUNTRY LOVE
Side 1:
Rhinestone Cowboy
I Really Had a Ball Last Night
Some Broken Hearts Never Mend
Ruby, Don't Take Your Love to Town
I'm So Lonesome I Could Cry
Sea of Heartbreak
Release Me
Side 2:
Blue Bayou
Lucille
Jambalaya
I Recall a Gypsy Woman
Funny Familiar Forgotten Feelings
Oh Lonesome Me
I Can't Stop Loving You
Six Days on the Road
RCA Victor PL28530
1983

12" 33rpm vinyl
AS LONG AS I HAVE YOU
Side 1:
When the Music Stops
Te Voglio Mi Amor (If You Want My Love)
I Can See Purple
Love Keeps Making Me Blue
As Long As I Have You
You Can Always Ring My Number
Side 2:
With Every Beat of My Heart
Head Over Heels
1-2-3 (Get Ready for Love)
Higher On Your Love
Baby I'm Burning
RCA Victor PL70047
1983

CD
WELCOME TO MY MUSIC
Is This the Way to Amarillo?
Sweet September
One Dance with You
Come with Me to Paradise
I Did What I Did for Maria
Going to Havana
Kiss in the Night
Coming Home
Torero
Island in the Sun
September Love
Tomorrow Manana Manana
Moonlight and Roses
White 261842
1991

CD
WELCOME TO MY MUSIC 2
You Are My Darling
Las Vegas
Down in Mexico
Darling Tomorrow
Passion
In San Jose
Avenues and Alleyways
It Happened in Sevilla
She Took Me to the Mardi Gras
Night After Night
Spanish Eddie
The Summer Rain
Arrivederci
White 74321 11012-2
1992

CD
IN LOVE AGAIN
Come Back Diana
Don't Go Down to Reno
Knocking On Your Door
Solitaire
Dancing in the Sunshine
One More Time
Jenny My Love
Lonely Nights
Sweet Angel in Blue
My Little Latin Lover
Too Young
Got to Be Mine
White 74321 15936-2
1993

CD
CALYPSO AND RUM
Dreaming of Natalie
Calypso and Rum
A Morning in December
Moon Over Napoli
Wild Wild Woman
Hasta Manana
My Hawaiian Girl
Kiss Me Marie Elena
Broken Dreams
Silver Moon
Give Me Back My Heart
Memories of Monte Carlo
White 74321 21771-2
1994

CD
THIS IS YOUR DAY
Oh Mi Amor
Mona Lisa's Smile
Sweet Romantic Blue Eyes
Never
Too Many Times
Love for Eternity
I'm a Lucky Man
How Much You Mean to Me
All Over the World
My Summer Lady
Something in Your Eyes
This Is Your Day
Intercord 845.281, 7243 4 84388 2 9
1996

CD
TIME FOR LOVE
Never Say Auf Wiedersehn
Best Ingredients
Closer to Heaven
Germany
You Give Good Love
Right Side Up
Only Time Will Tell
Love Without Tears
Easy On Yourself
Time for Love
Sweet September
I Did What I Did for Maria
Is This the Way to Amarillo?
EMI 7243 4 97887 2 5
1998

CD
THE GREATEST HOLLYWOOD MOVIE SONGS
You Light Up My Life
(I've Had) The Time of My Life
Say You, Say Me
I Just Called to Say I Love You
You Take My Breath Away
The Shadow of Your Smile
Raindrops Keep Falling on My Head
Arthur's Theme (The Best That You Can Do)
Born Free
Three Coins in a Fountain
A Whole New World
Days of Wine and Roses
Evergreen
The Way We Were
All the Way
Edel 0058692ERE
1999

CD
WEINACHTEN MIT TONY CHRISTIE
Santa Claus Is Coming to Town
Winter Wonderland
O Tannenbaum / O Christmas Tree
I'll Be Home for Christmas
Merry Christmas Everyone
The Christmas Song (Chestnuts Roasting on an Open Fire)
Let It Snow! Let It Snow! Let It Snow!
Last Christmas
Silent Night, Holy Night
A Winter's Tale
Jingle Bells
Blue Christmas
White Christmas
Rockin' Around the Christmas Tree
Have Yourself a Merry Little Christmas
Da Music B000071X04
2001

CD
WORLD HITS and LOVE SONGS
The Eyes of a Woman in Love
Baby Come Back
What a Crazy Summer
Our Love Is Forever
Only a Heartache
Wind Beneath My Wings
Avenues and Alleyways
Las Vegas
Don't Go Down to Reno
Sweet September
I Did What I Did for Maria
Is This the Way to Amarillo?
Voice B00006191V
2002

CD
DEFINITIVE COLLECTION
Is This the Way to Amarillo? (Hermes
House Band feat Tony Christie)
Avenues and Alleyways
Las Vegas
Solitaire
Happy Birthday Baby
I Did What I Did for Maria
Drive Safely Darlin'
On This Night of a Thousand Stars
Daddy Don't You Walk So Fast
Most Beautiful Girl
Don't Go Down to Reno
The Way We Were
So Deep Is the Night
Didn't We?
You've Lost That Loving Feelin'
Home Loving Man
Vienna Sunday
Loving You
Almost in Love
Street of Broken Dreams
Is This the Way to Amarillo?
Universal 9827867
2005

CD
NOW'S THE TIME
Now's the Time
Money Spider
7 Hills (featuring Roisin Murphy)
Nobody in the World
Steal the Sun
Longing for You Baby
Get Christie
Too Much of the Sun
Key of U
Workin' Overtime
I Thank You
Something Better
Acid Jazz AJXCD249
2011

CD
BEST OF TONY CHRISTIE
DIE GROßTEN HITS AUF 50
JAHREN
Northern Lights (Shine for You)
If Only I Knew
Nothing Left to Lose
Let's Get Together Again
Hungry Years
I Can't Lie to Me Anymore
Company Like Yours
Wild Ones
Stupid Thing
Dancing Days
Valentine
In the Arms of Angels
Is This the Way to Amarillo?
Avenues and Alleyways
Las Vegas
Solitaire
I Did What I Did for Maria
Daddy Don't You Walk So Fast
Happy Birthday Baby
You've Lost That Loving Feeling
Now's the Time
Workin' Overtime
Born to Cry
Danger Is a Woman in Love
Telamo 405380420001
2012

CD
Tony Christie and Ranagri
THE GREAT IRISH SONGBOOK
Cliffs of Doneen
On Raglan Road
The Banks of the Lee
Spancil Hill
Star of the County Down
When You Were Sweet Sixteen
Lord Franklin
She Moved Through the Fair
Carrickfergus
The Black Velvet Band
Wild Mountain Thyme
The Parting Glass
Stockfisch 357.4087.2 WRASS 336
2015

CD
50 GOLDEN GREATS
CD1
(Is This the Way to) Amarillo?
Every Word She Said
My Prayer
Las Vegas
Life's Too Good to Waste
Love and Rainy Weather
Born to Cry
I Did What I Did for Maria
Happy Birthday Baby
Home Loving Man
Drive Safely Darlin'
My Sweet Lord
God Bless Joanna
Solitaire
Just the Two of Us
Walk Like a Panther (with The All Seeing I)
So Deep Is the Night
CD2
Avenues and Alleyways
Now's the Time
All I Ever Care About Is You
Don't Go Down to Reno
Say No More
On Broadway
Star of the County Down

Daddy Don't You Walk So Fast
When Will I Ever Love Again
Turn Around
Smile a Little Smile for Me
Key of U
Didn't We?
Working Overtime
Carrickfergus
Most Beautiful Girl
I Need You
CD3
Early Morning Memphis
Just Like Yesterday
Hangin' Around
Have You Ever Been to Georgia?
Dancing Days
Drift Away
Wild Is the Wind
Stupid Thing
Tequila Sunrise
Only Ones Who Know
Wild Ones
Louise
I Surrender
You Are My Lifeline
Damned
When All Is Said and Done
Wrasse WRASS344
2015

ALBUMS
(Selected releases never released in UK or Germany)

BULGARIA
12" 33rpm vinyl
**RECITAL AT THE FESTIVAL
'THE GOLDEN ORPHEUS 72'**
Side 1:
Las Vegas
Have You Ever Been to Georgia?
Don't Go Down to Georgia
I Did What I Did for Maria
(You're Love Keeps Lifting Me)
Higher and Higher
My Way
Side 2:
(Is This the Way to) Amarillo?
Gioulia
Hey Jude
So Deep Is the Night
BTA 1380
1972

SPAIN
12" 33rpm vinyl
NO VAYAS A RENO
Side 1:
Don't Go Down to Reno
A House Is Not a Home
Avenues and Alleyways
God Bless Joanna
My Love Song
So Deep Is the Night
Side 2:
You've Lost That Loving Feeling
Daddy Don't You Walk So Fast
Is This the Way to Amarillo
Life Without You
Solitaire
On Broadway
MCA S-26.184
1973

TONY CHRISTIE
WOULD LIKE TO THANK

With special thanks to our Earth Angels:
Yvonne Clapperton, Martyn Young, John and Sylvia Stannier,
John and Iris Taylor, Richard Eldridge

To the people who have been prominent in my business life:
Margaret and Ray Smythe
Harvey Lisberg
Danny Betesh
Mitch Murray
Peter Callander
Brian Berg
Jackie Joseph
Paul Spraggon
Chris Weller
Jackie Gill
John Craig
Kelvin Teal
Vinesh Patel
Jack White
Jerry Toger
Max and Gundel Schautzer
Carmen Nebel and Norbert
Tessy Schulz
Ian and Jo Ashbridge
Chris Davies
Roger Partridge
David Shaw
Chris Greenhalgh
Geoff Littlefield
Christopher Riddle
Jan Stephan
Chris Berry
David Burrill
and a very special thank you to Leba and Neil Sedaka

A NOTE FROM CHRIS BERRY

Tony is one of the finest recording artists in the world and writing his autobiography with him has been both an honour and a very real pleasure. We have laughed, there has been emotion, there has also been single malt whiskey, but most of all there has been friendship. Tony has been a chart topper all around the world, he has played amazing venues, he has reinvented himself for new audiences and will of course always be linked with 'Amarillo', but he is most of all a kind, considerate man who still enjoys a pint of real ale with the lads in his local.

Tony is revered as 'the gentleman of pop music' in central Europe where his career saw its second wave in the 1980s and 1990s before the phenomenal success of 'Amarillo' and his *Definitive Collection* in the UK saw he and his lovely wife Sue return from Spain. For me, his recording career since 'coming home' has brought about some of his finest work on the albums *Made in Sheffield*, *Now's the Time* and *The Great Irish Songbook*, the latter with the wonderful Ranagri, but his back catalogue, including 'Avenues and Alleyways', 'I Did What I Did for Maria' and 'Don't Go Down to Reno' all written by the immensely successful songwriting duo of Mitch Murray and Peter Callendar, is as good as any.

The really wonderful thing about Tony, that I found in working with him, Sue and his son Sean, is that he is untouched by success. I don't mean he hasn't enjoyed himself at times, bought the Rollers, had a nice time, but that he has remained true to himself. He is a very natural man, quiet away from the stage, screen and studio. There's still the Yorkshireman there, that element that all of us true Yorkshiremen have — a certain belligerence, that we want to remain who we are — but there is also the beating heart of a family man who has fought for his own and succeeded.

Tony will tell of being fortunate, that each time he has needed it something has come along, but he's also worked the shifts, served his time. His voice remains his most powerful weapon and whether that has been in singing songs like 'Sweet September' and 'Kiss in the Night' for his European audiences, or 'Happy Birthday Baby', which should have been a hit in the UK, or fantastic numbers like 'Danger Is a Womanin Love' and 'Now's the Time', more recently, he's still got it.

What he also has is good humour and a good heart.

Much love to you Tony and to Sue, Sean and your lovely family. It has been great writing the book with and for you. Now let's crack open another bottle of Dalwhinnie!

Chris x

Chris Berry is from the north of England and lives near Leeds. He is a writer and performer. Feature writer for the Yorkshire Post *for 20 years, author of several biographies and crime fiction, singer-songwriter, both as a solo artist and with his Chris Berry Band. He's a keen sportsman and currently runs several distances from parkrun to half marathons. Born in Kingston upon Hull, he is a staunch Yorkshireman.*

Also by Chris Berry

FICTION
TOUGH SEASON *Crime Thriller*

NON FICTION
TONY CHRISTIE The Song Interpreter
JOE LONGTHORNE The Official Autobiography
SUGAR IN THE MORNING Joe Longthorne
LES BATTERSBY & ME Bruce Jones
BOXSTER'S STORY The Truth Behind the Bull
THE J.D. IRELAND STORY

www.chrisberry.tv

FANS OF TONY CHRISTIE

Danni Niels Andersen

Howard Attew

Madeline Ballantine

Brenda Battle

David John and Sharon Baxter

Neil Geordieboy Beaton

Laura-Ann Smeaton and
Bethany Smeaton

Wayne Briggs

Veronica Broome

In memory of Jim Buckley

Gordon Bussey

Gavin Craig Carroll

Jack & Elaine Chittleborough

Susan Cole

Gary Coleman

Chris Conlan

Chris & June Cooper

Chris Cooper

Maurice and Lily Dance

Paul Davies

Andrew Dawson

Mary Deighton

Carl Difazio

Andy Dixon

Elsie May Doody

Christine Dossor

Lin Ellis

Liz Fairclough

Dave Fishwick

Jennifer Fleming

Garry Gibson

Josef Giehrl

Jack Gillespie

James Green

May Greene

Andrea Häckert

Christine Hainsworth

Trevor Gordon Hancox

Dot Harrison

Kevin Harrop

The Hawkes family

Richard Hawkins

Connie Healy

Melanie Heinrichs

Marilyn Henderson

Gillian L Heys

Palle Hichmann

Valerie Higham

Debbie & Mark Hill

Ida Hodson

Rose Holland

Diane Hollyman

Nigel Hunt

Mr B V Jackson

Ian Jackson

Bethany Flora Ann James

Steve James

John Jeffcote

Irene Joyce

Audrey Kitchen

Rosalyne Kitching

Joyce Kwan

Jessie Lockett

Carol Loughton

Brian and Anne March

Jim Mantz

Keith Markham

Josephine Marshall
(nee Maude)

Simon McLean

Alan McNamara

Elaine McWattie

Ingrid Meeser

Kevin Megson

Helen Meredith

Carola Migalk

Shaida Mohamedbhai

George Michael Mosley

Shaida Mohamedbhai

Jackie Mulrane

Alexander Neu

Joan and Alf Newey

Sandra Nixon

John Norton

Reinhard Obetzhauser

Beate Okunowski

Gwendoline Peel

Tony Phillips

Loretta Piczenik

Mary Rose Littlewood
and Brian Platts

Wendy Porter

Anne Preston MBE

Carol Ramshaw

William Robinson

Janet Salmon

Colin Sayce

Sebastian Schreiter

Joan Senior

Alan & Karen Selby

Joan Senior

Karen Short

Jill Dodge and Jane Smeaton

Margaret & Ray Smyth

Susan Stanley

David Staniforth

Steeplejack

Geraldine Stevens

Pauline Taylor

Christine Taylor

Paul Taylor

Alison Thom

Eileen Thorpe

Angelika Treichel

Ros Turner

Kathy Wagle

Angie Ward

Heike Wesener

Eileen Whalley

Barbara Wheat

Elizabeth Wheat

Darcie Leigh Wilders

Eileen and Malcolm Williams

Claire & David Wilson

Roger D Wilson

Elke Wohlzufrieden

Martin and Trudy Yates

Ian and Julia

for more information and regular updates visit

www.tonychristie.com

www.greatnorthernbooks.co.uk